I0984809

*The American
Immigration Collection*

Americans
in
Process

A Study of Our Citizens
of Oriental Ancestry

WILLIAM CARLSON SMITH

Arno Press and The New York Times

NEW YORK 1970

Reprint Edition 1970 by Arno Press Inc.

LC# 76-129413
ISBN 0-405-00567-9

The American Immigration Collection—Series II
ISBN for complete set 0-405-00543-1

Manufactured in the United States of America

AMERICANS IN PROCESS

AMERICANS IN PROCESS

A STUDY OF OUR CITIZENS OF ORIENTAL ANCESTRY

by

WILLIAM CARLSON SMITH, Ph.D.

Professor of Sociology

Linfield College

INTRODUCTION

by

ROMANZO ADAMS, Ph.D.

Professor of Sociology

University of Hawaii

EDWARDS BROTHERS, INC.

ANN ARBOR, MICHIGAN

1937

PRINTED IN U.S.A.

Lithoprinted by Edwards Brothers, Inc., Lithoprinters and Publishers
Ann Arbor, Michigan, 1937

PREFACE

This study of the second generation of oriental ancestry had its inception in the Survey of Race Relations on the Pacific Coast which was directed by Dr. Robert E. Park of the department of sociology of the University of Chicago. The author is deeply indebted to Dr. Park for valuable counsel, particularly in the early stages of the project. The author is also indebted to all other participants in the Survey whose documents he was permitted to use as they were distributed by the central office.

The scene shifts to the Hawaiian Islands where the project was continued. Acknowledgment is made to Dr. Arthur L. Dean, then president of the University of Hawaii, for many courtesies extended by the University which greatly aided the study; to the Institute of Pacific Relations for a grant-in-aid and to the secretaries J. Merle Davis and Charles F. Loomis for counsel and encouragement; and to the Institute of Social and Religious Research of New York City for a subsidy which made possible the continuance of the undertaking. The list of those who contributed to this study is too long to publish, but we cannot overlook, in particular, Mr. Oren E. Long, Superintendent of Public Instruction, Benjamin O. Wist, Dean of the School of Education of the University of Hawaii, and Miles E. Carey, Principal of McKinley High School of Honolulu, without whose coöperation the project would have been seriously hampered. Grateful acknowledgment is made to Dr. Andrew W. Lind of the department of sociology of the University of Hawaii for placing valuable research data at the disposal of the writer. But more than to anyone else in the Territory of

v

Hawaii the author is indebted to Dr. Romanzo Adams of
the University of Hawaii whose counsel, based on his
rich experience in the Islands, has been invaluable.
Finally, we must not forget the many members of the
second generation of oriental ancestry, both on the
Coast and in Hawaii, who furnished the many life histories and other data on which the volume is largely
based. None of these contributors, however, are to
be held responsible for shortcomings of the study.
          Certain serious difficulties were en-
countered in the organization of this monograph--pos-
sibly the scope is too extensive. Conceivably four
distinct monographs could have been prepared: The
Japanese in Hawaii, The Chinese in Hawaii, The Japanese in Continental United States, and The Chinese in
Continental United States. Although simpler this
would have necessitated considerable duplication.
While the present procedure has avoided a degree of
repetition it has, at times, been necessary in order
to make comparisons and contrasts.
          This report should have been published
earlier but the "modified prosperity" of the past few
years made that impossible. It is now issued in the
hope that it will lead to a better understanding not
only of the American-born children of oriental ancestry but also of the native born of other ancestries
who now constitute about one fourth of our entire
population.

                              William C. Smith

TABLE OF CONTENTS

INTRODUCTION

America has received immigrants from many lands. These immigrants have differed more or less widely from the people of the old American stock and they have differed widely among themselves in cultural traditions and in racial traits. Sometimes they have been received with appreciation, sometimes with tolerance, and sometimes with antagonism, but America has never made a serious effort to understand them. Even when we have recognized the existence of certain problems of maladjustment among the immigrants, the common assumption has been that no special maladjustment would carry over to the second generation. We have had confidence in the character of our institutions; we believed that they were able to create an effective society out of peoples assembled from many sources.

This attitude was the natural result of our earlier experience. Most of our earlier immigrants were not greatly different from us in culture and they were of the same or closely related racial stocks. Moreover, America of the earlier period gave to these immigrants about the same type of economic opportunity that the people of the old stock had enjoyed. Large numbers became farm owners, skilled workers, or small tradesmen in the pioneer West. In the circumstances they adopted American ways and developed American attitudes rather promptly. It was not so much that they learned from the older Americans as that they responded to a similar situation in a similar way. They were Americanized by the same social forces that made the American type in the beginning; they had the experiences of pioneer life.

If this somewhat idealized account is
not true in complete detail, it is true nevertheless
that the exceptions were not important enough to affect the general attitude of the American people as
a whole. We were well satisfied with our experience;
the immigrants were pleased and their children were
good Americans. Of course, we referred to the second and even to the third generations as Norwegian,
German, or whatever their ancestors were. Probably
they spoke another language as well as English.
Other old country customs were maintained. We were
able to identify the American-born with their immigrant ancestors for a long time. But we did not
think of these things as lessening their Americanism.
If certain old-country customs were transplanted to
America, we tended to think of the procedure not as
a lessening of Americanism, but as an enrichment of
our culture. We did not define Americanism narrow-
ly. The general trend of life among the immigrants
and their children appeared to be satisfactory.

More recently our immigrants have
come from other sources, or in larger numbers from
sources of little importance formerly. Many of the
later immigrants represent cultural traditions that
differ from ours by a very wide margin and some of
them possess physical racial traits which identify
them. Such immigrants might be expected to adopt
American ways and develop American attitudes more
slowly even if they enjoyed as great opportunities
as did the earlier immigrants. It is less easy for
the Italians or the Poles to learn the English language and to adopt American customs generally than
it is for the Germans or the Scandinavians, and the
obstacles that lie in the way of the Chinese and the
Japanese are still greater. Of even greater importance, so far as the outcome is concerned, is the
fact that the recent economic situation in America
has been such that the immigrants have not had the
appropriate opportunity. The modern industrial
worker does not commonly enjoy much contact with

Americans of the old stock, nor does he get the experience essential to the development of similar
traits of character. If there is some adverse discrimination based on race this works toward a still
further narrowing of experience and of sympathy.

There is another complicating factor.
We are faced by the necessity of redefining America.
Formerly America was predominantly agricultural and
rural, but it is becoming industrial and urban.
Those American traits that represent the old pioneer
life are undergoing modification and new urban
traits, ultimately to be regarded as American, are
in process of development. The present situation
for the more recent peasant immigrants to American
cities is largely one of cultural disorganization;
they are not maintaining their old culture effectively, they have not become the possessors of the
old American culture, they have not achieved a new
culture--they are just "getting by." Still we may
believe, counting time by generations, that they and
their descendants will make important and worthy
contributions to the Americanism that is to be.

But for the present, there seems to
be no well-defined tendency among these newer immigrant peoples in the direction of Americanism--the
Americanism of tradition. Hence there is a growing
apprehension lest they remain permanently foreign
or lest they create in America some new system antagonistic to what we prize as the real achievement
of America.

Democracy is jeopardized directly by
the failure of immigrant groups to achieve economic
and social equality, and indirectly through the
tendency of any under-privileged group to pull the
next group with which it competes down to its own
level. Moreover, the clash of opposing customs, and
of divergent ethical and esthetic standards impedes
social processes in a society organized on a democratic basis. Evidently our complacency is not war-
ranted and Americans are slowly developing a new

set of attitudes toward the immigrant.

Among the immigrants whose presence
has excited greatest apprehension are those from
Asia, notably the Chinese and the Japanese. The
problem of assimilation in the case of these people
is complicated by race differences. There is no
question as to the innate capacity of Chinese and
Japanese to master the technique of American economic life and of modern science, to acquire the
finest of our intellectual and spiritual possessions, or to participate fruitfully in the political
activities of a democratic community. They can do
all of these things if America gives them opportunity for the appropriate types of social contact and
of experience.

It is just here that the question of
race comes in. Race means a group of physical
traits--color, stature, features, etc.,--that make
possible popular identification and classification.
A democracy is a society of open classes, that is,
of classes that one may enter or leave rather freely according to his personal abilities and interests. The son of a small farmer becomes an industrial magnate, the son of a common laborer becomes
a member of a learned profession, or the son of a
man of great distinction may return to an humble
calling. To the extent that the physical marks of
race are made to serve as a basis for social classification and to open or close the doors of opportunity, there is a tendency toward a system of
closed classes--caste.

America, out of long years of experi-
ence with two races, the American Indian and the en-
slaved Negro, has developed certain unfortunate beliefs and attitudes relative to race. The real
question is not one of the capacity of the Orientals, but of our ability to give them a fair opportunity. Will we let them participate in the common
life of America with opportunity to win good will,
power, and honor according to merit or will we erect
racial barriers?

Of course, some barriers must exist
for the first generation. Cultural differences are
very real and somewhat persistent, but they may be
obliterated in a generation or two. The peculiarity
of racial traits is that they are quite permanent.
If some type of adverse discrimination comes to be
based on racial traits there is no easy way to
escape from it. The passing of generations does not
solve the problem as it does where culture traits
alone are concerned.

In view of this situation it is im-
portant that America should understand the young men
and women of Oriental ancestry who have been born in
our own country. Their problems are not automatically solved by time. These young people are American citizens. They are disposed to be loyal citizens. Many of them are familiar with our history
and our literature and they respond enthusiastically
and with sincerity to the appeal of the fine things
in the American tradition but they are more than a
little anxious as to whether they will be admitted
to full participation as Americans according to
merit.

No matter what one's views may be
relative to the wisdom or unwisdom of our former
immigration policy, these young people of American
birth and Oriental ancestry are a part of us. Most
of them will remain and also their children and
their children's children. They are ambitious,
alert, intelligent. They are securing an American
education. If America means opportunity they are
preparing to make full use of that opportunity. No
mean success will satisfy them. Their faces are
definitely set toward the winning of a superior
economic status. Many of them are ambitious for
recognition in the fields of art, science, and
scholarship. They would enter fully into the
spiritual heritage of America and enrich it from
Oriental sources.

Whether they shall make their due

contribution to American life or whether they shall
be an irritant depends largely on the way Americans
of the older stock meet them. Americans will play
their part the better if there is not only good will
but understanding.

Dr. Smith, after six years in California, has spent about three years in a study of
the second generation Oriental in Hawaii. This
comparative study has distinct advantages, not the
least important of which is that it secures evidence
to show that the response of these young people is
not rigidly controlled by some inborn racial traits,
but that their behavior and attitudes are largely
influenced by local social environmental factors.
They will become what America makes them.

Dr. Smith has given some attention to
the more commonly considered facts of the situation
such as numbers, geographic distribution, and occupational activities, but his principal interest
lies in another field. He is concerned with the
more intimate aspects of experience. He undertakes
to discover the meaning of the multiplied personal
contacts made in the home, in the school, on the
playground, in church, in business, and in polite
society and also the significance of such barriers
as may limit contacts.

His data show how preëxisting atti-
tudes limit or facilitate contacts and how the experiences derived from such contacts result in attitudes which condition further contacts. If we are
to understand these youth of Oriental ancestry we
must see their experience from the inside, that is,
from their own point of view.

Personal contacts of a friendly and
confidential sort with numerous students and other
young people supply part of the data, but Dr. Smith
makes much use of personal life histories of which
he has collected some fifteen hundred. From a reading of a considerable number of these histories, the
present writer is convinced of their sincerity and

that a fair proportion of them are very valuable
documents in that they reveal not only the various
types of situation in which these young people find
themselves, but also their reactions in terms of
behavior and attitude.

Dr. Smith has used the life histories
as wholes in reaching his conclusions and he has
presented to the reader considerable parts in the
form of excerpts. Even these detached excerpts go
far toward making the young people understandable.
The interpretations are sympathetic and intelligent.
A wide reading of this volume will help toward the
development of a sound public opinion relative to
Americans of Oriental ancestry.

Romanzo Adams

Chapter I

ORIENTAL HERITAGES TRANSPLANTED TO AMERICA

Every human group, in the course of its experience, has developed a certain fund of values peculiar to itself, such as moral and religious ideas, family organization, industrial and technical practices, political ideas, educational ideas and practices, and a set of attitudes toward these values. The totality of these sentiments and practices, these memories and traditions, constitute the heritages--the cultural baggage--of the immigrant who comes to America. These immigrant heritages set off the newcomer from others in America; he has standards and practices which differ from ours.

The immigrant cannot divest himself of these heritages as he disembarks at the port of entry; they have shaped his life in the homeland and their influence will persist even in the new country.[1] These standards and practices have, in the main, been acquired in intimate relationships in the home and in the village; hence they have become deeply rooted in his life. In these small groups, with their face-to-face relationships, the rules of conduct are sacred and must not be questioned. When a person goes into another group with different standards, it becomes a matter of conscience whether he will cling to the old code or adopt a new one. A young Japanese woman came to the United States and married. After the marriage the couple lived with an American woman. The Japanese husband worked at night and the young wife was greatly disturbed as to what course to follow.

Mother (the American woman) objected to my sitting up
to await his (husband's) return. This troubled me greatly; for
in Japan it is considered lazy and disgraceful for a wife to
sleep while her husband is working. Night after night I lay
with wide-open eyes, wondering whom it was my duty to obey--
my far-away mother, who knew Japanese customs, or the honored
new mother, who was teaching me the ways of America.[2]

These heritages, evolved from the simple
life of the homeland village, are tenacious. Much
immigrant behavior cannot be explained apart from
these old-world traditions. In a crisis situation,
particularly, there is a tendency to react on the
basis of traditional standards.

Certain of these heritages are transmitted
to the children who are born and reared in America.
It is because of their contacts with the old-world
heritages in the immigrant home and community that
the American-born youth differ from typical American
children. Contacts with these heritages bring many
problems into the lives of the young people. A serious situation arises when children, reared in immigrant homes, break from these traditions before they
have acquired American standards and behavior patterns.

A thorough discussion of oriental heritages
would require several volumes, an undertaking quite
beyond the scope of this monograph. We shall limit
ourselves to the presentation of a few samples, as
it were, which will give a background for the study
of our American citizens of oriental ancestry.

A. Transplanted Chinese Heritages

Organizations. Immigrants to America, no
matter what their origin, tend to transplant their
organizations and institutions and carry them on, as
nearly as possible, as they did in the homeland. Organizations, however, which functioned efficiently

in the old country will not necessarily fit American
conditions and immigrants develop new agencies to
cope with the new problems. Village and district organizations were common in China. With such a background the Chinese in certain areas organized the
immigrants from the same village or district. To be
sure, these organizations inevitably differed from
those in the Orient. In the early days of Chinese
settlement, the six most important district organizations united and formed the "Six Companies"[3] with
headquarters in San Francisco. This more-inclusive
organization is distinctly a product of American
conditions. It developed as a defense measure
against the harsh treatment accorded the Chinese in
California. In China the "tong" was a society made
up of a kinship group, but on the Pacific Coast it
took over certain elements from the Chinese guild
system and the Hong Tuck Tong became the cigar makers' union. Most tongs perform useful functions.
They serve as business and social clubs or mutual-
benefit associations. The denial of participation
in American life, however, has led to the development of notoriously anti-social activities on the
part of certain tongs; they have developed in ways
entirely foreign to China.[4] For instance, the dis-
proportion in the numbers of the sexes and the ban
on marriage with white women have led to the importation of prostitutes. The owner of a "slave girl,"
however, cannot cope with the police and the mis-
sions[5] single-handedly. The tong steps in to aid
him and becomes a vice insurance society.[6] In
Hawaii, where conditions differ markedly from those
on the Coast, there is no tong in the San Francisco
sense; tong wars are unknown in the Islands.

Familism. In the Orient, and particularly
in China, the family is of far greater importance
than in the Occident. The Chinese live, move, and
have their being in the family.

According to blood the person is assigned position and status. In the blood-group he achieves recognition and fixes his standards of personal behavior. In that group his wishes secure satisfaction, and according to its norms he organizes his wishes into his dominant life-scheme. Blood sets the limits beyond which the person does not wander in his efforts or objectives.[7]

Apart from the family the person is nothing. "He who is cut off from it is an outcast and a vagabond. There is no new circle which he can enter."[8] Familism dominates a man's economic activities. A man never becomes precisely his own master; he is always bound by the family group.[9]

Since a person is completely dependent upon the family group, filial piety is an inevitable outcome. This results in certain types of behavior toward those who are in a specific relationship, or who occupy a certain status, and it determines the reciprocal obligations of others with reference to oneself. Filial piety is not merely a matter of form or etiquette; it is a tremendous force in the motivation of conduct.[10]

When the Chinese came to America, they brought their family heritages and carried on the ancestral customs so far as possible, but the new environment was not conducive to a continuance of the traditional order. Great changes in their family organization were inevitable. The fact that it was largely a movement of male workers in the prime of life was highly significant. This disparity in the sex distribution made it impossible for all men to marry. The fewness of the Chinese women in Hawaii led some to marry Hawaiian or part-Hawaiian wives. In these unions where race lines were crossed, it was impossible for a husband to set up a household like that in his homeland because his wife was of alien culture and was ignorant of the practices of the Orient. Furthermore, far away from the home environment, the old codes no longer controlled

them. Hence, their behavior, directed by impulse
rather than by social tradition, tended to become
individualistic.[11]

Ancestor Worship. Closely linked with familism is the practice of ancestor worship which
unites the present members of the community with
those who have passed on. For many centuries this
has been the one spiritual force that has moulded
Chinese life in its every aspect.

There is no other in the region of belief that would
take its place for a moment. A man, for example, may worship
the idols or not; he may profess a belief in them or he may
express his utter scepticism about them, and no one cares a
button what he thinks. Let a man, however, neglect the worship of the dead, and he is looked upon with the utmost scorn,
both by his own kindred and also by his neighbors. The bitter-
est taunt that the Chinese can hurl against the convert to
Christianity, and the one that stings him most, is the sneer-
ing statement that he has no ancestors.[12]

When the Chinese migrated to America, they
could not break completely with the past that bound
them to their dead ancestors. Shrines and ancestral
tablets were set up in their houses. They were,
however, far removed from the ancestral halls and
graves of their fathers, and under these conditions
ancestor worship could not have the same significance.
Since they were detached from the old environment,
the group pressure was released and they tended to
conform less meticulously to the ancient codes.

Marriage. When a Chinese boy attains maturity he may not decide whether he shall marry or remain single.[13] "Very likely he was betrothed in in-
fancy or early childhood, and. . . . long before the
boy is his own master he may have a wife."[14] Marriage
is not a personal matter but is purely and simply a
concern of the family. "Often the real motive for

hastening the wedding is the felt need in the boy's
family of an additional servant, which need will be
supplied by the introduction of a new bride." [15]
Marriage is arranged by a match-maker or go-between.
The two persons concerned never meet during the be-
trothal negotiations and usually see each other for
the first time on the wedding day.[16] Their wishes
are not considered and their consent is not necessary.

The old practices could not be followed in
their entirety in America, yet many Chinese parents
have endeavored to follow the oriental pattern. An
American-born Chinese, a high-school graduate, had
chosen the girl he wanted but his old-fashioned
mother refused her consent and hired a "go-between"
to arrange a marriage with the daughter of a life-
long friend of hers. The boy had seen the girl only
once, but the situation was such that he had to consent. The girl's parents were willing and accepted
the gifts sent by the boy's mother. The "go-between"
arranged the day, and all was settled.

Separation of the Sexes. The oriental practice of keeping the two sexes separate has been
transplanted to America. Usually they eat at separate tables; at times separate dining rooms have
been provided. Chinese parents do not want their
daughters to associate with boys or become friendly
with them. This, however, cannot be rigidly en-
forced as in the Orient. The sexes mingle in the
schools and the young people begin to follow the example set by American youth.

Male Superiority. In the Chinese system,
males are usually given a position of superiority.
The boy "is welcomed to a household with a wild delight, to which it is wholly impossible for an Occidental to do any justice." [17] On the other hand,
"The Chinese girl. . . . is very likely to be unwel-
come though this is by no means invariably the

case."[18] Daughters are regarded as transients who
eventually will lose membership in their father's
family by marriage; they are liabilities because
they leave as soon as they become economically valuable. Furthermore, many carry dowries with them to
their new homes. Hence the saying, "There is no
thief like a family of five daughters, and the term
'lose-money goods' is jestingly applied to girls."[19]

In considerable measure the idea of male
superiority has been transplanted to America. The
higher value placed on the male sex is revealed by
the fact that some baby girls are neglected while
nothing is left undone for a male child. Boys give
status, and a man with several sons has a high standing in the community. Commonly authority rests
with the father. [20]

New Year Celebration. Although official
China, in her desire to keep pace with other nations,
with a stroke of the pen discarded the old planetary
system of reckoning time and adopted the Gregorian
calendar, yet the masses, with their reverence for
the past, did not see fit to throw away the venerable custom of celebrating the passing of the old
year and the coming in of the new. It is the time
when absent relatives return home; it is a time of
feasting and rejoicing. Certain articles of food
are as inseparably associated with this celebration
as roast turkey and mince pie with a New England
Thanksgiving. In addition to the feasting there is
an abundance of noise; firecrackers, large and small,
are exploded everywhere both by day and by night.

The Chinese in America make much of their
New Year celebration.

Tomorrow night will be happy New Year to many of our
people, to the toilers in the fields, to the workers in the
shops, and to those who know no holiday except at New Year.
Precious tablets and exquisite tapestries that have been
tucked away for months will be proudly exhibited to friends

and well wishers. Favorite silk pieces with tiny glittering
mirrors and golden dragons will be spread over teakwood chairs
and tables. The children will be thoroughly washed with hot
water fragrant with smelling leaves and will be properly dolled
up in an atmosphere of immaculate cleanliness while the older
folks will wear a visage of good cheer. Tea will be served
and oh,--the eats. Dinner on New Year's eve and the four days
following is fit for a king. "Eat heavy" seems to be the slogan and they certainly avail themselves of the opportunity to
"eat heavy" as this is one time during the year when they can
let loose and eat merrily, fully and heartily, especially
after debts have been settled[21] and prosperity looms ahead.[22]

Gambling. "Gambling is deeply rooted in the
folkways of the Cantonese, and most Chinese peasants
learned to gamble before they came to this country."[23]

Gambling is, indeed, a very marked feature of Chinese
life. A child buying a cake will often go double or quits
with the stall keeper, to see if he is to have two cakes or
nothing, the question being settled by a throw of dice in a
bowl. Of the interval allowed for meals, a gang of coolies
will devote a portion to a game of cards. . . . There are also
various games played with chequers. . . . and there is
chess. . . . In all of these the money element comes in.[24]

A cursory examination of police records
shows that gambling flourishes among the Chinese immigrants in America. A police officer in California
said, "It's as natural for the Chinaman to gamble as
for a baby to drink milk."[25] In certain towns of
northern California the commercialized gambling of
the Chinese is highly organized and constitutes an
important part of the business of the community. In
some places the gambling is conducted in camouflaged
stores which are stocked with canned goods and other
wares, while in other instances there is no attempt
at disguise.[26]

B. Transplanted Japanese Heritages

The Japanese, like the Chinese, have transplanted many of their heritages to America and have
followed the old-world patterns as closely as possible in the new environment. In certain plantation
communities of Hawaii, where the Japanese were in
the majority, many of the old forms were continued.
The following document reveals some of the oriental
customs followed in a plantation home.

When Akiyoshi Nakai was born in 1906. . . . there was
great rejoicing, as is always the case when the first son of
the family is born. All the neighbors came to congratulate
the family bringing with them eggs or fish for the mother and
cloth or blankets for the infant son. On the third day, there
was held an informal tea party, where the sages of the camp
gathered to suggest names for the boy, names that meant valor,
strength, wisdom, sunshine, etc. Finally, the parents agreed
on "Akiyoshi," the Japanese characters of which mean "the
breath of autumn." On the thirty-first day, there was a great
celebration. There were all sorts of Japanese delicacies;
sushi (rice cake), kamaboko (fish cake), and above all, raw
fish and sake (rice beer), the essentials of any Japanese
feast. The guests squatted on the floor and ate anything they
wanted of food placed on a low table before them. The guests,
most of whom were men (there were few women in those days)
drank until one o'clock the next morning, singing and dancing
to the music which the happy mother played on the samisen (the
Japanese three-stringed guitar). The baby was fed with a
grain of rice on the hundred-and-tenth day, and this commenced
his eating of other foods besides milk. On the following May 5,
the day of the Boy's Festival, called Tango or Sekku, the parents displayed many flags on which were drawn heroes of Japan
and many large cloth carp were attached to tall bamboo poles.
These carp and flags were given by friends as a token of their
wish that the boy would grow big and strong, and follow the
ideals of Bushido like the Samurai of old; and that he would
have the persistence and perseverance of the carp which goes
up rapids and even climbs falls. The parents celebrated his

first birthday by distributing the <u>mochi</u> (pounded rice) to
their friends and by an informal tea to which were invited
only the more intimate friends. On the whole, they were very
happy on the plantation. They were prosperous and contented.
They knew all the people of the camp intimately and were on
very friendly terms with everyone. Moreover, the parents did
not miss very much of Japan, except some relatives, for the
camp was a small Japan itself transplanted to a plantation in
Hawaii.[27]

   <u>Family System</u>. In Japan the family, though
it does not have such wide ramifications in the social body as in China, exercises a great influence;
it has shaped the forms in which the nation's political life has been cast; it is the real foundation of
Japanese social organization; it controls much of
the routine of life; it is a dominant influence in
behavior.

   When members of the family were so closely
bound together, filial piety came to be the supreme
virtue. This was not merely a matter of certain obligations of the child to parent or grandparent, but
it included reverential service to the dead ancestors and the behavior of the individuals with reference to the entire family group. This gave a minimum of freedom to the individual members; no one
could conduct himself according to his own inclina-
tions. Minute rules governed all. But even in this
state of subjection there was some compensation because of the mutual helpfulness. Each member of the
household was obligated to assist the others, and in
turn could expect protection and aid.[28]

   Despite the different conditions in America,
the Japanese family heritages exert a powerful influence. In the midst of disorganizing influences
there is a remarkable family solidarity. Mutual
helpfulness is evident on every hand.[29] Even though
many of the native-born youth find themselves widely
at variance with the ideas of the immigrant generation, they are bound to their parents with a loyalty

the Occidental cannot understand. The immigrants
pay considerable attention to the family name and
family traditions. The honor of the family must be
upheld, even at great sacrifice.[30]
          Pride and honor have been factors in holding
down the number of expatriations from Japan; a failure to have the American-born children properly registered has been a source of embarrassment to the
families in Japan. When students of oriental ancestry in Hawaii have been advised to leave educational institutions on account of poor scholastic
standing, they have pleaded for permission to continue; a failure would disgrace the family name. A
failure in any line is not simply an individual matter; it is of great concern to the entire family.[31]
          Changes in the traditional family system,
however, have been inevitable. As the immigrants
from Japan have gone to different places to work,
much of the old life has been broken off; they have
been confused and bewildered. Their time has not
been their own, so they could not carry on those
leisurely activities and ceremonials as in Japan.
Arranged marriages have been successful in Japan because of the pressure of public opinion. The young
wife has been controlled and directed by her mother-
in-law and she has had meager opportunity to break
with tradition. The family council, supported by
traditions reaching back into the hoary past, has
been an important agency of control.[32] But grand-
fathers, uncles, and mothers-in-law did not come to
America to set up the family councils. In America
such councils, with relatives coming from great dis-
tances, was out of the question.

          Ancestor Worship. The world at large knows
Japan as Buddhistic in religion, but, according to
Lafcadio Hearn, "The real religion of Japan, the re-
ligion still professed in one form or another, by
the entire nation is. . . . 'Ancestor-worship.'"[33]
He also states that not only government, but almost

everything in Japanese society, derives directly or indirectly from this ancestor cult.[34] The whole family system is indissolubly bound up with ancestor worship.[35] The Japanese family has been and still is, in large measure, a religious group shaped and dominated primarily by the requirements of ancestor worship. The welfare of the household depended upon the observance of the ancestral cult. This made it obligatory upon the eldest son to marry in order to continue the ancestral line unbroken. To die without a male heir to perform the necessary rites was an outrage against his ancestors. Because of this a man could divorce a barren wife, take a concubine, or might even resort to adoption. If a man had daughters but no son, he might adopt a husband for his eldest daughter. The son-in-law could then perform the customary rites. Since daughters were expected to marry into other families, they were in no position to perpetuate the family cult.[36]

Male Superiority. In the Japanese family group, all must obey the head who may be the grandfather, the father, or the eldest son. In certain instances, when the head of the household dies, his brother assumes headship of the family and rules the widow and her children until the eldest son attains his majority.[37] The females of all ages in the household are subservient to the males.

The man takes precedence everywhere, and the woman must serve him. At meals the woman must first wait on her husband and then she herself may eat. When the guests come, the husband is the chief entertainer and the wife takes a back seat and says little. On passing through a door, entering a train or carriage, etc., the husband always precedes his wife. When walking on the street together she does not walk by his side, but comes along behind. The men do not intend to mistreat the women; they simply take what they regard their due as the head of the family.[38]

The Japanese immigrants have transplanted
the idea of male superiority to America. Character-
istically the immigrant women have taken a secondary
place and have deferred to the men. "At the sight
of a man the women bend their bodies stiffly from
the waist up, accompanying the gesture with a fold-
ing of the hands and a lowering of the eyes. In
Bly, California, the male is lord."[39] The idea of
male superiority manifests itself in many ways. In
a certain community on the Pacific Coast report has
it that the Japanese call the doctor more promptly
for the boys than for the girls. Japanese parents
have often revealed keen disappointment at the birth
of a girl.[40] A college boy in Hawaii wrote of his
home:

My father's dominant position was evident at home.
He was the boss and had his own way, while the other members
of the family had to do just as he said. He practised the custom of old Japan, where the father was supreme in the house.
We had to obey his orders whether they were good or not. My
mother, on the other hand, was a very lovable woman. She
worked hard and no matter how she was imposed upon, she was
always obedient to father. . . . At times, when father was
drunk, she was subjected to extreme cruelty but she never said
a word. She carried out the custom of old Japan that a wife
should obey and be loyal to the husband at any cost.[41]

Separation of the Sexes. The Japanese parents endeavor to keep the two sexes apart, according to the practice of the Orient. A college girl
wrote:

Many Japanese parents will not let their daughters do
certain things; they will not permit them to go out with boys.
If they go to a movie, they must go with girls. The girls,
however, do not say anything; they just accept the situation.
I feel the home restraints to a considerable degree and at
times I get wrought up about it. My mother permits me to go
out with a group, but not with a boy friend.[42]

This segregation of the young people has interfered
with programs of the young people's societies in
some churches. The parents, however, are unable to
enforce this regulation. The young people have
mingled freely in the schools. They have observed
the American young people and are unwilling to be
forced into a situation where they appear peculiar.

Marriage Arrangements in Japan. Since the
perpetuation of the ancestor cult is fundamental,
the question of marriage cannot be entrusted to the
young people themselves. The wishes of the persons
concerned must not be permitted to thwart the requirements of the household religion. All matters
relative to marriage must be decided by the family.

The young man and woman have nothing whatever to do
with the match-making. . . . Whenever the parents of a young
man think their son old enough to get married, they secure the
services of some friend, who acts as a "go-between." It is
the duty of this party to search out a suitable girl and win
the consent of her parents. . . . While this is going on, it
is not likely that either of the young people is aware of it,
but as soon as the parents have arranged matters to their own
satisfaction they are informed. It often happens that the man
has never seen his bride until the wedding day.[43]

This being the practice, arrangements of the
parents are usually accepted as a matter of course
and no questions are raised.

"Etsuko," mother said very gently, "the gods have been
kind to you, and your destiny as a bride has been decided.
Your honorable brother and your venerable kindred have given
much thought to your future. It is proper that you should express your gratitude to the Honorable All."
I made a long, low bow, touching my forehead to the
floor. Then I went out and returned to my desk and my writing.
I had no thought of asking, "Who is it?" I did not think of
my engagement as a personal matter at all. It was a family

affair. Like every Japanese girl, I had known from babyhood
that sometime, as a matter of course, I was to marry; but that
was a far-away necessity to be considered when the time came.
I did not look forward to it. I did not dread it. I did not
think of it at all.[44]

Under such a system, marriage is purely and
simply a business arrangement. "Sentimental or romantic considerations have no part in it."[45]

It was not a question of affection, but of religious
duty; and to think otherwise was impious. Affection might and
ought to spring from the relation. But any affection powerful
enough to endanger the cohesion of the family would be condemned. A wife might therefore be divorced because her husband had become too much attached to her.[46]

Marriage Arrangements in America. More in
Hawaii than in continental United States, the Japanese immigrants have adhered to the custom of parentally-arranged marriages. A college girl in
Hawaii reveals the fact:

My parents are quite arbitrary in their ideas concerning matrimony. It would break their hearts if I married
on my own initiative; it would be the final act of filial disloyalty. They suspect that thoughts of marriage are current
in my mind and they try to question me in their quiet dignified
manner. My parents believe that because I am so young and in-
experienced they should select a life partner for me and I
should approve their choices.[47]

Chapter II

HAWAII VERSUS THE PACIFIC COAST

This monograph is a study of our American
citizens of oriental ancestry in two areas--the Pacific Coast states and the Hawaiian Islands. That
the reader may have a better understanding of these
young people in the two areas, it will be a distinct
advantage to present certain differences between
Hawaii and the Pacific Coast at the very outset.
This will serve as a frame of reference for the interpretation of differences in behavior.

Hawaii differs markedly from the Pacific
Coast.[1] The most casual observation will confirm
this.[2] In this connection a few of the most striking differences that touch the Americans of oriental
ancestry will be considered. Other differences
stand out in the discussions of the various subjects
in this monograph.

Minimum of Prejudice in Hawaii. The attitudes of the white people and the treatment they accord members of oriental groups in the two areas
stand out in striking contrast. The resultant reactions of the Orientals to these differences in stim-
uli also vary markedly. Visitors from the Pacific
Coast who spend a few days in the Islands often
comment on the friendly relations existing between
the races. With almost monotonous regularity they
tell Honolulu gatherings, usually attended by members of several races, that the people of Hawaii
have solved all race problems and have conclusively
demonstrated that the different races can live together amicably. But Hawaii is neither California

nor Washington, and all too often the tourists do
not fully appreciate the real situation. Their eyes
are set to recognize behavior characteristic of the
Pacific Coast, but since that is not in evidence
they are prone to conclude that all is harmonious
and there is no prejudice or discrimination. An
American sociologist who had spent several years
among the Negroes in the southern states said, "Hu-
manly speaking, you have no race prejudice in Hawaii." On the whole, it may be said that in Hawaii
the several races are living together in relationships characterized by a high degree of harmony and
friendliness. The differences in attitudes in the
two areas are disclosed through the experiences and
reactions of those who have gone from one area to
the other. On his first visit to Honolulu, a California-born Japanese wrote: "The greatest surprise
by far was the general cosmopolitan air of the city.
Here two cultures meet, the one from the Orient and
the other from the Occident. . . . This is one place
where the appellation, 'The Land Where Hatred Ex-
pires,' may sincerely be applied."[3] On the other
hand, persons who have gone to the Pacific Coast
have had unpleasant experiences. A Japanese college
boy reported the treatment he received.

> The most important thing I learned, while I was in
> San Francisco, was the attitude of the white people there to-
> ward the Japanese. Before I went to San Francisco, I heard
> various rumors about the treatment of Japanese in California
> by the Whites. But I didn't realize the true situation until
> I had personal experience. I went to a barber to get my hair
> trimmed and on entering the shop, one of the barbers approached
> me and asked my nationality. I answered that I was Japanese.
> As soon as he heard that I was of the yellow race, he drove me
> out of the place as if he were driving away a cat or a dog. I
> never felt so cheap as when I was treated this way by this
> animal who wore the face of a man.[4]

          In Hawaii this would not happen. We must

not conclude, however, that there is no prejudice in
Hawaii. In Honolulu the majority of the barbers are
Japanese women, while in California the majority are
white men. This fact alone changes the situation,
because the Orientals are not dependent upon the Occidentals for such service. In Honolulu, however,
Orientals are actually served by white barbers.[5] In
Hawaii there is, without question, less prejudice
than on the Pacific Coast. In many theaters on the
Coast Orientals are given none but the most undesirable seats. In Hawaii it is quite the custom for
them to attend theaters without differential treatment; to be guests at hotels without discrimination;
to participate in formal social events along with
Whites, as at the Governor's Reception or the Japanese Consul General's Reception. The fact that
there is no prejudice or should be none in Hawaii is
a matter of tradition and principle which practically all members of the community feel bound to maintain. This is a creed to which many, especially the
leading spokesmen for Hawaii, subscribe, even though
in practice they find it difficult. Governor Farrington,[6] in season and out of season, proclaimed
that there was no race problem in Hawaii. The relative absence of prejudice in Hawaii may be illustrated by the fact that the Central Y.M.C.A. in
Honolulu at one time employed a Japanese college
student to supervise a group of white boys in a summer camp. Managing a group of boys is no easy matter, but this Japanese succeeded even with white
boys.[7]

There is, nevertheless, a certain amount of
prejudice against the Japanese in Hawaii, but it is
against them as a class rather than as a race. It
seems that all who have come to Hawaii as plantation
laborers, no matter what their origin, encounter a
certain amount of prejudice. Probably there is less
prejudice against the Japanese than there is within
their own group--that is, between the Japanese
proper and the Okinawans of the Lu-chu Islands.

There is apparently no greater antagonism between
the different races of Hawaii than there is between
the Hakka and Punti groups from the province of
Kwangtung in China. On several issues, the Chinese
in Honolulu have aligned themselves as Hakka versus
Punti. There is no such profound distinction between the Caucasians and any of the other racial
groups in Hawaii as that between the Eta[8] and the
other classes in Japan.

An Anglo-Saxon college girl in Hawaii has
portrayed some of the prejudice.

There was one other source of conflict at high school,
and that was at election time. We Haoles[9] were never able to
elect those we nominated, and thus there were very few white
students in office. I remember we often used to vote twice,
for in those days we voted by showing hands or by standing,
and we were willing to run the risk of being reprimanded for
it. The main injustice was that the Orientals always voted
for non-white students. The Japanese and Chinese were not especially fond of each other but, strange to say, they always
voted for each other, that is, a Chinese would vote for a Japanese and vice-versa, rather than for a white student. It
angered the Haoles, for we felt that the Orientals were doing
this merely to anger us. It was really they who drew the
line. Another trick they used, or at least we thought they
did, was to split the white vote. We would nominate a white
student, then an Oriental would be nominated. If the Orientals thought our candidate had a good chance, they would nominate another fairly popular Haole. The Haoles then split
their vote while the Orientals voted as a solid bloc for the
Oriental, no matter if he were Japanese or Chinese. The main
trouble was that not all the Haoles could see through this
trick.[10]

The two years at high school showed me that even
though we were in classes together, some pupils felt quite
strongly against children of other races. There was an effort
to keep Orientals out of the dramatic club and I remember the
principal berating us soundly for it. This, however, did no

good as it only made many of us down on him; we considered him
pro-oriental. We were tired of the teachers telling us how desirable the oriental students were. It was the teachers in
their clumsy way of trying to set things right that made
things very much worse. The next year the club took in Orientals and for some time I heard it did nothing. However, I can
say nothing as to whether it was due to lack of coöperation between races, for I left and went to a different high school.[11]

        In all probability the conduct of the orien-
tal pupils was a reaction to the attitude of the
Caucasians. The Occidentals, in drawing a line
against the Orientals, aroused such resentment that
they were actually barred from elective offices.
Those of oriental ancestry do not always attempt to
dominate because of superior numbers. On the contrary, any white student who shows a friendly attitude toward them is usually given more than his
share of consideration. In the spring of 1928, in
this same school, an Anglo-Saxon girl, who had been
friendly to the Chinese and Japanese, was elected by
an overwhelming majority to the vice-presidency of
the student body. Unbeknown to her she was also
elected to another office in one of the important
organizations of the school. Any white pupil who
would make headway in such a school must be acceptable to those of oriental ancestry.

                Intermingling of Races.
        (1) In Hawaii. In the Territory the various
races intermingle freely and a white person will not
be ostracized if he shows himself friendly to the
Orientals. Even Japanese and Koreans may be friendly in the Islands. But then in this respect, one
must speak guardedly, for the relations between the
races often appear more friendly than they actually
are. A Korean college girl gives an insight into
the situation.

        I have had contact with other racial groups such as
the Filipinos, the Japanese, Chinese, Hawaiians, Haoles,

Portuguese, etc., but I have never been very intimate with
them. When I see them I do not ignore them, I laugh, joke,
and associate with them, but still I am not intimate with them.
We different races may be said to be living in harmony, in
brotherliness with one another, but still I feel the racial
antagonism. Even in our University, there is racial antagonism
veiled behind smiles and friendship. We are mere acquaintances,
not friends. The Haoles do not care a bit for the Orientals.
The Hawaiians on the other hand do not like the Whites. Every
day, I hear remarks about racial antagonism. We try to mix socially, but always the same crowd gathers for a real good time.
The great majority stays away and sneers at such gatherings.[12]

   (2) <u>On the Pacific Coast</u>. In California,
white men who have shown friendliness to the Orientals have been made uncomfortable. Opprobrious
epithets such as "white Jap" have been common.
Nevertheless, there have been instances of interracial friendships. In a comparatively isolated
community in southern California, where the Japanese
were in the majority, a white girl and a Japanese
girl were chums. The fact that the white girl's
father was the manager of a fish cannery, owned and
operated by Japanese, doubtless had some influence.
Moreover, since there were few white families in the
community, the Japanese girl was probably more attractive than the white girls. Furthermore, the
white girl was in no danger of social ostracism because of her friendship with a girl of oriental ancestry.

   In California, it is not merely the white
and the yellow who do not mingle, but the different
groups of oriental ancestry tend to stand aloof from
each other. In one of the large universities the
Japanese and Chinese would have nothing to do with
each other. One Japanese girl who associated somewhat with a Chinese was ostracized by her own group.

   <u>Attitude Toward Intermarriage</u>. On the Pacific Coast there is a strong sentiment against

intermarriage and several states prohibit such unions. Persons who marry outside their own racial
groups are usually ostracized. A white woman in
California said:

> Fifteen years ago when I married, prejudice was at
> its height. Because of my marriage to a Japanese, my family
> was "frozen out" by the white people, and I have been moving
> away from the Whites more and more ever since. I now live in
> a Japanese district and I wouldn't live near a white person.
> Of course, I am not prejudiced against the Japanese or else I
> would not have married one.[13]

In Hawaii, where the races intermingle quite
freely, there is a more liberal attitude toward intermarriage. There is no legal bar against such unions and those who marry outside do not suffer ostracism.

The Hawaiian people, doubtless, have influenced the attitudes toward intermarriage.[14] Race
mixtures ordinarily come on the fringes; the undesirable elements usually mix their blood. With the
Hawaiians, however, it has been different. In the
early days of European contact, King Kamehameha I
gave women of royal lineage to become wives of white
men. This set the stamp of approval upon intermarriage and has influenced all the groups in the
Territory.

Attitude toward Racial Hybrids. The attitude toward intermarriage has reacted favorably on
the persons of mixed blood in Hawaii. The status of
the mixed-bloods may be considered both cause and effect of the tolerant spirit.[15] No stigma is attached
to a mixture of blood and very few hesitate to talk
about their mixed ancestry; many speak of it with a
sense of pride. Many hybrids occupy positions of
prominence in Hawaii and, to a number, a mixture of
Chinese and Hawaiian blood has been a distinct advantage. In 1926 the first pure Chinese were

elected to office in Hawaii. Prior to this, several
Chinese-Hawaiians had held governmental positions.
These distinctions had come because their Hawaiian
blood had made them acceptable to the voters, a high
percentage of whom were Hawaiians. The mixed-bloods
are, in considerable measure, responsible for the
interracial harmony. A Chinese-Hawaiian can mingle
freely with both the Chinese and Hawaiians and both
groups will unite in the support of such a person.
In the opinion of a teacher in the Territorial Normal School in Honolulu, problems of discipline would
be greatly complicated if the mixed-bloods were elim-
inated from the institution. The majority of offices in the student organizations were held by hybrids. If a person with Chinese, Hawaiian, and
Scotch blood was president of the students' association, all three groups would consider themselves
represented. Furthermore, the other groups such as
the Portuguese and Japanese would be more whole-
hearted in their support of such a cosmopolite than
of a pure-blood representative of any single group.[16]

     Effects of Differences in Conditions. Be-
cause of these marked contrasts in conditions, there
are striking differences between the Americans of
oriental ancestry in the two areas. When those of
the younger generation go from one area to the other,
they comment on these differences. Some young Japanese in California maintain that the behavior of
those who come from Hawaii is at such great variance
with their own that it gives the whole Japanese community an unsavory reputation.

     (1) Retention of Heritages. The young peo-
ple of Hawaii retain more of the oriental heritages.
They have no aversion to wearing oriental costumes
on certain occasions and appear to be perfectly at
ease when so dressed. At one of the California universities the Cosmopolitan Club was making plans for
a public program in which the different groups were

to dress in national garb. Those of oriental ancestry were so reluctant to appear thus that it was
only after much diplomacy and persuasion that their
consent was secured. In Hawaii, the young people do
not hesitate to talk about things oriental, for
there is slight danger of being held up to ridicule.
In California they do not want to appear interested
in the Orient lest that be considered un-American.

(2) <u>More Philosophical Attitude in Hawaii</u>.
The Americans of oriental ancestry on the Coast have
been under great tension and a number have become
bitter. A college girl in California speaks for a
large number.

Oftentimes I would be greeted by such complimentary
appellations as "Jap," "skibee," "Chink," and "yellow dog," and
some bold rascal would even fling stones at me. These thought-
less cruelties, which were like knife stabs into my heart, especially painful because of my extreme timidity and sensitive-
ness, made me shrink from walking along the street alone. At
times, I would be filled with hatred against America and Americans, and at times, I wished that I had been born a white
person so that I should not have to encounter any affronts.[17]

On the whole it may be said that the Americans of oriental ancestry in Hawaii take a more
philosophical attitude toward the whole situation
than do those on the Coast. They are less perturbed;
they have met the whites in many lines of endeavor
and, where they have had an equal chance, have won
their full share of honors. In many instances they
have won more than their share, even against heavy
odds; they have learned through actual experience
that white people are not necessarily unbeatable.

It so happened this year, 1927, that a Haole girl received the honor of being valedictorian in a graduating class
of three hundred. One of her Japanese friends approached her
and said with great seriousness and dignity, "You should be

very proud of the fact that you are the first Haole in eleven
years to receive that honor."[18]

A high school girl made this observation.

Look at the annual oratorical contest sponsored by
the Anti-Saloon League. Who are the people that enter these
contests? Who march out with glorious victory? I am proud to
say that the Orientals have always taken the honorable places.[19]

As far as I know the first place for the last three
or four years was taken by the Japanese boys and girls.[20]

This philosophical attitude makes an indelible impression. The young people of oriental
parentage in Honolulu behave as if they actually belonged to the community; in California many appear
timid and ill-at-ease. It has been noted that several from Hawaii have been able to gain a more ready
entrée into the white group in California than those
born in the state. The Hawaiian-reared are so natural in their behavior that certain white Americans
recognize in them likenesses to themselves and accept them. A white boy in a California college gave
his reaction to a Chinese boy from Hawaii. In doing
so, he referred to a number of Orientals he had
known in high school and college and observed how
uneasy and self-conscious other Orientals had been.
But this Hawaiian boy was an exception; he seemed
perfectly at ease under all circumstances.

Since October of this year "Beans" has been a member
of the Sigma Phi Alpha fraternity. This is not my fraternity,
but I know many of its members very intimately and "Beans"
holds a position in the group which has absolutely no race
consciousness. This seems to me significant of the attitude
of college students in general toward Orientals. This year also he tried out and was admitted to the debating society of
which I am a member. . . . "Beans" owes his success to his
forcing the students to accept him on terms of equality.[21]

Chapter III

POPULATION FACTORS AND RACE RELATIONS

An adequate understanding of the American
citizens of oriental ancestry and their problems of
adjustment makes necessary a consideration of number, composition, and distribution of the oriental
population. Since those of American birth are so
closely linked with the immigrant generation, the
data for both groups must be considered.

A. Orientals in the Population

In Continental United States. Table I presents the distribution of the Chinese and Japanese

Table I

CHINESE AND JAPANESE IN CONTINENTAL UNITED STATES
COMPARED WITH THE TOTAL POPULATION, BY NUMBER AND
PER CENT, 1860-1930

Year	Chinese	Japanese	Total Chinese and Japanese	Total Population	Per Cent of Total
1860	34,933	--	34,933	31,443,321	00.11
1870	63,199	55	63,254	38,558,371	00.17
1880	105,465	148	105,613	50,155,783	00.21
1890	107,488	2,039	109,527	62,947,714	00.18
1900	89,863	24,326	114,189	75,994,575	00.15
1910	71,531	72,157	143,688	91,972,266	00.16
1920	61,639	111,010	172,649	105,710,620	00.17
1930	74,954	138,834	213,788	122,775,046	00.17

Data from the United States Census

in continental United States from 1860 to 1930.

According to Table I, the Chinese and Japanese constituted less than two-tenths of one per cent of the total population of continental United States in 1930.

Table II presents the data for the three Pacific Coast states.

Chart I presents the distribution of the Chinese[1] in the three Pacific Coast states and in the remainder of continental United States for the decades 1860 - 1930. This chart shows that in 1860 all the Chinese were concentrated in California from which they gradually dispersed to the other coast states and to areas farther east. This, however, is not entirely accurate even though the census of 1860 reports a total Chinese population of 34,933 in the United States and also gives an identical number for the Chinese in California. A closer examination of the census reports reveals the fact that the Chinese were counted and reported separately only in the state of California. Footnotes indicate that several hundred Chinese, enumerated with the white population, were resident in Oregon and a few in other states.[2] In 1930, the Chinese percentage in California increased while that of the other two Coast states decreased.

Since the oriental group in continental United States, except for 1880, has constituted less than two-tenths of one per cent of the total population (Table I), it would have been a negligible quantity were it not for the fact that the Orientals have been concentrated largely on the Pacific Coast, and particularly in California where they have assumed considerable importance. Since California has been the area of greatest concentration, this explains in large measure why this state has been in the forefront of the anti-oriental agitation. A closer study of the California data reveals still other factors. At first the Chinese went in large numbers to the gold-mining regions from which they

Table II

CHINESE AND JAPANESE IN THE PACIFIC COAST STATES

1860–1930

Year	CHINESE				JAPANESE			
	Washington	Oregon	California	Total	Washington	Oregon	California	Total
1860	---	---	34,933	34,933	---	---	---	00
1870	234	3,330	49,277	52,841	---	---	33	33
1880	3,186	9,510	75,132	87,828	1	2	86	89
1890	3,260	9,540	72,472	85,272	360	25	1,147	1,532
1900	3,629	10,397	75,753	89,779	5,617	2,501	10,151	18,269
1910	2,709	7,363	36,248	46,420	12,929	3,148	41,356	57,433
1920	2,363	3,090	28,812	34,265	17,387	4,151	71,952	93,490
1930	2,195	2,075	37,361	41,631	17,837	4,958	97,456	120,251

Data from the United States Census

CHART I

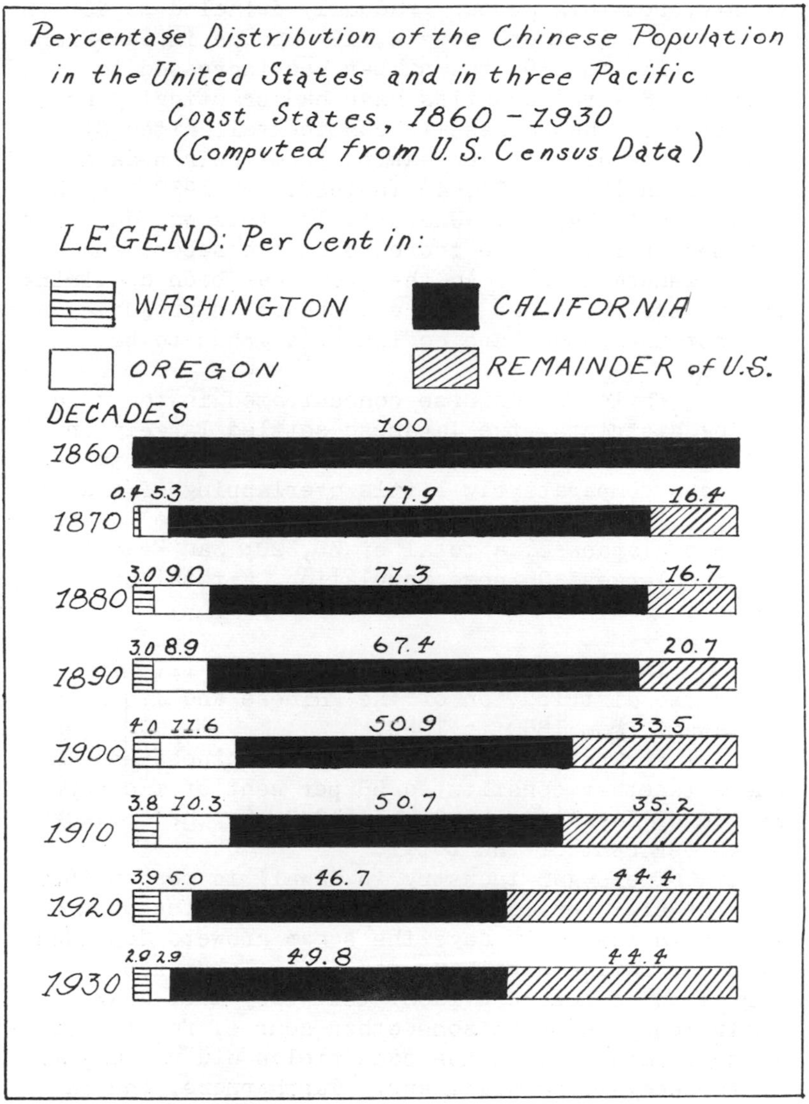

Percentage Distribution of the Chinese Population
in the United States and in three Pacific
Coast States, 1860 – 1930
(Computed from U. S. Census Data)

LEGEND: Per Cent in:

| | WASHINGTON | | CALIFORNIA |
| | OREGON | | REMAINDER of U.S. |

DECADES

1860   100

1870   0.4 5.3   77.9   16.4

1880   3.0 9.0   71.3   16.7

1890   3.0 8.9   67.4   20.7

1900   4.0 11.6   50.9   33.5

1910   3.8 10.3   50.7   35.2

1920   3.9 5.0   46.7   44.4

1930   2.9 2.9   49.8   44.4

gradually dispersed. In 1860 the 2,392 Chinese made
up 22.1 per cent of the total population of Placer
County, but this number gradually dwindled to 405 in
1930. In 1860 there were 2,719 Chinese in San Francisco while in 1890 the number had increased to
25,833. Several counties have had practically no
Orientals. The Chinese in continental United States
have been gradually decreasing from their peak at
107,488 in 1890 to 61,649 in 1920. In 1930 they had
increased to 74,954. Undoubtedly, this was due, for
the most part, to the increase in the second and
third generations.[3] As the group has been declining
in numbers there has been a decrease in prejudice
against them; they are no longer a group to be
feared.

     While the Chinese concentrated in the gold-
mining districts, the Japanese settled largely in
the agricultural areas, with the result that there
has been comparatively little overlapping of the two
groups. In 1930 Los Angeles County had the largest
group of Japanese, a total of 35,390; San Francisco
had the largest Chinese population, a total of
16,303.

     In the Hawaiian Islands. Table III pre-
sents the distribution of the Chinese and Japanese
in Hawaii from 1860 to 1930.

     According to Table III, the Chinese and Jap-
anese together constituted 56 per cent of the population of Hawaii in 1900. In 1930 they had receded
to 45 per cent of the total.

     The sugar industry in Hawaii is responsible
for the high percentage of Orientals in the population. In the early days the sugar growers depended
upon the native Hawaiians for their labor supply.
Very soon it became evident that they must draw
their man power from some other source, for the continuous hard work in the cane fields did not appeal
to the easy-going Hawaiians. Furthermore, the Hawaiians were not sufficient in numbers to supply the

demand. Attempts were made to secure South Sea Is-
landers as well as Europeans but with limited success, except for a considerable number of Portuguese. After exploring various possibilities and
trying several experiments, the Orient was found to
offer the best solution to the labor problem.

Chinese and Japanese came in large numbers
to work on the sugar plantations, but for a number
of years they have been dwindling. In 1897 the
Chinese were at their peak with 8,114, but in 1934
there were only 618 of their men left on the plantations. The peak year of the Japanese was in 1908
with 32,771, but in 1930 their numbers had been reduced to 8,956 men. From this point the Japanese

Table III

CHINESE AND JAPANESE IN HAWAII COMPARED WITH
THE TOTAL POPULATION, BY NUMBER AND BY PER
CENT, 1860-1930

Year	Chinese	Japanese	Total Orientals	Total Population	Per Cent of Total Population
1860	600	---	600	69,800	00.86
1872	2,038	---	2,038	56,897	03.58
1884	18,254	116	18,370	80,578	22.80
1890	16,752	12,610	29,362	89,990	32.63
1900	25,767	61,111	86,878	154,001	56.41
1910	21,674	79,675	101,349	191,909	52.81
1920	23,507	109,274	132,781	255,912	51.89
1930	27,179	139,631	166,810	368,336	45.29
1936	27,495	149,886	177,381	393,277	45.10

Data for 1860-1890 from Romanzo Adams, The Peoples of Hawaii, pp. 7-8; for 1900-
1930 from the United States Census; for June 30, 1936, from Annual Report of the
Governor of Hawaii, 1936, p. 31.

gradually increased until they reached 10,717 in
1934. This was due to an increase in the number of
American-born workers. In 1905 the Koreans had
4,946, but in 1932 only 442 of their men were in the
sugar industry.[4] The Koreans likewise increased to
522 in 1934.

Composition of Population and Race Relations. Numbers and the composition of a population
as to race or ancestry are important factors affecting race relations. In the areas where the oriental
groups have been highly concentrated, intense prejudices have developed. There is little prejudice
where the Orientals are too few to enter into active
competition with the Whites. They may, to be sure,
be present in large numbers without prejudice being
directed against them, provided they enter into a
relationship of mutualism whereby they perform the
unattractive labor that is avoided by the dominant
group.[5] If the intruding group is large and does
not accept without question a position of inferiority, resentment tends to arise.[6]

An examination of the census figures shows
that the population of Hawaii is more heterogeneous
than that of the Pacific Coast and the white or
Caucasian group is in the minority. On the Pacific
Coast in 1920 the white group constituted more than
95 per cent of the total population. The Indian
group, which has been small and segregated in areas
where it in no way comes into direct competition
with the Whites, may be dropped from the picture so
far as race relationships are concerned. The Negro
group has been increasing and in recent years has
received some attention. Since the Chinese and Japanese have been the largest non-white groups, it has
been easy to focus attention upon them. Probably
the fact that there are several different ancestral
groups in Hawaii instead of two has been a distinct
advantage; it has not been easy to single out·any
one group for attack.

Sex Distribution. The sex distribution of a
group is a factor of considerable social significance.
Chart II, presenting the sex distribution, shows
that the proportion of males, particularly among the
Chinese, is exceedingly high but is gradually approaching an equilibrium.[7] Deaths among the older

CHART II

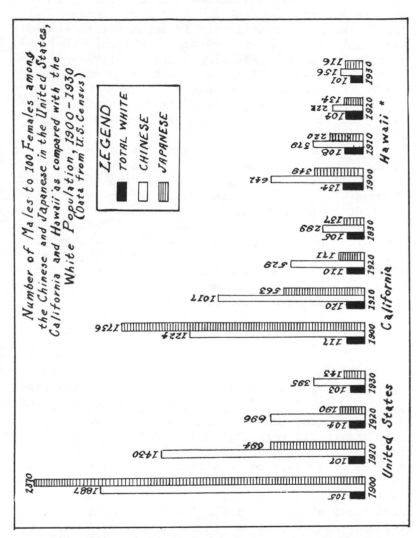

*The Portuguese are selected as a basis of comparison for Hawaii because they are more normally distributed as to the sexes. Since the "Other Caucasian" group contains a large number of men in the army and navy, it is not a good basis. In 1900 "Caucasian" is used. This included Portuguese, Anglo-Saxon, and Spanish. The army group at that time was comparatively small.

Chinese immigrants and the return to China of a number are tending to equalize the sexes. Another factor, however, is retarding this trend toward a balance between the sexes. A number of Chinese males,
born in China but possessing American citizenship because their reputed fathers were born in the United
States, are entering the country in spite of the exclusion laws. Among the Japanese the imbalance between the sexes is gradually giving way to a normal
distribution.

        The excess of males among the Chinese has,
without doubt, had its effect upon race relationships. It has been responsible for some of the bitterness against the dominant white group and has also affected the behavior of the Chinese in ways that
have given them unfavorable publicity.[8] Because of
the larger proportion of women among the Japanese,
they have been able to live more normally. In Hawaii the sexes have been more nearly balanced and
this, doubtless, has had a bearing on the better relations which have prevailed there.

        Marital Conditions. Closely related to the
sex distribution is the marital condition of a population. According to the 1920 census, 24,782 Chinese males fifteen years old and over in continental
United States were married, but there were only
3,046 married females in the same age group. In the
earlier decades the disparity was even greater. In
1930 the totals were 23,868 and 5,574 which indicates a trend toward a better balance. A few Chinese men have married outside their own groups, but
that number is comparatively small. The conclusion
is inevitable that a large number of the men have
kept their wives in China. The Japanese have maintained a better balance; in 1920 there were 31,250
married males to 22,193 married females. In 1930
the figures were 29,401 males and 23,930 females in
this same group.

        In Hawaii there is a better balance. In

1930 there were 5,037 married Chinese males fifteen years of age and over and 3,212 married females in the same age group. In 1920 there were 5,460 married males and 2,416 married females. In 1910 there were 5,674 married males and 1,555 married females. In the early decades, when there was a wide disparity, a considerable number of the men had wives in China. Because wives of their own kind were not to be had, a few hundred Chinese immigrants married non-Chinese women, the majority of whom were Hawaiian and part-Hawaiian.[9]

The Japanese in Hawaii have maintained a better balance than the Chinese. In 1910 there were 19,746 married Japanese males fifteen years of age and over and 13,968 married females in the same age group. In 1920 there were 25,279 married males and 22,373 married females. In 1930 the figures were 24,415 males and 23,257 females. Prior to the passage of the Immigration Law of 1924, the Japanese could secure wives from their own country with a minimum of difficulty. Because of this situation there have been comparatively few outmarriages among the Japanese of Hawaii.

Because of the disparity between the sexes a considerable number of American-born women have married immigrant men much older than themselves. This has brought a problem to the citizen-born men, particularly among the Chinese; it has reduced the number of potential wives. Furthermore, the disparity of the sexes has been accentuated because many Chinese men have brought their sons to America, while they have left their daughters with their wives in China. Some few married outside; that, however, is no easy matter, particularly on the Pacific Coast, because of prejudice. Restrictive legislation has made the condition all the more acute; alien women may not be brought from the Orient and several states prohibit intermarriage with the Whites. This situation practically forces a number of men into a celibate life. The Chinese-American

Citizens' Alliance has made efforts to have the Immigration Law of 1924 amended to permit American
citizens of Chinese ancestry to bring alien wives
from China.[10] In February, 1926, February, 1928, and
March, 1930, spokesmen for the Chinese-Americans
presented their case to the Congressional Committee
on Immigration and Naturalization.

Among the Japanese, the situation is less
acute. Since the immigrant Japanese brought wives
in large numbers, the young men are more favorably
situated with reference to marriage than the young
Chinese. Since the Japanese immigration to Hawaii
began much earlier than to the Coast, the wives had
been coming for a longer period. The group in Hawaii is older and more of the native-born girls have
reached the marriageable age. Because of the relatively large number of women in Hawaii a number of
men on the Coast are looking to the Territory for
wives. Advertisements appear in the Honolulu newspapers from time to time from men on the Coast. It
is no easy problem to solve, however, for the Hawaiian-born girls are not greatly interested in going to the Coast as picture brides.

Age Distribution. The age distribution of a
population is an important factor. The situation in
California is presented by Table IV.

Age distribution has a direct bearing upon
race relationships. An examination of the census
data reveals the fact that the Chinese group for
some time was coming to be more and more one of men
above middle age. According to Table IV, the percentage of Chinese above forty-five in 1920 was
much larger than that of the total population. As
this group has advanced in age, there has been a
progressive withdrawal from active competition with
the white group and there has been a corresponding
decline in ill-feeling. The figures for 1930 indicate that the age distribution of the Chinese group
is now practically identical with that of the total

Table IV

AGE DISTRIBUTION OF THE CHINESE AND JAPANESE
COMPARED WITH THE TOTAL POPULATION OF CALI-
FORNIA BY PER CENT, 1920, 1930

Age Period	Per Cent Distribution					
	Chinese		Japanese		Total Population	
	1920	1930	1920	1930	1920	1930
Under 5 years	5.7	8.9	18.3	12.9	8.0	7.1
5-9 years	5.1	9.2	7.6	17.2	8.2	8.2
10-14 years	4.0	6.2	2.6	11.0	7.6	7.5
15-19 years	5.2	7.4	3.9	5.8	7.1	7.6
20-44 years	35.7	42.0	55.6	33.8	42.6	42.0
45 and over	43.9	24.2	11.8	19.2	26.2	27.3

Data from the United States Census

population. Because of the scarcity of Chinese
women, the increase by births has been small and
there has been no need for propaganda to restrict
the group further. In the Japanese group the percentage of children under five years of age was unusually high in 1920 and that particular age group
figured prominently when the agitation for exclusion
was at its height. The birth-rate was high because
a considerable number of women of child-bearing age
had arrived from Japan within the preceding decade.
Propagandists seized upon this as conclusive proof
that it was only a matter of time until the white
people would be crowded out of California.[11] "Here
was an oriental invasion from within which might
overwhelm the white supremacy of the Pacific Coast,
for these California-born Japanese children were
citizens by birthright, regardless of the fact that
their parents could not be naturalized."[12]

The age distribution for Hawaii as presented
in Table V is more nearly normal, and this is undoubtedly one factor in the better relationships
which prevail in the Territory.

Factors in Race Relations. The Census figures on distribution and concentration and on sex
and marital status of the Orientals, however, do not
tell the whole story with reference to race relationships. It is necessary to analyze and compare other

Table V

AGE DISTRIBUTION OF THE CHINESE AND JAPANESE COMPARED
WITH THE PORTUGUESE* IN HAWAII BY PER CENT, 1920, 1930

| Age Period | Per Cent Distribution | | | | | |
| | Chinese | | Japanese | | Portuguese* | |
	1920	1930	1920	1930	1920	1930
Under 5 years	12.2	12.4	17.2	15.6	17.6	12.0
5-9 years	10.7	13.1	12.4	16.7	15.8	13.4
10-14 years	8.4	11.4	7.9	13.3	13.2	13.8
15-19 years	8.1	9.5	7.2	9.4	11.1	12.4
20-44 years	27.6	29.3	40.7	28.0	30.6	35.1
45 and over	33.0	24.4	14.7	17.1	11.8	13.5

* The Portuguese group is chosen as a basis of comparison
because it is the most nearly normal as to age distribution.
The "Other Caucasian" group includes a large number of men in
military and naval service and is not normal. The total population does not provide a suitable basis because of the large
number of Filipino men who are working on the plantations. The
large number of Chinese and Japanese in the total population
also produce a wide deflection from a normal age distribution.

Data from the United States Census

factors in the different areas in order to understand the differences. The fact that there has been
so little feeling or prejudice against the Orientals
in Hawaii is doubtless due, in considerable measure,
to the absence of a class of poor whites in direct
competition with the Orientals. In a measure, the
Portuguese are comparable to the poor whites in such
places as South Africa and the West Indies. The
Portuguese, who are classified as Caucasians but not
ordinarily considered as Haole, are in more direct
competition with the Orientals than are the Haoles.
Since they came to the plantations as contract laborers and have not as yet risen to a position where
they may ignore the Orientals, they give evidence of
more feeling against the Orientals than do the
Haoles. This prejudice has not yet been highly developed, probably because the Portuguese are not of
American stock and have but recently come from the
plantation. The sugar planters are not in competition with the Orientals. Moreover, there is as yet
no active competition between the children of oriental immigrants and those of the Haoles. In California, the Japanese have competed with the small,
independent white farmers and have aroused their ill
will. In Hawaii, where the large plantation system
is in operation, there is no opportunity to compete
with the white planters. In the Islands there has
been no competition between oriental and white laborers, but in many places on the Pacific Coast there
has been competition in the labor market; this has
led to serious conflict situations, for instance, in
the fruit and melon areas of California and the lum-
ber regions of the northwest coast. There has been,
and still is, a certain amount of competition in the
small businesses and in the skilled occupations in
Hawaii.[13] One observer, who has spent a number of
years in Hawaii, is of the opinion that prejudice is
on the increase, due to the keener competition of
the Orientals as they become better educated and
more Americanized. [14]

The New England missionary element has been
an important factor in race relationships in Hawaii.
The sugar industry is largely controlled by the descendants of the old missionaries, and, even though
they are interested in dividends, they appear to be
more humanitarian than many captains of industry on
the mainland. Over against this Puritan leaven in
Hawaii was the Irish influence in the early days of
California. The early history of California indicates that a large number of restless, discontented,
adventurous Irish rushed into the gold fields in
1849 and shortly thereafter. They were recent immigrants from Ireland and came with many hatreds and
complexes which were soon directed against the Chinese. They were leaders in the anti-Chinese agitation and have been prominent ever since in the anti-
Asiatic movement.

Of all influences in Hawaii, probably the
native Hawaiians have been the most potent; they
have served as a catalytic agent in the laboratory
of race relationships. According to Dr. Palmer:

> In explanation of this happy situation, it must al-
> ways be remembered that the basic race, the Hawaiian, though
> brown of skin, was royal in rank. The Hawaiian has never been
> a slave. He gave the Islands their kings and queens and has
> no sense of racial inferiority because of the color of his
> skin. Consequently, when other brown-skinned peoples came,
> they found no predetermined social prejudice already estab-
> lished against them. They were received on their own merits
> and had to start with no advance handicap of racial antipathy.[15]

Furthermore, the multiplicity of races in
Hawaii has been a factor of no small significance.
In the early days of California, the Chinese were
the outstanding group of different race. Hence it
was easy to focus the attack upon one single point.
Later the Japanese were the target. In Hawaii the
several races and race mixtures have made it impossible to direct any concerted attack upon any single
group.[16]

B. The American-Born Group

To give the American-born citizens of oriental ancestry their proper setting against this background, certain statistical data relative to them will be presented at this point. These figures aid in understanding the problems they have to face in making adjustments to life in America.

Total American-Born Group. Table VI gives the totals for the American-born Chinese and Japanese by decades since 1890.

Table VI

AMERICAN-BORN CHINESE AND JAPANESE IN THE UNITED STATES, 1890-1930

Continental United States

	1890	1900	1910	1920	1930
Chinese	2,930	9,010	14,935	18,532	30,868
Japanese	118	269	4,502	29,672	68,357

Hawaii

	1890	1900	1910	1920	1930
Chinese		4,021	7,195	12,342	19,711
Japanese	1,701*	8,881	19,889	48,586	91,185
Totals	4,749	22,181	46,521	109,132	210,121

*The American-born group was not segregated into Chinese and Japanese in the census of 1890.

Data from the United States Census

Table VI shows that in 1930 there were 99,225 American-born Chinese and Japanese in continental United States and 110,896 in Hawaii, a total of 210,121. In 1890 the total was 4,749.

Third-Generation Group. There is now a considerable group of native-born of native parentage.
Since the Chinese came to America earlier than the
Japanese, there are more American-born Chinese in
the higher age-groups. In Hawaii there could be a
few native-born Chinese eighty-four years old in
1937. Because of this, the third-generation group
is much larger among the Chinese than among the Japanese. Those of the third generation tend to be
farther removed from the immigrant group and are on
the whole more thoroughly occidentalized.[17] The data
for this group are presented in Table VII.

Table VII

NATIVE-BORN CHINESE AND JAPANESE WITH NATIVE-BORN
PARENTS IN THE UNITED STATES, 1900-1930

| | Continental United States | | Hawaii | | |
	Chinese	Japanese	Chinese	Japanese	Total
1900	245	32	---*	---	277
1910	738	44	237	29	1,048
1920	2,391	212	1,303	326	4,232
1930	4,325	839	4,582	4,289	14,035

*The Hawaiian data are not available by groups for 1900.

Data from the United States Census.

Intermediate Group. There is another group
of considerable size which is midway between, namely
the native born of mixed parentage who have one
foreign-born parent. Table VIII sets forth the figures for this group.

Position of American-Born Group. Chart III shows what percentage the American-born Chinese and Japanese are of the total for each of these groups. An examination of this chart shows that the percentage of the native-born Chinese group was in 1890 only 3.3 per cent of the total in continental United States, while in 1930 it was 41.2 per cent. The Japanese increase has been more rapid in the same period. In Hawaii the native-born have formed a larger percentage in both groups than in the United States proper, due to the higher percentage of women of child-bearing age in Hawaii. Chart III shows clearly that the older generation is gradually receding from the picture while the native-born generation is coming more and more into prominence.

Table VIII

NATIVE-BORN CHINESE AND JAPANESE WITH ONE FOREIGN-BORN PARENT IN THE UNITED STATES, 1900-1930

	Continental United States		Hawaii		
	Chinese	Japanese	Chinese	Japanese	Total
1900	1,003	33	---*	---	1,036
1910	2,121	145	839	96	3,201
1920	4,189	512	2,710	1,513	4,735
1930	8,409	2,481	5,252	9,950	17,683

*The Hawaiian data are not available by groups for 1900.

Data from the United States Census.

The American-born generation is a complicating factor in race relationships. The Chinese and Japanese immigrants to America have been given a status of inferiority and have been required to do the drudgery. Because of differences in language

and cultural background, comparatively few of the
immigrant generation have been able to rise very far.
But the second generation is coming to be rather
thoroughly Americanized, ambitious, and desirous of
acquiring a status superior to that held by their
parents; they are not following in the footsteps of
the older generation. The dominant white group, in
large measure, is unwilling to accede to the demands
of this younger group which has the inescapable
racial marks of the older generation. As these ambitious and hopeful young Americans endeavor to make
a place for themselves, what will be the outcome?
Will they become assimilated and gradually become
lost in the American group or will they become a
sort of racial caste, in American but not of
America?[18]

CHART III

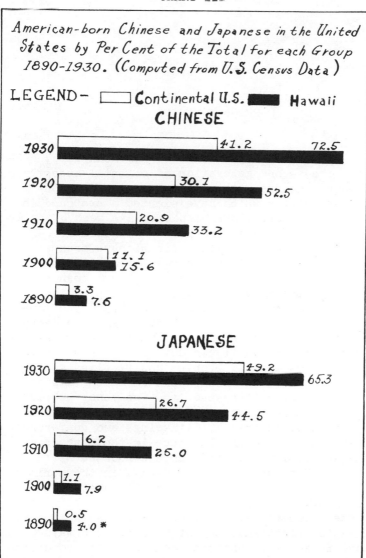

American-born Chinese and Japanese in the United States by Per Cent of the Total for each Group 1890-1930. (Computed from U.S. Census Data)

LEGEND— ☐ Continental U.S. ■ Hawaii

CHINESE

1930 — 41.2 — 72.5
1920 — 30.1 — 52.5
1910 — 20.9 — 33.2
1900 — 11.1 — 15.6
1890 — 3.3 — 7.6

JAPANESE

1930 — 49.2 — 65.3
1920 — 26.7 — 44.5
1910 — 6.2 — 25.0
1900 — 1.1 — 7.9
1890 — 0.5 — 4.0 *

*Estimate. In 1890 the American-born group in Hawaii was not segregated into Chinese and Japanese.

Chapter IV

THE AGRICULTURAL SITUATION IN HAWAII
PRIOR TO 1932[1]

In making adjustments to American life, members of the second generation of oriental ancestry have made contacts with a number of institutionalized activities which have exerted a profound influence upon them. These impacts have been of prime importance in their occupational adjustments.

The vocational situation with reference to agriculture in Hawaii has changed greatly within the past few years. In fact, the change has been so marked that the year 1932 may be considered the close of an epoch in the industrial history of the Territory. In keeping with this, we shall endeavor to describe the agricultural situation as it was prior to 1932 and as it has developed since then.

The vocational problem has received considerable attention. Newspapers in editorials and news columns have discussed it. The young people have had certain organizations in which this has been the major interest. Gatherings and conferences have assigned considerable space in their programs to the subject. In a conference conducted by the Y.M.C.A. of the University of Hawaii in the spring of 1928, the men were asked to submit questions for discussion. The majority submitted had a bearing upon the occupational problem.[2] Since sugar production is the basic industry of Hawaii, it always finds a place in such discussions. In fact, the vocational problems of the younger generation cannot possibly be understood apart from it.

Working Conditions on the Plantations. The
majority of the oriental laborers who migrated to
Hawaii prior to the annexation, came under an en-
forceable-contract system. That conditions were not
entirely satisfactory under the contractual relationship may be assumed from the fact that thousands
of Japanese on the island of Oahu marched into Honolulu immediately after the archipelago had been annexed to the United States. The majority returned
to the plantations, but they went as free persons;
the enforceable labor contracts adopted under the
monarchy became invalid. Labor conditions were improved; annexation brought the Islands under the
Chinese Exclusion Act, thereby cutting off a labor
supply. At the same time the sugar industry was
stimulated as it came under the American protective
tariff.[3] The following statement by a Japanese college boy in Hawaii, even though somewhat dramatic,
gives an idea of the feeling of release when the
contract expired. Since this boy was born after the
annexation and knew nothing of the conditions existing prior to 1898, it may be assumed that the feeling toward the contract system had been of sufficient importance to be handed down as one of the important experiences of the family and had been portrayed quite vividly to him.

Thirty-five years ago a company of ambitious young
men and women bade farewell to their kindred and sailed from
the port of Kobe, Japan. After a tedious journey of over a
month, they reached Hawaii, a land destined to become their
adopted home. Soon after landing, they were driven to a little plantation village where they were put to work for three
years. This period was more than sufficient to break down
these young people, both physically and spiritually. Quar-
tered in crude shacks, they labored day after day like mules.
Early in the morning when the stars were still visible they
packed their implements and went into the yet uncultivated
land to remove stones and stumps. All day long they toiled
under the hot tropic sky and when the sun hid behind the

heights of Mauna Kea their weary legs carried their exhausted
bodies homeward. Life was dull and monotonous to these pioneers of the Hawaiian sugar industry; their only consolation
was to receive their pay of twelve dollars at the end of each
month. Many of them intended to escape from this miserable
bondage, but the iron hands of the plantation were over them.
Totally betrayed in all their expectations, they were compelled
to dramatize the life of the slaves during the days of Lincoln.
Yet nature was sympathetic toward these unfortunate victims of
the cold-blooded plantation system, and then came the day when
the contract expired--a day, perhaps more memorable to them
than January 1, 1863, when the Emancipation Proclamation was
issued. Free from all restraints, they chose their own
courses. Many who had saved enough money, immediately returned to their motherland. Still a large number decided to
remain and acquire a sufficiently large fortune which would
enable them to spend their old age in leisure in Japan.[4]

   Remuneration on the Plantations. There has
been considerable discussion of the low wages paid
on the plantations, but often an erroneous impression has been given when the basic wage has been referred to as if that were the total wage. There is
a basic wage of one dollar per day guaranteed to all
workers. In addition to this, all day laborers who
have worked twenty-three days or more in a month receive a bonus of ten per cent. There is also an additional bonus on a sliding scale when the raw sugar
price for the month averages five cents per pound or
more. According to the Hawaiian Sugar Planters' Association, about ninety-five per cent of all the day
workers perform their duties under some form of contract, which is in reality a piece-work system. In
this way they are enabled to earn two or three times
the basic wage.[5] Furthermore, the sugar planters
guarantee work throughout the entire year. In addition to the wages, the plantations provide free
housing, free water, free fuel, and free medical attention for the worker and his family. Nurseries,
kindergartens, and recreation facilities are also

provided free of charge by some. In many places
milk is supplied at a price below that of the commercial dairies. "Staple foods and the necessities
of life are sold to employees at cost by the plantation stores. In most of these stores not even the
overhead expense is figured into the price. Articles in the general stock which do not come within
the necessity class are sold at normal prices."[6]
The workers are not obliged to buy from the company
stores. In all plantation towns, independent deal-
ers are permitted to compete for trade. Doubtless's,
the dissatisfaction is increased when the Orientals
read the newspaper reports giving the profits of the
plantations. Early in 1928 a Japanese newspaper
carried the headline, "Twenty-Three Plantations'
Profits Amount to Ten Millions." The news article
under this heading gave a list of plantations taken
from the Manual of Hawaiian Securities which showed
percentages of profit ranging from 1.5 to 33.0 per
cent. While it would require an expert accountant
to analyze and interpret the figures, they do not
seek such analyses but draw their own conclusions.
Furthermore, they have ample opportunity to observe
the unequal distribution of income between the management and the laborers.

Probably many Orientals, as well as others,
are unreasonable in their demands. It may be impossible to grant all they ask, for certain plantations in the Territory have been operated at a loss.
Hawaii is not well adapted to sugar production and
the producers must carry on their operations under
great handicaps.[7] The land areas are limited and
much is rocky and uneven. This necessitates large
expenditures in placing the soil under cultivation.
Inadequate rainfall in certain areas has necessitated
the construction of expensive irrigation systems.[8]
According to the Governor's Report for 1927,[9] the
approximate investment in irrigation equipment--
ditches, wells, pumps, and power plants for the
Territory reached a total of $28,499,000.[10] It is

not the geographical and climatic conditions, but
the Republican party with its protective tariff
which has been the determinative factor.[11] This entire situation reacts upon the sugar-men and makes
them uneasy; it places serious limitations upon what
they may do with reference to the wage problem.[12]

    Control of the Sugar Industry. The sugar
industry of Hawaii is controlled from the top; it is
an autocratic and paternalistic organization which
has in no way been touched by the idea of "democracy in industry."[13] This system has developed unrest
and dissatisfaction in the workers from the Orient.
According to an editorial in a Japanese newspaper,

        Hawaii is built upon an antiquated economic system
within a modern government. She is cursed with coolieism in
a twentieth century democracy. . . . A small group of experts,
controlled by a smaller group of capitalists, directs the
great mass of coolie laborers, who, for the sake of verbal
gentility, are called "plantation workers." And there is not
much room for the substantial middle class people in between. . . . For the mass of the people, it is either enlist-
ment, if they are fortunate, into the small group of experts,
or degeneration into the big field of plantation labor. The
capitalists being Americans. . . . naturally give their preference of better jobs to the whites, leaving the mass labor
for the other races.[14]

    Resulting Disappointments. Many Orientals
had come to Hawaii with the idea that America was a
land of golden opportunity. But in all too many instances the actuality did not measure up to the
ideal and bitter disappointment was in store for
them. One of the heaviest crosses to bear was the
loss of status. In the Orient, and particularly in
Japan, social distinctions are quite marked. In the
Orient, the wage worker is assigned a low status,
while the person who owns and tills his own soil has
a much higher standing.[15] When those who had

standing in the Orient came to Hawaii and were assigned the lowest position in the social scale--that
of the common laborer on the plantations--they reacted against this. If the economic situation had
measured up to their expectations, making possible a
return to the Orient to enhance their social status,
they doubtless would have endured a distasteful condition temporarily.

A. Factors Turning the Second Generation Away from the Sugar Industry

Attitude and Advice of Parents. Several factors have conspired to turn the American-born generation of oriental ancestry away from the sugar
plantations. The hopes of many parents were blasted
and they developed an antagonistic attitude against
the entire system. This feeling they conveyed to
their children in no uncertain terms. In Hawaii
some think that it is possible to deal with the second generation without considering the experiences
of their parents on the plantations. But these memories and vicarious experiences, handed down by the
parental group, are a part of the social heritage
which must be considered; it is absolutely necessary
to consider the total situation to which they respond.

Furthermore, many parents have definitely
advised their children to leave the sugar plantations. A Japanese college girl said that her father
called her to his death bed and advised her to be
somebody other than an ordinary person working in
the cane fields. It was then and there she decided
to become a teacher. Many parents have been willing to make great sacrifices for their children,
provided they would turn their backs upon the plantation. Some parents have not only advised but
have adopted certain devices in order to develop attitudes antagonistic to the sugar plantations in

their children. The following document shows the
method adopted by one Japanese.

>Father made up his mind to send his children to school
>so far as he possibly could. Yet he had no idea of forcing us.
>Instead he employed different methods which made us want to go
>to school. We were made to work in the cane fields at a very
>early age. Every Saturday father would wait for us to return
>from the Japanese School and would take us to the field. We
>believed, at that time, that he was not very kind--our neigh-
>bors always did the hard work and the children the easiest
>part, while we had to go through the whole process. Brother
>was made to stand behind the plow as soon as he was tall
>enough to guide the implement. After a day's work in the
>fields dad used to ask: "Are you tired? Would you want to
>work in the fields when you are old enough to leave school?
>You can earn about fifty cents for what you did today. Per-
>haps in years to come you will be earning one dollar a day."
>Sometimes he used to say, "Isn't Miss Kojima (one of the pio-
>neers in the teaching profession) lucky? She works from nine
>to two and gets eighty dollars per month. Her Saturdays and
>Sundays are free. She needs never complain about soiled hands
>and scratched arms." He sent me to work as a housemaid one
>summer and this experience made me dislike such employment.
>In fact, my father did everything in his power to make us
>realize that going to school would be to our advantage.[16]

Democratic Ideas of the Schools. The
schools of Hawaii have been an important factor in
turning the youth away from the basic industry. The
schools, in considerable measure, have placed emphasis upon an idealistic democracy. When the pupils
have left the schools to make places for themselves
in the industrial life of the community, they have
come face to face with an autocratic regime in
which democratic ideas are a misfit.[17]

White Attitude toward Manual Labor. The attitude of the white people toward manual labor in
Hawaii is an important element in the situation.

They sneer at a white man who does anything with his
hands. This is strikingly set forth by a white
teacher in the Territory.

When I was principal of the high school, we carried
on some school gardening. But vegetables will not grow merely on water--they need fertilizer. Since we had no lawn mower
for the school yard, I would let horses come in to crop the
grass and in the morning we would gather the fertilizer they
left. One day I attended a committee meeting which was making
plans for a county fair. Senator_____ was there and in the
midst of the deliberations turned to me and said, "Of course
you'll be there with the horse dung!" He looked down on me
because I gathered that fertilizer for our school garden. Much
is said in Hawaii about the unwillingness of the young Orientals to do manual labor. Many of the Whites blame the young
people and blame the schools in part, but they forget about
their own attitudes.[18]

There are many salesmen in Honolulu on low salaries
who look down on manual work of any kind. One young clerk, at
the end of his day, went to a store to buy a pair of shoes to
be worn at a dance that evening. He asked to have them delivered, but was told that it was too late to make a delivery.
Nevertheless he insisted that they be sent; he was too proud
to carry a parcel like that on the car. There are men in this
city who would not be seen carrying home a loaf of bread on
the street car. There are even school principals in the Territory who will not carry anything into the school buildings.
They will drive to school and then have pupils carry their
parcels, for which they pay them. What may one expect from
the young Orientals when the leaders in the white community
betray such an attitude![19]

Many white people indoctrinate their children
quite early with the idea that manual labor should
be avoided. This is disclosed by a public-school
teacher.

The Caucasians progressed in their school work because

they had a better understanding of the language. They felt
superior to the others and did not wish to clean the erasers,
boards or room; they disliked the idea of pulling weeds or
cleaning the school yard. I received many notes from mothers
saying that they did not send their children to school to
sweep the floors or clean erasers, or worst of all to clean
the yard. In the worst case I had, I first answered the notes
verbally. I talked to the boy and tried to make him realize
that it was only one of his school duties to help keep the
room tidy and clean and at that special time, to keep our section of the yard free of stones and weeds. He couldn't see it
at all and his mother couldn't see it either. One day the
mother came to see me. She was going to see that I was dis-
missed. After a long and heated argument, I asked her, "Are
you an American?" "Of course I am," was the emphatic reply.
"Well, you are the narrowest-minded American I have ever seen,"
I answered. That ended it all. The woman never spoke another
word but in a few minutes turned and went home. Her son continued to do everything the other pupils did--even to pulling
weeds. Nothing more was said about it.[20]

The children of immigrants, no matter what
their origin, are eager to cast off the heritages of
their parents and take on everything American. The
white people are accepted as Americans par ex-
cellence--the patterns to be followed. But these
white models do not work in the cane fields. Why,
then, should the sons of Orientals jeopardize their
Americanism by doing such work?

B. Movement to Attract Youth to
the Plantations

Propaganda. A considerable amount of propaganda has been carried on and many things have been
done in an attempt to attract the young people to
the plantations. Some propagandists have been optimistic about their movement, but many of the youth
of oriental ancestry have sneered at it. Governor

Farrington used his influence to create an interest
in agriculture. But not even the eloquent words of
the Chief Executive could change their attitude. On
August 6, 1928, the Governor delivered an address at
a session of the Territorial Conference of Social
Workers in which he stressed the necessity of directing the youth back to agriculture. This was followed
by a discussion when a young Chinese said: "You
cannot force the oriental youth with a high school
education to go back to the plantations; he will not
do it. We realize that our parents started on the
plantations, but you cannot expect us to go back. I
am an Oriental and I am speaking from the standpoint
of the Oriental who has been educated." Many of the
younger generation have spoken emphatically on this
subject. The following letter from a Japanese was
refused publication by one of the American daily
papers, but was published in a Japanese daily in
Honolulu. The letter is self-explanatory.

Will you kindly allow me space in your paper to answer a statement made at a recent meeting of the Conference of
New Americans held in Honolulu? One of the speakers, a well-
known and prominent member of the community and a Caucasian,
in the course of an address to these young American citizens
of Japanese ancestry, declared that many a good American plantation worker had been spoiled to make a poor dentist, or
words to that effect. The speaker implied, and was so understood by his audience, that the younger generation of Japanese
should be content to work on the plantations as their fathers
had worked, and that any effort to raise their status to that
of the professional class was a mistaken effort because they
are incapable of making good as dentists, doctors, or in similar lines of work.

I am a dentist myself; one of the younger generation
of American citizens of Japanese ancestry against whom this
attack was made, and in common with hundreds of others in my
class I deeply resent the unjust and insulting charge that I
am unfit for this kind of work and would make a better

plantation laborer than I do a dentist. . . . We do not look
down upon labor as degrading, for it has been by honest and
faithful labor well performed that our parents have built up
the great industries of Hawaii. And in the doing of their
work they have laid the foundations for our work, which comes
after them. We would be going backward if we did not strive
to better our condition in life and help to realize the driv-
ing purpose that spurred our parents on to greater effort in
our behalf.

        The wealthy Caucasians who own the big industries of
Hawaii can appreciate and understand the sentiments that moved
the lowly laborers to urge their children on to greater efforts, for they themselves have the same regard for their children, sending them to universities and to foreign countries to
complete their education, expecting them to carry on and to
improve upon the work of their fathers. How can they then
have the heart to discourage the young Orientals, who are trying their best to live up to their responsibilities as American citizens and to be worthy of the trust placed in them by
their parents? . . . .

        I have had no trouble in making good as a dentist.
In fact I am sure I make a better showing as a dentist than I
would make as a plantation laborer. And the same is true of
my professional associates. There is still plenty of room for
more, not only in this profession but in many others. And if
the authorities would weed out those who are practicing without a license and without a proper education and training
there would be room for still more. The young Americans of
Japanese ancestry have a long way to go yet before they over-
crowd the professions, for the Japanese form one of the largest groups in the Territory, and they are still far short of
their quota in the professions.

        The plantations cannot expect to attract the young
people until they can offer them as great advantages as are
now offered in the professions and in commercial lines. If
they had a gold mine of opportunities there, as some of the
enthusiastic propagandists would lead us to believe, they

would not have to launch an intensive advertising campaign. . . .

I readily concede that conditions on the plantations are better than they used to be. But they are not good enough to form an inducement to young Americans. My friends can not under any circumstances be content to compete with the cheap labor that is imported every month from the Orient, and they would not be content to replace this labor even at a considerably higher wage, unless there was an opportunity for continued advancement, with plenty of room at the top, and a real chance to work their way up to positions of trust and responsibility.

I am not an economist, and I do not pretend to know how this can be done. It is a problem that is up to the plantations to solve. But until they solve it satisfactorily there is no use in trying to drag the younger generation of Americans of Japanese ancestry back to plantation jobs, for they will not stand it.

To young men who are proficient in dentistry and in other professions, as well as those who have been well educated along commercial lines, the whole world is open and the field of opportunities is unlimited. While we prefer to stay in Hawaii and do our part toward building up the Territory, we are ready and equipped to go to any quarter of the globe where opportunity beckons, if there ever comes a time when the local field is overcrowded and there are no more opportunities here. As plantation laborers there would be no field open to us except the local labor field, where we would be chained to the soil like chattels.

I am proud of my American birth and citizenship because of the opportunities they bring me for self-development and for actual service to society. I have always been willing to do my part, and when the nation was calling upon its manhood to defend the flag, I was one of those who willingly gave my service to my country. I think I made a good soldier, just as I have made a good dentist. I have a right to resent being told that I am not fit for anything but a plantation laborer![22]

The Schools. In recent years the schools
have been making a serious attempt to interest pupils in agriculture and certain plantations have coöperated by letting out small acreages to boys on
contract. The movement, however, has not made any
great headway. [23] There has been little interest in
this movement chiefly because it has been an effort
to interest boys in agriculture, not as independent
farmers but as laborers.

The whole educational system, from kindergar-
ten through the university, has made no great impression. [24] The University of Hawaii has an agricultural course, but the registration has been comparatively light. Out of a total of 236 Japanese students in 1927-1928, only eighteen or 7.6 per cent
were registered in agriculture; out of 110 Chinese,
ten or 9.0 per cent were registered in this course.[25]
In the senior class of 1928, eight of a total of
ninety-three were registered in the agricultural
course.[26] In 1930-1931 the figures were as follows:
twenty-two or 6.0 per cent from a total of 365 Japanese, and six or 2.6 per cent from a group of 228
Chinese.

Conclusions. The conclusion is inevitable
that getting the younger generation back to the soil
is not a mere matter of developing certain skills;
it is a matter of developing attitudes, and that is
a far bigger problem. To be sure, conditions on the
plantations have improved greatly in recent years,
but many early experiences have made indelible impressions and have been important factors in shaping
attitudes toward the entire system. A considerable
number have begun to reflect upon the situation and
cannot be induced to return to the plantations unless great changes are made. It is very doubtful if
the Korean college boy, who wrote the following
statement, could be attracted to the cane fields so
long as these memories persist.

Among the Koreans in the camp, there were only five women. The daily routine was the same all the month through; there was no change in anything. The plantation's head foreman, or the big _luna_ as he is commonly called, and the camp boss who were of Caucasian race, were very rough and cruel fellows. They came to the camp every morning on horseback with their long snakelike leather whips and raised the "dickens" with the laborers for the least mistake. These two men were terrors to the people of the camp. I was terribly afraid of them and whenever they came to the camp, I ran and hid myself until they went away. I thought that they were some sort of demons or terrible gods, such as found in the Korean fairy tales.[27]

Certain changes are gradually coming through the substitution of the piece-wage and crop-contract for the wage system. On a few sugar plantations there has been something approaching a leasehold tenant system and it is quite significant that the sons of lease-holders have shown a greater tendency to remain on the soil.[28] Opportunity for initiative and independence undoubtedly would bring great changes. Dr. A. L. Dean wrote in a letter that about five per cent of the boys were looking forward to agriculture. "It is a somewhat striking coincidence," he wrote, "which may or may not mean something, that the five per cent of boys desiring to take up agricultural work coincides pretty closely with the percentage of persons in agriculture as independent agriculturists or as _lunas_ (foremen) and the like. This suggests that if the agricultural work can be put upon a basis in which individual initiative and independence can play an important part, a larger proportion of the boys would, doubtless, look to agriculture as a future."[29]

Changes will come very slowly because of the conditions peculiar to Hawaii. The development of the sugar industry has called for large capital outlays which could not be handled as well by small independent producers.[30] The expensive irrigation

systems and sugar mills, doubtless, can be provided
and operated more efficiently under the present system.[31] The present organization has made possible
great improvements in methods of production through
the employment of specialists and experts for carrying on research and experimental work. The large
plantation under one management, which can plan on
an extensive scale, can use the equipment to the
best advantage. If a group of independent farmers
should desire to harvest their cane at the most advantageous season, the mill would be overtaxed.
Furthermore, a tradition has grown up with the sugar
culture which will not change readily. Many of the
producers are sensitive and stand strongly against
any proposed innovations.

Available evidence seems to indicate that
the traditional plantation system of Hawaii cannot
be maintained on the basis of citizen labor with an
American standard of living.[32] So long as an adequate supply of cheap labor can be secured, the plantation management will make little adjustment. For
a considerable period of time, the Philippines have
supplied a sufficient number. But Hawaii must take
California into consideration. A large number of
Filipinos have been leaving Hawaii for the Coast
every year. Many have had the mainland as their ultimate destination and have used Hawaii as a relay
station to earn money for continuing the journey.
California, however, has not been satisfied with the
arrangement.

Paul Scharrenberg, secretary of the California State Federation of Labor, indicated in an
article that the Filipinos were replacing white
workers on the Coast. When local workmen raise questions about this situation, "no explanation is forth-
coming except the bold statement that the Hawaiian
sugar planters must have cheap labor to continue in
business. Such an explanation does not explain anything but brings forth resentful inquiries about the
legal status of the Filipino, the reason for his

migration and the possibility of putting an end to a situation that is rapidly forcing another unwanted, unassimilable alien group on California and other western states."[33]

On September 23, 1927, the annual convention of the California State Federation of Labor passed a resolution urging Congress to place the same restrictions on the immigration of Filipinos that apply to other Asiatics. The Federation also favored immediate independence for the Philippine Islands.[34] On October 3, 1927, the annual convention of the American Federation of Labor adopted a resolution in favor of Filipino exclusion. On May 19, 1928, Congressman Welch of California introduced a bill in Congress to exclude the Filipinos from the United States. On May 15, 1929, the California legislature passed a resolution urging Congress to exclude Filipinos from the United States or at least to restrict their immigration. This was approved by the California Senate without debate. On March 24, 1934, Congress approved a bill providing for the exclusion of the Filipinos, except for an annual quota of fifty. The introduction of the Welch bill in Congress caused considerable uneasiness among the sugar planters of Hawaii. Not all in Hawaii have been opposed to closing the doors against the Filipinos. A candidate for the mayoralty of Honolulu in 1928 stood strongly against unrestricted immigration of laborers with a low standard of living. Several candidates for the territorial legislature opposed further migration from the Philippines. An editorial in a Chinese paper in Honolulu favored exclusion on the ground that the influx was creating both a labor situation and a serious social problem. A Japanese paper in Honolulu considered exclusion to be the solution of the employment problems of the American-born Japanese. In the opinion of this editor a stoppage of this cheap labor supply will tend to break up the large holdings of the sugar planters into small independent farms which would attract the

young Japanese. The New Freedom, an independent
newspaper in Honolulu, on November 30, 1928, expressed itself strongly in favor of exclusion.
        With the stoppage of Filipino immigration
considerable readjustment will become necessary.
This may bring sufficient change to attract the second generation of oriental ancestry to the soil.
For some time many of the planters have considered
these young people a problem--a veritable drug on
the market. Wallace M. Alexander, president of
Alexander and Baldwin, a corporation which controls
a number of sugar plantations, made a statement at
a meeting of the directors of the Honolulu Chamber
of Commerce, a portion of which we quote.

        One of the greatest problems we will have to meet
within the next five or six years, is that of what to do with
the second generation of Orientals here. It is also going to
be one of California's problems, although upon a smaller
scale. Nevertheless, what we are going to do with these young
students of Japanese and Chinese ancestry, who were born under
the American flag, and apparently to all the rights of citizenship, is a problem that is going to tax our greatest efforts.
There is no solution that I can see other than in some way
spreading the American citizens of foreign ancestry throughout
the United States. The problem as I see it will involve the
distributing of this population throughout the United States
rather than confining it to the Pacific Coast and the Territory of Hawaii.[35]

Mr. Alexander's idea had the approval of a considerable number of the sugar men, but, since the agitation for disbarment of the Filipinos assumed a serious aspect in 1928, they began to modify their
views; they may need the second generation in a few
years. The riots between the Whites and the Filipinos in the Santa Clara and Pajaro Valleys of California in January, 1930, brought no joy to the sugar
planters of Hawaii.
        With these facts in view, it is not

surprising that the young people have sought opportunities in the cities. Much uncertainty has hung over the choice of a vocation, but the majority have been determined not to choose the plantation. A Chinese college boy in Hawaii told about his day of decision. "Graduation brought me to the crossing of the roads. On the left the sign read, 'To the Cane Fields,' and on the right, in radiating rays, it spelled 'Higher Education.' In the fall the guiding hand of fate landed me in high school." In all probability he did not leave this choice blindly to fate, but with wide open eyes, he turned the hand in the desired direction.

Furthermore, the young people have had sufficient data at hand to calculate with reasonable certainty where they would be ten or even twenty years hence if they worked on the plantations. In the city, on the contrary, there has been uncertainty but a chance. A number of young men, particularly among the Chinese, have occupied positions of importance and have received good incomes.[36] If several have succeeded, many others would be unwilling to admit that they could not do likewise. They preferred to take a gambler's chance in the city; they might rise far above anything possible on the plantation. If they failed in the attempt, they would have the satisfaction of having tried.

Other Agricultural Opportunities. Pineapple culture, a comparatively recent development, differs considerably from the sugar industry which has traditions extending almost a century into the past.[37] A considerable number of pineapples are grown by independent producers on small acreages. They, however, are not able to operate as efficiently as the large growers who conduct an experiment station in connection with the University of Hawaii. Even then, the independence has attracted a considerable number of Japanese growers. Pineapple culture is more seasonal than sugar, but the wages are usually

higher. Since the heavy canning season falls in the
three summer months, which synchronizes with the
school vacations, large numbers of pupils work in
the canneries and thus labor disorganization is ob-
viated. There is no feeling of antagonism toward
the pineapple industry such as there is against almost everything connected with sugar.

There are certain limited agricultural opportunities in Hawaii aside from sugar and pineapples. Since these minor industries are not conducted on a large scale, there is more room for individual initiative. In the Kona district, coffee, cotton,
oranges, avocados, and macadamia nuts are grown. Experiments are being carried on with a view to further agricultural developments in the district.
There is a considerable amount of rice grown in the
Territory, but this industry receives very little
attention. J. M. Westgate, Director of the United
States Experiment Station, in Hawaii, has made sug-
gestions to the younger Chinese relative to the
growing of minor crops, especially the litchi nuts.

Migration to continental United States to
engage in agriculture has been urged upon the young
Japanese of Hawaii by certain men. After spending
several months in California in 1927, Rev. Takie
Okumura of Honolulu advised young Japanese to go
there and take up agriculture on a five-to-ten acre
scale. The Hawaii Club of San Francisco, made up of
Hawaiian-born Japanese, addressed their own group in
the Territory in their Bulletin of October, 1925,
setting forth the opportunities in California. They
urged the young men not to be satisfied as mere
laborers but to become bosses, lessees, or landown-
ers themselves. In this way they would be able to
provide opportunities for a considerable number of
workers from Hawaii.

Chapter V

THE AGRICULTURAL SITUATION IN HAWAII
SUBSEQUENT TO 1932[1]

Objective Factors in the Situation. In the
autumn of 1932 the Hawaiian Sugar Planters Association ceased to encourage the immigration of Filipinos and since that time only a negligible number
have arrived. On the other hand, there has been a
continuous return movement of the workers to their
homelands, the plantations paying the return passage
of those who had fulfilled their labor contracts and,
through contributions to the bureau of Social Service, paying indirectly the passage of several thousand in Honolulu who had not kept their contracts
but who wished to return. There has been, therefore,
a marked decrease in the number of Filipinos employed on the sugar-cane plantations. On June 30,
1932, the Filipino men on the plantations reached
their maximum at 34,915 while on June 30, 1934, they
numbered about 29,321, a decrease of 5,594 in two
years. Due to the great reduction in pineapple production that has occurred on account of the depression, the employment of Filipinos in the pineapple
fields has undoubtedly decreased in a higher ratio.[2]
To make good the loss of Filipino laborers,
there has been an increasing employment of young men
born in the Territory, mainly Japanese, but some
Portuguese and others are included. The extent of
the increase since 1932 is made evident by Table IX.
Since there has been no new immigration, these increases represent an increasing employment of Hawaiian-born men. Moreover, there has been a continued decrease in the number of aliens employed

65

because of old age, death, and departures from the
Islands. In the two years, 1932-1934, the Territory
lost 2,168 alien Japanese--all ages--by excess of
departures to foreign ports over arrivals. It appears, therefore, that the employment of Hawaiian-
born Japanese has been sufficient to make good the
loss of some six or seven hundred alien Japanese a
year and to provide an increase of more than 1,300
men in the two years. The decrease in the total
number of men employed on the plantations in 1934 is
undoubtedly due to the operation of the Jones-
Costigan Act which requires a decrease in sugar production.

Table X, which classifies the workers according to citizenship, reveals the movement of the
non-citizens away from and of the American citizens
to the plantations. There was an increase of 19.4
per cent in the Portuguese citizens on the plantations, a 54.0 per cent increase in the Chinese group,
227.8 per cent among the Koreans, and 248.9 per cent
among the Japanese. Undoubtedly the increase among
the Japanese is most significant because of the size
of that group.

The increased employment of the native-born
is not fully reflected in the statistics relative to
the men. While a considerable number of minors are
rated as men, there is an increasing number of regularly employed boys too young and too small to be
counted as men. According to Table IX, the number
of such decreased considerably after 1932. The
variation in numbers of employed school children
probably has no significance except that when the
plantations are oversupplied with men they are able
to employ fewer minors. The slump in pineapple production in 1932 and 1933 threw many workers out of
jobs. The sugar plantations relieved the unemployment situation in a measure by hiring extra men, and
this probably decreased the employment of school
children. By 1933, departures of Filipinos made it
possible to employ more school children. The

Table IX*

EMPLOYEES ON THE SUGAR CANE PLANTATIONS OF HAWAII BY ANCESTRY, 1920-1934

MEN	1920	1923	1924	1926	1928	1929	1930	1931	1932	1933	1934
Hawaiian and Part-Hawaiian	1,322	677	645	591	568	574	557	639	615	800	857
Portuguese	3,086	1,943	1,804	1,691	1,675	1,682	1,730	1,987	2,202	2,174	2,263
Porto Rican	1,422	1,126	1,072	1,104	816	810	842	808	797	846	834
Spanish	313	104	89	75	74	76	80	89	90	94	91
Other Caucasian	896	1,188	1,151	1,217	1,292	1,269	1,269	925	900	936	977
Chinese	2,578	1,484	1,394	1,280	1,058	946	805	787	706	666	613
Japanese	19,474	13,436	12,781	11,899	9,849	9,197	8,956	9,062	9,395	10,217	10,717
Korean	1,982	1,063	990	715	571	520	484	468	442	458	522
Filipino	13,061	20,743	19,475	25,390	32,149	34,345	34,706	34,301	34,915	31,818	29,321
All others	373	238	198	197	247	160	145	68	65	63	55
Total men	44,307	42,001	39,599	44,159	48,279	49,579	49,532	49,134	49,947	48,072	46,255
Women	Included above	5,294	3,250	2,667	1,928	1,733	1,477	1,502	1,480	1,552	1,608
School Children		3,930	4,400	3,890	5,938	4,889	4,724	5,290	2,754	4,636	4,870
Regular minors		688	704	676	485	461	384	485	811	1,292	1,163
Emergency, part-time		-	-	-	-	-	-	-	-	-	370
Total women and children	-	7,912	8,354	7,233	8,351	7,083	6,585	7,277	5,045	8,967	8,011
Total employees	44,307	49,913	47,953	51,392	56,630	56,662	56,117	56,411	54,992	57,039	54,266

*Table prepared by Dr. Romenzo Adams.

Data from the Annual Reports of the Governor of Hawaii

Governor's Report enumerates 1,487 emergency, or
part-time workers for 1933. The ancestry is not
given but since 1,338 were returned as "non-citizen"
it may be assumed that they were mainly Filipinos.
By 1934 most of these, all but 370, had returned to
the Philippines or had been placed on the regular
payrolls. The significant point is the increase of
regularly employed minors from 384 in 1930 to 1,292
in 1933. In view of the changing attitudes both of
parents and children,[3] we may expect a considerable
number of these minors to remain on the plantations
and be counted as men in a few years.

When the young men and boys who have been
entering plantation service shall have added five or
six years to their ages and when a considerable number of them shall have married and established homes,
a new type of society will be created on the planta-
tion--a society more American in character and one
that will be more satisfying to the Hawaiian-born
generation.[4] Needless to say, the technique of
labor management will change to fit the character of
the native-born workers.[5] Even now changes are being made, but without public announcement. It may
be said, however, that in the past techniques developed more or less naturally in response to the
requirements in dealing with immigrant men, most of
whom could speak no English except for the commonly
used pidgin.[6]

Plantation Policies and Worker Attitudes.
Thus far we have considered the statistical and more
or less external factors in the situation. We may
now turn to the policies of the plantations and the
attitudes of the workers.

For several years prior to 1932 the plantation managers and the capitalists prominent in the
control of the plantations were giving considerable
attention to the situation as it was developing. On
the one hand, it was becoming evident that the native-born were becoming too numerous to find

Table X

ORIENTAL AND PORTUGUESE WORKERS ON THE SUGAR PLANTATIONS BY CITIZENSHIP, 1931-1934

Racial Ancestry	1931*		1932		1933		1934		Increase in Citizens 1931-1934	Per Cent Increase over 1931
	American Citizens	Non-Citizens	American Citizens	Non-Citizens	American Citizens	Non-Citizens	American Citizens	Non-Citizens		
MEN										
Chinese	74	713	77	629	96	570	114	504	40	54.0
Japanese	1,199	7,063	2,448	6,947	3,485	6,732	4,183	6,534	2,984	248.9
Koreans	18	450	19	423	41	417	55	467	41	227.8
Portuguese	1,651	336	1,674	348	1,880	294	1,971	292	320	19.4
**WOMEN **										
Japanese	208	999	258	989	418	879	516	826	308	148.1

*The workers were not classified by citizenship prior to 1931 in the Governor's Reports.
**The data are available only for the Japanese women and "all others."

Data from Annual Reports of the Governor of Hawaii.

employment unless considerable numbers entered plantation service. The social, economic, and political
problems involved in the presence of a large unemployed population were considered. On the other
hand, there was the increasing sentiment of Americans favorable to Philippine independence and the
growing desire on the part of Californians to prohibit Filipino immigration. While there was a possibility that such immigration might be prohibited
for continental United States and permitted under
regulation for Hawaii, any request for such special
treatment of Hawaii tended to be embarrassing since
it seemed to give support to the view held by many
on the mainland that Hawaii is not a part of the
United States. On this point the people of Hawaii
are very sensitive.[7]

        In connection with the so-called Ala Moana
rape case and the Massie-Fortescue murder case in
1931, the territory received much unfavorable publicity on the mainland. Some maintained that the
territorial government had broken down and should be
set aside in favor of rule by a commission in which
the Army and Navy departments would play a major
part. Bills were introduced in Congress to appoint
a non-resident of the Territory to the governorship.
In response to a Senate Resolution of January 11,
1932, requesting data on law enforcement in Hawaii,
Assistant Attorney General Seth W. Richardson was
sent to the Islands. His investigation resulted in
a voluminous report on conditions in the Territory.[8]
Hawaii was plainly on the defensive. The Governor
devoted the first seven pages of his 1932 report to
a defense.[9]

        This setting was unpropitious for seeking
special favors. Hawaii could not afford to arouse
antagonism on the mainland, and particularly in
California at such a critical time. Mr. Richardson
recommended that no more common labor be imported.
Had the planters opposed this, resentment in Congress might have brought "grave consequences."

Furthermore, they had not forgotten the fruitless
commission sent to Washington in 1921 in an attempt
to amend the immigration law to permit the importation of Chinese coolies.

Evidently there would be advantages if laborers could be found elsewhere. Porto Rico was
again investigated and found to be a possible source.
There were, however, reasons for not desiring Porto
Ricans. They had been tried before and, relative to
numbers, they burden the jails, charities, courts,
and prisons more than any other group in the Territory.

This situation inevitably forced the planters to consider the source of labor at their very
doors--the native-born young men of whom there were
practically enough to meet the needs, unless emigration should be too heavy. The problem here concerned the attitudes of the young men and the social
groups to which they belonged. Could they be induced to accept service on terms that were possible
and reasonable considering the price of sugar and
other factors?

Changes in Attitudes of the Young Men. There
is no adequate information available, but from
scraps of information pieced together from several
sources it may be inferred that about 1930 or possibly earlier the managers, quite generally, began to
study this question and to experiment for the purpose of bringing about a modification of attitude on
the part of the laborers and their sons. It is
probable that they began to see the handwriting on
the wall as California was bestirring herself more
and more against the Filipinos. California had
barred the Chinese and Japanese. Could they expect
the Filipinos to be an exception? The planters began to do things to make the laborer's position one
of greater dignity. More opportunity--at least a
little more opportunity--was given to Japanese men
to rise to positions a little above that of common

labor. Well-devised plans for training boys for the
work were used and the schools coöperated. It is
becoming evident that the managers, in considerable
measure, have convinced the workers that henceforth
there is to be a happier situation for the ordinary
laborer on the plantation. This they have done by
word and by deed.[10]

Doubtless a factor in the modification of
attitudes has been the increase of understanding
among the immigrant parents--especially among the
Japanese. Prior to (we may say 1928) there were
many factors in the local situation that tended to
mislead the Japanese immigrants relative to the opportunities that could reasonably be expected for
their sons.[11] When the situation began to change in
such a way as to reveal the fallacies involved in
their great expectations, they showed unusual capacity for reflection and for readjustment of attitude
on the basis of the realities. Young university men
who have gone to the plantations in recent years are
meeting with a different sort of experience from
that of the men who went out six to ten years ago,
and their evaluation of the situation is markedly
different.

To be sure the depression is a factor. The
opportunity to find non-plantation jobs is greatly
reduced. Honolulu had fewer people in 1934 than in
1932. California is no longer a "Land of Promise."
One might take the view that recent tendencies are
mere depression phenomena, but that is an inadequate
explanation. Undoubtedly, the depression hastened a
movement that was already in process. The answer,
of course, must be postponed for several years until
business conditions improve. Probably the movement
of citizens of oriental ancestry to the mainland will
be resumed when employment conditions on the Coast
become better. It is improbable, however, that the
movement will assume the proportions almost inevitable if Filipino immigration were continued as in
the last decade or in sufficient volume to meet
plantation needs.

<u>Changes in Attitudes of the Planters</u>. There
have been marked changes in attitude on the part of
the immigrant Orientals and their sons, but it has
not been a one-sided affair; the planters have made
almost unbelievable changes in a comparatively short
time.

During the period prior to 1852 the few
small sugar-cane plantations depended on native labor. In the twenty-four year period from 1852 to
1876 about 2,600 Chinese men were brought in, and
most of them served only for the contract period,
three to five years. During this period the laborers were mainly Hawaiian. Since 1876 the main re-
liance has been on imported labor and, up to 1932,
there was an almost steady importation of men to
provide for the growth of the industry, to take the
places of laborers who died or retired because of
age or other disability, and to replace those who
left the Islands or who quit plantation employment
to enter other occupations. The action of the plantation people in 1932 in stopping such importations
marks the end of an era extending over a period of
more than a half century. The old system had become
a tradition and until the leaders began to think
seriously about the matter it was regarded as permanent or, at least, one destined to be continued for
a long time.

In the early Twenties the big effort was to
secure legislation at Washington authorizing the importation of Chinese for a term of service as plantation workers or as servants, and for their return
to China after their term of service was completed
or when they broke their contracts. The planters
made representations to Congress that there was an
acute labor shortage in the Territory. The plantation strike in 1920 resulted in a loss of workers.
The Filipino and Japanese workers asked for certain
changes in working conditions but the planters
turned a deaf ear. After the strike had dragged on
for some months, a committee of representative

citizens proposed a plan for settlement, but the
planters rejected it.   The strike finally collapsed,
but the morale of the workers was broken.   Many left
the plantations and those who remained were listless
in their work.   The planters learned nothing from
the experience.   Workers' grievances would not be
considered.   The solution was at hand in the importation of Chinese coolies on short terms.   If they requested changes in the system, they could be deported.

          For decades the planters did not have to
think seriously about the labor situation.   At first
they secured an ample supply of Chinese and Portuguese.   When the Chinese were excluded the Japanese
supplied the deficiency, and when the Japanese immigration was stopped they tapped the Philippine
reservoir.   At first they recruited Filipino workers
and provided their passage to Hawaii, but in 1925
the planters discontinued the recruiting and paying
of transportation costs, and endeavored to control
the movement.   This, however, did not stop the Filipinos.[12] Many were impatient with the small allot-
ment of steerage space on the regular steamers and
in 1927 two vessels chartered by Filipino workers
docked in Honolulu.

          Under such conditions, why should the plant-
ers think seriously about the labor situation?   Why
should they pay any attention to the native-born sons
of Orientals who had not made satisfactory occupational adjustments?[13] Would not sheer economic necessity force them, willy-nilly, back to the plantations?[14] In the main, the planter attitude was a
negative one; nothing would be done to attract the
native-born youth.   No serious thought was given to
the development of a school system that would function efficiently under island conditions.   On the
contrary, impediments of different kinds should be
used to restrict access to educational opportunities,
such as fees, tuition, and a reduction in curricular
offerings.[15] This created resentment and a greater

determination to acquire an education that would
lead away from the plantation. Trade and vocational
education was concerned with the development of
skills while attitudes were ignored. Now that more
attention is paid to attitudes, skills come more
readily as by-products and the success quotient has
been raised to the advantage of all concerned. But
the upshot of it all is that the planters were finally forced to face the issue. Mr. Richardson
stated in his report:

> Many persons believe, however, that if Congress defi-
> nitely, if not completely, restricted all the importation of
> foreign labor, and pointed its legislation toward ultimate
> prohibition of such immigration, the seriousness of the situa-
> tion would be brought home to all groups in the islands, to
> the end that the problem would be thus more speedily settled.[16]

Ten or fifteen years ago, no one with any
knowledge of plantation conditions would have predicted such a marked change so soon. The sugar interests, in the past, have resented any suggested
change. This is well illustrated by an editorial,
"A Dangerous Theorist," in the Maui News of February 25, 1928, when it took up the cudgels against
Dr. Romanzo Adams of the University of Hawaii because of some experiments suggested in his pamphlet
on "The Education of the Boys of Hawaii and Their
Economic Outlook."[17] Dr. Adams suggested that experiments be conducted on two small plantations. Now
the experimental work is being carried on all over
the Territory. We have no accurate measure of the
influence of Dr. Adams' suggestion. Perhaps the
recent trends may best be regarded as responses to
the "logic of events." These changes are all the
more remarkable when we consider the traditions of
the sugar industry.[18] But it has happened, and such
radical changes tend to make one "optimistic about
the inevitable."

Chapter VI

OPPORTUNITIES IN TRADES AND PROFESSIONS
IN HAWAII

Skilled Hand Vocations. For some time the
majority of the boys of oriental ancestry have been
choosing the skilled vocations. Trades such as
those of carpenter, automobile mechanic, electrician,
or machinist do not restrict them to any single area;
they are useful anywhere.[1] Furthermore, these occupations provide a better income and give higher
status. Of great importance is the fact that many
can be their own bosses. The rise of commercial
aviation and the new developments in the wireless
field have begun to attract some. A considerable
number are turning to engineering and other closely
allied activities.[2] A Japanese high school boy on
one of the islands said that it was his one and only
ambition to become the Edison of the next generation.

A number of Japanese girls have turned to
the barber's trade. The Japanese practically control the barber shops in Honolulu. According to the
President of the Japanese Barbers' Association, in
the spring of 1928, there were 127 men (all Japanese-
born) who operated shops and fifty-five women (mostly American-born). There was a total of 173 American-born Japanese women barbers in the city and only
three American-born men.

The Business World. The business world is
attracting a goodly number, wherein Hawaii offers
considerable opportunity. The comparative absence
of race prejudice in Hawaii as compared with the Pacific Coast makes it possible for more Orientals to
be employed in business establishments conducted by

white people. The leading dry goods store in Honolulu employs several oriental salespeople. The head
of a commercial college in Honolulu informed the
writer that she had no difficulty in placing oriental students in positions. The majority of them, to
be sure, were at a disadvantage in situations where
the English language was important, but in certain
kinds of office work they were superior to the Occidentals. They are, however, not on a parity with
those of north-European ancestry; they are usually
paid a lower salary for the same work and the opportunities for advancement are more limited.[3]

Some thought has been given to the development of new industrial opportunities in Hawaii
through the utilization on a commercial basis of
certain unused products for local consumption.[4]
The Nippu Jiji has stressed the development of small
industries as a solution to the employment problem
of the young Japanese and has reported several successful undertakings. One ingenious Japanese in
Honolulu began to make shoes for workingmen from old
automobile tires. With this cheap, yet durable,
footgear he developed a good trade as did also several competitors who entered the same field. The
Honolulu Chamber of Commerce, after a study of the
situation, concluded that a large number of small
manufacturing businesses would not be profitable;
ocean freights are cheap and goods can be shipped
from the Coast to Hilo almost as cheaply as from
Honolulu. Any industry to be profitable must be big
enough to compete in the world markets. In 1927
two island manufacturers began to do a considerable
business on the mainland. Industries with such pos-
siblities are to be encouraged. Early in 1928 Captain Robert Dollar addressed a gathering in Honolulu
at which he suggested the establishment of a rubber
factory. He said that his ships transported the raw
rubber from Singapore to Los Angeles and then carried the finished automobile tires back to the
Orient. He also suggested that raw silk brought

from Japan might be worked into finished products in
Hawaii as well as in southern California.

   <u>Medicine and Dentistry</u>. The professions,
particularly medicine and dentistry, have attracted
so many that there is danger of overcrowding in these
fields.[5] In Hawaii, where the race lines are not
sharply drawn, the dentists and doctors are not restricted to their own groups. An oriental physician
in Honolulu has a clientele which is largely white
and mostly from the upper economic class. No stigma
is attached to the person who is attended by an
oriental doctor in Hawaii.
   A number choose the medical profession because of its attractiveness as compared with plantation work; some select this because of the social
position it confers; but, at least, one Japanese
boy in Hawaii, who had passed through a process of
disillusionment and had begun to reflect on plantation conditions, made this choice because of a desire to help his people. Through the practice of
medicine he could give his people service which men
of other races would not give them, but probably the
fact that the medical profession gave considerable
assurance of financial security was an important
factor. Had he chosen the legal profession in order
to seek justice in the courts for the Japanese, he
would be more restricted in his activities and could
not be as independent in raising his voice in behalf
of his fellows.

   <u>The Legal Profession</u>. The legal profession
attracts a few. Here they encounter difficulty, for
their practice in the courts is seriously limited.
Chinese and Japanese usually employ white attorneys;
the probability of winning their cases is enhanced
because judge and jury may be prejudiced against an
oriental lawyer. Hence their activities are largely
confined to giving advice and drawing up legal
papers.[6] A few turn to that profession from

altruistic motives; they wish to secure justice for
those who have suffered at the hands of the Whites.
Some legally-trained Chinese are planning to carve
out their careers in China.

Teaching. The vocation of teaching attracts
a considerable number.[7] This is primarily the
woman's profession. Out of a total of 700 boys at
McKinley High School, Honolulu, in the spring of
1927, only twenty-one expressed a desire to become
teachers. Table IX, based on the figures released
by the Registrar of the University of Hawaii for
1927-1928, shows the registrants in courses in education.

Table X, based on registration figures from
the Territorial Normal School,[8] throws further light
on the situation.

Table IX

REGISTRATIONS BY ANCESTRY AND SEX, WITH PERCENTAGES
OF WOMEN IN EACH GROUP, FOR COURSE IN
EDUCATION, UNIVERSITY OF HAWAII,
1927-1928*

Ancestry	Total	Men	Women	Per Cent Women
Hawaiian and Part-Hawaiian	30	7	23	76.6
Anglo-Saxon	32	2	30	93.8
Portuguese	7	2	5	71.4
Chinese	38	7	31	81.6
Japanese	63	37	26	41.2
Others	4	2	2	50.0
Totals	174	57	117	61.5

*The data for 1927-1928 were secured when the writer had ac-
cess to the records at the University of Hawaii in 1929. Later
data have not been available.

Data from the Registrar, University of Hawaii

Table X

REGISTRATIONS BY ANCESTRY AND SEX, WITH PERCENTAGE OF WOMEN IN
EACH GROUP, IN TERRITORIAL NORMAL SCHOOL, HONOLULU, 1925-1929

Ancestry	1925-1926			1927-1928			1928-1929		
	Total Number	Men	Wo-men	Per Cent Women	Total Number	Men	Wo-men	Per Cent Women	Total Number	Men	Wo-men	Per Cent Women
Hawaiian and Part-Hawaiian	111	7	104	93.7	88	7	81	92.0	114	16	98	86.0
Anglo-Saxon	28	3	25	89.3	23	2	21	91.3	14	0	14	100.0
Portuguese	44	8	36	81.8	39	8	31	79.5	39	5	34	87.2
Chinese	96	10	86	89.6	75	3	72	96.0	89	14	75	84.3
Japanese	168	69	99	58.9	91	22	69	75.8	114	19	95	83.3
Others	13	2	11	84.6	20	3	17	85.0	29	8	21	72.4
Totals	460	99	361	78.5	336	45	291	86.6	399	62	337	84.5

Data from the Registrar, Territorial Normal School.

Of a total registration of 460 at the Normal School in 1926, ninety-nine of whom were men and 361 women, 21 per cent of the total were Chinese and 37 per cent Japanese. In September, 1927, on account of raising standards, the registration was reduced to 336 and, since special emphasis was placed upon English in an effort to counteract the pidgin,[9] the Japanese group was affected more than any other. In 1927-1928, the Japanese group dropped to 27 per cent while the Chinese made up 22 per cent of the entire student body. In 1928-1929 the total registrations increased to 399; the Chinese remained at 22 per cent; the Japanese made a slight increase, reaching almost 29 per cent.

These figures from the Normal School, together with those from the University, probably indicate that the Chinese and Anglo-Saxon men had opportunities in the commercial world, hence comparatively few turned to the teaching profession. In the Japanese group, which is not so well established economically, a larger percentage of the men turned to this vocation. According to Table IX, the Japanese formed the largest group in the course in education in the University. In this group 59 per cent were men, while in the Chinese group 18 per cent were men and among the Anglo-Saxons there were only 6 per cent.

There is comparatively little race discrimination in the public school system. All teachers for the entire Territory are appointed by the Superintendent of Public Instruction and any citizen, regardless of ancestry, is eligible provided the professional requirements are met. Since there is a regular salary schedule which applies to all without discrimination, this is one vocation where persons of oriental ancestry may receive the same salaries as those of north-European lineage. In the commercial world, it is an unwritten law that Anglo-Saxons are to receive higher salaries than Orientals or Portuguese for the same work. While

the teachers' salaries are comparatively low when
measured by an American standard of living, they are
high in comparison with the salaries in other positions open to Orientals. When compared with the
earnings of their parents on the plantations they
seen very high indeed. [10]

The teaching profession has been a boon to
the girls of oriental ancestry in Hawaii. It has
helped the women to break down hoary traditions
which have weighed heavily upon them; they have
come to be real persons with high status in their
communities. It is a real distinction for the
daughter of a lowly plantation worker to teach in
an American public school; it brings honor to the
entire family and inevitably the position of woman
is enhanced.

The economic factor is an important one in
directing many into the teaching profession in Hawaii. The following statement by a Japanese high
school girl is typical of a considerable number.

My first choice of a vocation was to become a school
teacher. My neighbors influenced me in this more than anything else. The neighbor had four girls who became school
teachers. At first they were very poor but since these girls
became teachers, they became happy and wealthy. At present
they have a large tract of land, a beautiful and comfortable
home located on an upland where one can get a beautiful view.
They also have an automobile and a telephone. [11]

One college girl related her experience as a
substitute teacher during her last two years in the
grammar grades for which she received three dollars
per day. She earned more than her father when he
worked for a daily wage in the cane field. By way
of contrast with the long days in the hot sun, the
sweat and the grime of the plantation, the working
conditions of the teacher are pleasant; the teachers
seemed to have a clean and easy life with short
hours and much leisure time. This has been an attractive force.

Some young people are influenced by altruistic motives; they want to be of service in training the children of their own groups to become useful American citizens. A Japanese boy, who chose the teaching profession because of economic considerations and as a stepping-stone to something better, gradually began to see possibilities for serving the people of Hawaii through this profession. A girl who had spent some time in Japan decided to return there as a teacher of English, with the hope of developing a better understanding between the youth of that country and Hawaii.

In certain cases, the teaching profession is, frankly and avowedly, to be used as a stepping-stone to something better. For some time it will provide economic security and enhance status. It is easier to advance from teaching than it is from certain other vocations. In some instances, the teaching profession has been a sort of catch-all for those who could not fit into other vocations or who found the requirements too rigid in other professions. One Chinese girl, in consultation with her mother, concluded not to be a stenographer because the work was tiresome and Orientals received less pay than Anglo-Saxons; a nurse's job was not an easy one; hence teaching was on the whole the best to choose. Conditions, however, have changed radically within the past few years as the requirements for teachers have become more rigid.

A number of girls have chosen teaching because of actual experiences in assisting their teachers and in substituting for those who were absent. This proved to be delightful and gave them an enhanced feeling of their own dignity and importance.

There is also another vital factor. In Hawaii, where the Orientals are in the majority and the contacts with white people are limited, the teacher occupies a strategic position. The children of oriental extraction are eager to become Americans, and the teacher is the one representative of the

American community with whom they make close contacts. She becomes the pattern for their Americanism. In the main, teachers are kind and helpful,
and thus the pupils idealize them, come under their
moral domination, and think of following their example vocationally.

The teaching profession in Hawaii, however,
is limited in the opportunities it offers. For many
years all the locally trained teachers were assured
of positions, in addition to which a considerable
number were brought from the mainland. The saturation point, however, has been reached and in 1928
not all the graduates of the Territorial Normal
School were absorbed by the school system.[12] Because of this situation the standards have been
gradually raised, and the high school pupils have
begun to hesitate. The 1931-1932 enrolment in the
Teachers College was 510. After a study of the employment situation, it was decided to reduce the enrolment below 300 for September, 1932, to a point
commensurate with the probable number of school positions in prospect for the graduates.[13] Some believe that there is discrimination against them.
They are right in a certain measure. There is discrimination against different groups in the commercial life of Hawaii and in the school system as well.
The important positions in the system will not be
held by Chinese or Japanese for some time to come,[14]
neither will the high schools be staffed by them in
the immediate future; they would encounter grave
difficulties on account of the attitudes of many
Anglo-Saxon pupils.

Nursing. Nursing offers some opportunities
for the girls, but in this they have encountered a
strong group pressure. In the Orient the nurse occupies a much lower social status than the teacher.
Teaching is held up as clean and easy while nursing
is said to be dirty, disagreeable, and hard. Because of this, many parents have stood strongly

against entrance into this profession.[15]

Conclusions. The vocational problems of the
younger generation in Hawaii are not easy of solution. The range of opportunities is limited. There
has been considerable discrimination against them,
enough to justify the views they have held. When a
certain high school teacher was asked to recommend a
chemist with certain qualifications, he suggested a
Chinese. The mere mention of an oriental name, however, ruled him out, although the boy was far superior to any white boy in the class. An elderly
Chinese business man stated that a number of Chinese
in a certain bank were doing work of a more or less
mechanical nature. They had no opportunity for advancement, while white boys came in and were advanced over them. In several instances white men
have been imported from the mainland and placed in
positions over competent Orientals who knew the
business and were acquainted with Island conditions.
Some employers have declared that since the Chinese
lacked initiative they could be used only for the
more or less mechanical work. A manager of an industrial establishment, who called his employees in
the higher positions his "cabinet," declared that he
was determined to keep it white. Another business
man said that he would not have an Oriental if he
could get a white man. An executive reported that
a man was being considered for a certain position,
but when the budget committee decided to drop the
salary to $75.00 they frankly said, "We'll have to
get an Oriental." A letter from a young Japanese is
typical of the situation in which many find themselves.

I am employed in a position where I must have a fairly accurate knowledge of the English language. I will say
that while I speak Japanese, I know very little about the
written language of that country. The position pays me fairly
well—enough to live on decently with a little left over every

month for the savings bank. Employed on exactly the same work
I am doing is a Caucasian who is paid ten dollars a week more
than I receive. Why? Are we not both Americans? I know that
I do my work as well as he does, and there are times—when he
is away on vacations, for instance—when I do his work as well
as my own, which would indicate that I am as capable as he.
The reason I do not receive as much as the white American is
because I'm a "Jap." I am not complaining. I know the custom
and do not rail against it.[16]

   Superficially it would appear that the various races in Hawaii live in perfect harmony. Beneath the surface, however, there is considerable
discrimination against the races of color in the occupational field. The Orientals are not promoted to
the more responsible positions. In the spring of
1927, the manager of one of the large business
houses in Honolulu addressed a group of college
Y.M.C.A. boys on the occupational outlook in Hawaii
for college-trained men of oriental ancestry. He
said that it depended on the individual how far he
could go and that he would be given opportunity for
advancement in accordance with his own abilities.
But he went on to say that he could not employ
Orientals to wait on the public in his office because that would result in a loss of business. It
has been quite common for speakers representing the
sugar industry to talk about the opportunities open
to the college-trained man of oriental ancestry who
would be willing to begin at the bottom and work up,
but when specific questions were directed at them
the replies would be more or less evasive.
   Executives, however, are not always free to
do as they please. The manager of a sugar plantation said that he would like to promote an Oriental
to a skilled job which would carry with it a promotion to the skilled workers' residential area.
"Then," he said, "I'll have to invite him to my home
on Sunday afternoons to play tennis with the other
upper-grade employees. But the chemist's wife may

object to this and dissensions may arise. The upshot of it all is that I cannot promote him."[17]
Many point to the building trades and say that the
Orientals have crowded the white men out so that on
the large construction jobs it becomes necessary to
bring skilled workers from the mainland. Because of
this they are giving preferential treatment to white
men in order to keep them in the Territory.

     With the marked change in attitude on the
part of the sugar planters since 1932, there will
probably be less discrimination against the American-
born group in other occupations as well. An important factor in the situation will be the decrease
in pressure upon the white-collar occupations, due
to the increasing attractiveness of plantation work.

Chapter VII

VOCATIONAL ADJUSTMENTS IN CONTINENTAL UNITED STATES

On the Pacific Coast there is more prejudice, but the second generation has a greater range of opportunities. The Japanese group on the Coast is younger and the second generation has not yet faced the vocational problems in the same measure as have the Japanese in Hawaii.[1] The anti-Chinese agitation, with its attendant violence[2] which began when gold mining was the chief occupation in California, drove the Chinese into a ghetto life in the various Chinatowns from which they have never fully emerged. Since the Chinese are of less importance in the commercial life of San Francisco than in Honolulu, the second generation is in a less advantageous position. Many Chinese on the Pacific Coast are pessimistic regarding the vocational adjustments of the American-born group.

For some time it has been apparent that, in the main, the young men of Chinese and Japanese ancestries were not interested in following the occupations of their fathers.[3] Like the children of other immigrants they have been desirous of turning to vocations that would afford a higher status. The rising generation has been avoiding certain of the occupations which engaged their immigrant parents, even though the remuneration has been higher than in certain other vocations open to them. A case in point is the field of domestic and personal service in which the Chinese immigrants in particular held a prominent place.[4] The final outcome, however, is at present a matter of speculation. Changes will

doubtless come as more of the younger generation begin to face realities. Already the young Japanese
are changing their ideas. According to an editorial,

> Out of all the trouble from the depression, we notice
> one thing and that is that more and more second generation mem-
> bers are entering domestic work for their living. In years
> gone by, the California raised girls have had the tendency of
> looking down upon domestic workers. They would have considered
> it an insult if anyone had offered them such employment. And
> this, despite the fact that their parents may be or have been
> domestic workers. In other words, white collar jobs was their
> ideal.[5]

Fishing. The Japanese have played an important part in the fishing industry of southern
California for a number of years. Out of 1,520 commercial fishermen licensed in Los Angeles County between April 1, 1923, and March 31, 1924, 47.9 per
cent were Japanese. In 1933-1934 the Japanese constituted 32 per cent of a total of 1,567. The group
has been decreasing because some of the old men have
died and others have returned to Japan while the native-born boys have not been filling the vacancies.[6]
The boys have not been attracted strongly to the
arduous task of fishing. Up to 1935 there were only
four American-born licensed fishermen among the Japanese.[7]

Agriculture. The Japanese immigrants in
particular have engaged in agriculture on the Pacific Coast. A number of these immigrants, as well
as some Americans, have urged the American-born
Japanese to turn to the soil.[8] Nevertheless, in
face of all this urging, the Japanese population has
been moving away from the rural districts to the
larger cities, especially to Los Angeles. The land
laws[9] have practically driven the aliens away from
the soil. The drab life of the immigrants in the
rural areas[10] has not appealed to the children, and

it is not surprising that many sons of Japanese
farmers have migrated to the cities. Nevertheless,
after some disillusionments in the city it is highly
probable that a considerable number will return to
the land.[11] The alien land laws do not affect them.
They have the advantage of the experience of the
older generation and by building wisely upon this,
there is reasonable assurance of success. Ichihashi
writes:

> The writer's own investigations of Japanese farming
> during the last two years do not lead him to conclude that the
> "too much Americanized" second-generation Japanese refuse to
> enter upon farming. On the contrary, quite a number of these
> have already commenced to seek their opportunity of earning a
> living in this industry,[12] and it is this fact that, in part,
> explains the continuation of Japanese farming in spite of the
> legal disabilities imposed upon the alien Japanese.[13]

Members of the younger generation, both Chinese and Japanese, have been turning to farming on
a scientific basis in California. The Native Sons
of the Golden State, an organization of California-
born Chinese, has been making a study of the opportunities in agriculture and has considered experimental work to place it on a sound basis. The
younger group will not carry on agricultural operations as did their fathers. The young Chinese in
southern California, who are raising asparagus, potatoes, and onions, hire Mexicans to do the heavy
work. Farming on the mainland is conducted on the
basis of relatively small, independent units where
each man is operator of his own farm instead of being merely a hired laborer. Additional laborers
are employed by many, but there is no great social
distance between manager and laborer; an industrious
worker of one year may be manager and employer the
next.

The fact that a considerable number of
Orientals, both alien and citizen, have engaged in

the produce business has stimulated agriculture.
Native-born men who have the right to buy or lease
land have been urged to become agriculturists to
raise the produce for the markets.[14]

Produce Business. When the Anti-Alien Land
Law of 1920 drove many Japanese into the cities,
particularly to Los Angeles, a considerable number
began to operate fruit and vegetable stands. The
Orientals have also been making headway in the wholesale produce business, and it is more than a local
trade; they have been shipping produce to the eastern markets. A considerable number of American-born
Chinese have been in this field and the younger
Japanese also have been drawn into it.[15] In Fresno,
California, a group of young Chinese have dominated
the produce business of the city and contiguous area
for some time.

Trade. In Los Angeles a considerable number of grocery stores are conducted by alien Japanese who cater to white trade. In Sacramento, a
number of Chinese, some of whom are American-born,
are in the grocery and meat business in the heart of
the city where they cater entirely to white trade.
The finest meat market in the city has been operated
by Chinese. The Japanese also have a number of
stores with white patronage, but except for their
art stores, they have not penetrated into the heart
of the retail area to the same degree as the Chinese.
In Tacoma, Washington, a Japanese has conducted a
ten-cent store in the white retail area and about
90 per cent of his customers have been white Americans. On the Pacific Coast the International Dollar
Stores, a chain system controlled by Chinese, are
located in the main retail districts and have practically all white customers.[16] In Sacramento, California, several Hawaiian-born Japanese are operating
garages and automobile repair shops which have a
considerable white patronage.[17] It seems that many

white people have no aversion to buying from Orientals; the relationship does not in any way assume
a social equality. So long as satisfactory service
is rendered and good value is received, there is no
objection. Probably, the politeness of the Oriental
in these relationships is a factor of considerable
importance. Some, however, have gone to great extremes in their efforts to keep white Americans from
having business relations with Orientals. A case in
point is the following letter written by the Secretary of the Anti-Oriental League of Americans.

We wrote you once before in regard to patronizing the
Orientals and we note that our outside representatives report
that an auto bearing licence No. 474-661, and registered in
your name has been noticed again parked in the neighborhood of
the Chinese Meat Markets and some one riding in said machine
purchased meat in a Chinese meat market. The Anti-Oriental
League of Americans has had faith in you as an American, among
Americans, living in America, the greatest country and the
best place to live in the world today. We felt that you acted the first time without thinking, as so many people have
done and that when we called your attention to the injustice
of your action, that you would leave the Chinese alone and
spend your money with your own race, the white people, from
whom you get it, as thousands of other good Americans are doing. I cannot understand how any man can get his money from
the white people and then deliberately turn it over to the
yellow, oriental Chinese, while the white people are in need
of your support. I want to advise you that we shall continue
to have confidence in you as an American who favors the white
man in preference to the yellow, until we find that you have
determined to continue patronizing the Chinese, and in that
case your name and address will appear in·the Oriental Menace
as one who favors Orientalism. Let your motto be "America for
Americans" and help keep California white.[18]

Employment by White People. Chinese or
Japanese girls on the Coast have been employed in
certain positions as "figure-heads," as they

themselves termed it, where they were required to
wear oriental costumes as "atmosphere."[19] In one exclusive importing house a girl, employed as "atmosphere," was given a trial in the office when
there was a shortage of help. At once she demonstrated her efficiency and was then accepted on the
same basis as the other employees. Girls of oriental parentage have been employed in the stockrooms
of several stores where they have not made contact
with customers. In the most exclusive dry-goods
store in a coast city, a girl of oriental ancestry
has been employed for some time as a saleslady. An
exclusive shop under Jewish management in San Francisco has employed several dainty Chinese salesgirls.
In the spring of 1928 the Pullman Company employed
three Chinese girls as "Pullman Maids" to wait on
the women passengers on a limited train between San
Francisco and Los Angeles. Plans were also made to
train Chinese girls to do manicuring on a limited
train between Chicago and the Coast. They also used
a number of Chinese boys on the club cars between
Chicago and the Coast. The Chicago and Alton Railway has used Japanese maids, dressed in kimonos, on
the "Alton Limited" between Chicago and St. Louis.
Hairdressing has been attracting a number of Chinese girls in San Francisco.[20]

　　　A number of young Orientals are employed in
banks and in other business houses such as credit
clothing establishments where they are expected to
bring trade from the groups they represent.[21] The
Oriental Branch of one of the big banks in San
Francisco has been managed by a Chinese woman while
all the tellers were Chinese girls. Establishments
engaged in trade with the Orient employ a number of
the second generation, especially in positions where
knowledge of an oriental language is required, but
comparatively few can meet that requirement.

　　　White people on the Coast resent the intru-
sion of persons of a different color into certain
employments. In one of the northwest cities, a girl

of oriental parentage, who had graduated from a
business college, won first place on a list of eli-
gibles through a competitive examination. She was
given a position in one of the municipal offices but
at first the white girls resented her presence. She
was placed at the bottom of the salary list. Advancement for her was a slow process, but gradually
her efficiency was recognized and the feeling
against her died away.

       Teaching. In continental United States very
few persons of oriental parentage are in the teaching profession.

       At present four Chinese ladies are employed in the
Los Angeles day schools, and one Japanese gentleman in the
evening high schools. All the ladies are elementary teachers,
while the young man is teaching a class in the Japanese language. The class started about two months ago in response to
demands made by foreign commerce representatives of steamship
companies and jobbers. . . . It might be added that no prejudice against these teachers has appeared. All cf them are
satisfactory teachers, and one young lady is a leader in the
large school in which she is located. The principal uses her
in enterprises requiring ability and administrative fore-
sight.[22]

In 1926 a Chinese girl was added to the teaching
staff of the Commodore Stockton Grammar School in
San Francisco where all the pupils are Chinese.
Since she could understand the Chinese children her
services were almost invaluable and she was made assistant to the principal. A second Chinese teacher
has since been employed in the same school. Two
Chinese teachers are employed in the Lincoln School
of Oakland, California, in a community where most of
the Chinese and Japanese children live. Both of
these teachers have had Chinese and white pupils in
their classes, and there has never been any difficulty with the other teachers, the community, or the

children. One has been employed since 1918 and the
other since 1926.[23] Seattle employs two oriental
clerks in the elementary schools, but no teachers
from this group. [24]

A number of school officials and executives
of the teachers' colleges on the Coast replied unanimously to letters of inquiry that there was practically no opportunity for teachers of oriental ancestry in the public schools.[25] Some, however, have
advocated that schools in the oriental areas of the
cities and in certain rural districts could make use
of Chinese and Japanese teachers to good advantage,
particularly in the lower grades.

Several persons of oriental ancestry have
applied for teaching positions but without success.
A Chinese girl, a graduate from a college in Oregon
with a major in education, sent her application to
many schools. She worked through teachers' agencies
and the placement bureau of the college. "I had,"
she said, "the best of recommendations; I had everything but the color." After receiving a favorable
reply to one application, she met the school officials only to be told that they had just filled
the position. A friend commented that the girl's
name did not betray her race, that she did not look
"Chinesey" and even though she had sent her photo-
graph, it is possible that the school officials did
not know she was Chinese until they met her. After
repeated attempts she decided to accept a business
position. [26] Another college girl in the northwest
was looking forward to the teaching profession, but
was none too hopeful. At the university appointment
office they even hesitated in giving her an application form because of the difficulty she would encounter. A girl of oriental ancestry in the Northwest was teaching stenography in a business college
where the majority of the students were white. A
private institution of this kind, however, differs
markedly from the public schools. In British
Columbia the teaching profession is practically

closed against those of oriental ancestry. A Chinese girl, the first to graduate from the Normal Training School, was offered a position by a school principal but the Board refused to ratify the appointment.

The number of students of oriental ancestry in the teacher-training institutions on the Pacific Coast is negligible, even though there is no restriction on their admission. In 1927-1928 one of the teachers' colleges in California had enrolled twenty Japanese and three Chinese. This institution gives two years of regular liberal arts work and many who pursue this course have no intention of making teaching their profession.

A number of Orientals are teaching in collegiate institutions on the mainland. The majority of them are foreign-born and are giving special courses that have a bearing on the Orient. Some who have distinguished themselves in other fields, such as chemistry or biology, have also received appointments. This being true, members of the second generation who make outstanding records should be able to secure positions of this nature.

Social Service. A few young women are planning to enter social service among their own people.[27] A Japanese college girl in California wrote of her decision to enter this field.

The reason why I decided to become a Y.W.C.A. secretary among the Japanese girls here in America is that I want to do something to help them. God knows how much we girls born in America of Japanese parentage need leaders and advisors. More than anything else in the world we need women who will show us the meaning of life and teach us how to live. It is life that we want, rich, full, free, and many-sided. Yes, it is life that we want, but we have been denied the chance to attain life in all its richness, fullness, and beauty. Like flowers whose growth has been retarded by lack of sunlight and air, so our development has been stunted by lack of sympathy and opportunities for self-realization.

In order to keep other girls from experiencing the bitter gnawing that I have felt in the absence of someone to whom I could turn for sympathy and advice, I want to become a woman to whom girls will feel free to unbosom themselves, a woman to whom they will come for guidance and comfort. Because fate has robbed us Japanese-American girls of part of the heritage of girlhood--the right to a mother's tender sympathy--our conception of life is often narrow and distorted. In our hunger and craving for life, we constantly grope for something, we know not what, and when we go on midnight joy rides or engage in petting parties, we are simply giving vent to the restlessness within us. Down in the soul of every girl is a yearning for truth and beauty and love, and I want to help the girls satisfy that yearning by carrying out the principles of the Y.W.C.A., which aim to respond to the fundamental needs of a girl, her respect for her body, the expansion of her mind, and the realization of her soul. I want to give the girls a glimpse of the soul of Japan, not only of the quaintness and exquisite art of the country, but that unflinching perseverance and dauntless courage of the Japanese people which have enabled them to rise in a few years to a world power. I want also to make the girls see the America that lies behind the front page of the newspaper, the America of Washington, of Lincoln, of Roosevelt--the real America with its spirit of liberty and justice to all. In us Japanese-Americans, in whom the East and West have met, I want to combine the best elements of both civilizations; in other words, I want to help develop personalities in whom the modesty and gentleness of the Japanese girl go hand in hand with the vivacity, the open-mindedness, and the big-heartedness of her American sister, so that we Japanese-Americans shall make of ourselves a people of whom both Japan and America will be proud.[28]

Library Work. A number of Japanese girls in California are taking courses in library training. One of them, after graduation from the Library Training School of Los Angeles, was employed by the public library.[29]

The Legal Profession. The legal profession
is attracting a few young men. The group is too
young, however, to have given this field a real test.
For several years the only Japanese in Los Angeles
who had been admitted to practice in the courts was
Hawaiian-born.

Medicine and Dentistry. On the Coast the
practice of the medical men and dentists is largely
restricted to members of their own race, except for
some of the recent immigrants from Europe as well as
the Mexicans and Filipinos. [30] Members of the second
generation encounter difficulties in the oriental
communities because they do not use the parental
languages sufficiently well to deal with their
clientele. In the middle West and East where race
lines are drawn less rigidly against the Orientals,
it is possible to serve white Americans. [31] For the
present the dentists and medical men have the least
difficulty in making adjustments; they can carry on
these professions in their own communities.

Other Professions. Engineers and certain
other specialists occupy no enviable position; the
opportunities offered for their talents in the
oriental communities are practically negligible.
They have to sell their services to American employers which is often difficult. A young Chinese
marine engineer in San Francisco secured employment
with a steamship line. He went to the vessel to begin his duties, whereupon the crew threatened to
strike; Orientals did the manual labor on the ship
but they were not acceptable as engineers. [32] A citizen of Chinese ancestry, who specialized in dairying
at the University of California and later completed
postgraduate work for the degree of Master of
Science at Iowa State College, served as an interpreter in the immigration station at San Francisco.
He was the only Chinese in his class at the California Agricultural College. All his classmates

were able to secure good positions, but he never had an opportunity to make use of his speciality. Since the Chinese have not engaged in dairying, he had to make his connections in the American community or not at all.

Exceptional Cases. There have been a number of exceptions. Probably after the anti-oriental feeling on the Coast has time to subside, there will be more opportunities. In Seattle a native-born Chinese architect has been employed by a white firm for more than fifteen years. He worked in the office and also went out to supervise construction projects where he dealt with white people. A Chinese, who became head draftsman in the office of a public utility in San Francisco, began as a draftsman and gradually worked up to the headship of the department where a number of white persons were under his direction. At first the white employees resented his presence but accommodations were gradually made. Several other Chinese and Japanese engineers are employed in California, both by public departments and by private concerns.

There are difficulties in making satisfactory vocational adjustments, but in a number of instances, it would appear that color or race is no bar. If a person is found who can do a certain job better than anyone else, he is selected no matter what the color may be.[33] If a mediocre person will fill the requirements, one with a white skin will likely be chosen. A case in point is that of a native-born Chinese girl on the Coast who was employed by an establishment which makes fancy neckwear, scarfs, handkerchiefs, shawls, and other silk novelties. They fill orders from big stores on the Coast, in Canada, in Chicago, and in New York. The Chinese girl was the designer and head of the shop where practically all the workers were white girls. She made frequent trips to Chicago, New York, and other cities in connection with the business. The best of

relationships seemed to prevail in the shop and in
the office. The manager spoke highly of her. She
stated that the manager treated her very well. Probably this man was particularly broadminded toward
Orientals; he was Jewish and had an Irish wife.
This girl, without doubt, was of a superior type.
She was the first Chinese girl to enter the state
university. In doing so she had to fight her way
against the opposition of her parents and the whole
Chinese community. She had been interested in art
while in high school and had become known for some
of her productions. She continued her art work in
the university and before graduation was offered a
position in the art department of one of the leading
dry-goods stores of the northwest where she was employed for seven years. When she left the department store, another Chinese girl was selected from a
field of forty applicants to fill the vacancy.

A third-generation Japanese girl, a talented
dancer, won much praise from the theatregoers for
her entertaining act at one of the large moving-
picture houses in Los Angeles. She was booked to
make a tour of the West Coast circuit after the completion of her engagement at the local theatre.[34]
Patrons of the moving-picture theatres, are, of
course, looking for something new and different and
do not draw rigid lines.

At one of the California universities a
Japanese girl was on the art staff of the college
humor magazine and the college annual for several
years. A number of her productions were reproduced
in national publications. In this particular activity her Japanese features did not interfere and
her work was accepted on its merits. A number of
Japanese musicians have been well received by American audiences. Artists, also, have been given recognition. It would seem that lines of demarcation
between races are less noticeable in the field of
the fine arts.

In certain instances, racial differences

prove to be assets of no small importance. A Chinese girl in California decided to enter the journalistic field where she hoped to capitalize her racial liabilities. Before graduation she contributed several articles to the largest daily paper in the city. Shortly after leaving the university she joined the reportorial staff of an American daily paper where she was employed for several years.[35]

Another Chinese girl in California came into prominence through the publication of an article on "The Sheiks of Chinatown" in one of the metropolitan daily papers. She could secure interesting materials not available to the ordinary white reporter. Furthermore, she could grasp the situation--she could see the salient features and write them interestingly. A California Japanese who was working for a doctorate in a large university was planning either to teach American history in Japan or oriental history in America, with a preference for the latter. At the outset he began to specialize in English, but even though he were superior in his English he would have great difficulty in securing a position to teach that subject. In teaching oriental history in America, his Japanese face will be an asset; it may create an impression that he is in a position to secure data on the Orient which are not readily accessible to one with Caucasian features.[36]

Chapter VIII

VOCATIONAL ADJUSTMENTS--CONCLUSIONS

What will be the solution to the vocational problems of our citizens of oriental ancestry? Kazuo Kawai, a young Japanese in California, wrote that there were three possible solutions, but each had its difficulties.

Accept Defeat. In the first place, they might adopt a defeatist attitude and say:

Why try to do anything at all? Probably we were meant to be just a servile class. We can't help it, so let's make the best of a bad bargain. . . .

I was urging a very close friend. . . . to go on to college. We were in high school together, and he made a name for himself by his outstanding abilities. But now he sees no use in continuing his studies. His attitude is "What's the use of going to college? I have a little fruit stand, and I give the American customers the kind of service they want. I have a comfortable income. I am happy. But you go to college and get a lot of theories that make you dissatisfied with the conditions of the Japanese here. You want to change things. But just the same, after graduation, you fellows all come around to my fruit store begging for a job."[1]

The young people on the Coast may operate the fruit stands and encounter no serious difficulties.[2] The Japanese, however, are highly sensitive and many consider such an occupation an admission of defeat. In Hawaii they may accept a position of inferiority and become plantation laborers. In that they will meet with no serious opposition; in fact,

they will have less difficulty than the young people
on the mainland in making their adjustments. A few
have accepted a defeatist philosophy and form a
shiftless and even criminal element in the various
communities.

        Find Places in Orient. In the second place,
the members of the American-born generation may go
to the Orient.[3] Of this proposal Mr. Kawai wrote:

        Most of us were born here, and we know no other coun-
try. This is "our country" right here. As to having advantage over the people in Japan, we have the wonderful advantage
of being quite unable to speak their language or read their
papers, of being totally ignorant of their customs, history or
traditions, of holding different ideals, of thinking in different ways. Yes, we have as much advantage over the people
in Japan as a deaf mute has over a man in possession of all
his faculties. An American would have an infinitely easier
time in Japan than we would, for they would excuse a foreigner
if he made mistakes, but we, with our Japanese names and faces,
would have to conform to their rigid standards or else be
"queer." As for advantage in education, with some of the universities over there like Imperial, Waseda, and others ranking
with the leading universities of the world, what chance have
we, products of the American rah-rah system, against their ma-
ture scholars? The trouble with us is that we have been too
thoroughly Americanized. We have attended American schools,
we speak English exclusively, we know practically nothing of
Japan except what an average American knows; our ideals, customs, mode of thinking, our whole psychology is American. Although physically we are Japanese, culturally we are Americans.
We simply are not capable of fitting into Japanese society, so
we are destined to remain here.[4]

        The majority of the young people both in
Hawaii and on the mainland prefer to stay in America.[5] Several have been offered positions in the
Orient, but after reflection have decided not to accept. On account of the conditions in America, a

considerable number are thinking about the Orient.
Some who have visited the Orient have been impressed
by certain conditions and have been fired with a desire to serve there; they have come to consider the
Orient from the point of view of missionary activity.   Others consider service in the Orient, if not
permanently then temporarily at least, in order to
promote a better feeling between America and the
Orient.   An editorial[6] suggested that a number of
college graduates go to Japan and other places in
the Orient as good-will missionaries.   In the East
they could be teachers of English and western history and also serve as preachers, doctors, chemists,
consuls, merchants, traders, and agricultural experts.   While carrying on these various activities,
they would be spreading the gospel of good will.
This editorial was doubtless inspired by an announcement made by the Doshisha University of Kyoto, Japan,
that a plan had been evolved whereby a number of
American-born Japanese would be added to the faculty
for a period of three years to teach English and
certain other subjects, while they were to have an
opportunity to study the Japanese language and culture.

The original plan of the Doshisha was aug-
mented by the Friend Peace Fellowships instituted by
Dr. and Mrs. Theodore Richards of Honolulu in 1928.
This arrangement is still in operation.[7]

The success of this Doshisha plan led to another development along identical lines.   Under the
Friend Peace Fellowships, two young college graduates of Chinese ancestry are sent to Yenching University, Peiping, China.[8]

There are certain opportunities in the industrial life of Japan, but there are many problems
connected therewith.   Japan is densely populated and
the competition for work is keen.   From several
sources has come the information that many graduates
of the Japanese universities are unable to secure
suitable employment in their own country.   Several

warnings have been issued that Japanese born and
reared in America should not go to Japan unless they
had sufficient funds or were assured of positions be-
forehand. This advice was given because there were
several destitute American-born college men in the
country who could not secure work.[9]

The young Chinese have been paying considerable attention to China, and many are planning to go
there for a life work. The annuals of the Chinese
Students' Alliance of Hawaii devote considerable
space to China and the opportunities there. They
tell about the undeveloped resources and the opportunities in the industrial field. In the present
period of transition they point to the unlimited
fields for service in teaching, in medicine, in politics, and in business. In addition to the immature
students, men of experience advise the young people
in both Hawaii and on the Coast to go to the Orient
to help build a new China. A number of Chinese, who
have visited their homeland, have brought back reports of opportunities for young men with American
training. On these visits they have seen several
American-born Chinese occupying good positions in
China. In this connection, we must consider the influence of Dr. Sun Yat Sen upon the young Chinese in
Hawaii. He was born of peasant parentage in a village near Canton, China. As a boy he went to Hawaii where he acquired an economic competence. Then
he returned to his own country where he became an
outstanding leader. Furthermore, an Hawaiian-born
son of a Chinese coolie holds a professorship in a
university in China. When sons of coolies, grown
up in their midst, have risen to positions of
eminence,[10] any consideration of a status of inferiority in America becomes all the more intolerable.
Not all American-reared Chinese can adjust themselves to the life of China. A Chinese woman took
her California-born daughter to China, while the
father and brother remained behind. The girl, anxious to return, wrote pleadingly to her teacher.

Gee, I am worried now because Chinese is so hard to
study and beside you have to memorize pages and pages. My
brother-in-law brought home some strawberry jam the other day
which is made by the Bakersfield Kern Grocery Store. Gee, I
nearly ate half of it already. When I'm eating it I feel as
if I'm eating lunch In Home Sweet Home. I feel so fine when I
see anything that came from America. I don't know why. Miss
Brown, dear, will you do me a favor? Do you meet my daddy often? If you do, will you please ask daddy whether I will get a
chance to go back to America or not?[11]

Remain in America. The third alternative is
as follows:

But others of our group intend to stay here and see
the thing through. We do not intend to succumb to our environment. We believe that our duty is to stay here and make
a distinctive contribution to American life just as other national groups have contributed to American life in the
past. . . . Our immediate outlook is of course very dark. But
our policy is to get the best education we can, to hold to the
highest ideals we know, and to keep ever before us the vision
of what we might accomplish, even though for a while we cannot find vocations befitting our abilities. Then we shall be
so dissatisfied with existing conditions that we shall be working continuously to change them. Only by such continuous hammering away will any change come about. Of course it is going
to be hard on the individual who will have to plug away at an
inferior position when he is really capable of something better. But this seems to be the only course which will bring
any ultimate improvement. And to the credit of the American-
born Japanese, many of them are following this policy and a
few of them are beginning to find their proper place in society.[12]

Emigration to Other Countries. In addition
to the three proposals of Kazuo Kawai, there is a
fourth possibility--that of going to other foreign
countries,[13] and this is receiving some attention.
Japanese newspapers, both in Hawaii and on the Coast,
have published materials on a colonization project

in Brazil. In 1925 the Japanese minister to that
country received an offer from the governor of the
state of Para on the Amazon River that if Japanese
were willing to come and develop some of the wild
lands, he would turn them over rent free. One paper
stated that the Brazilian Consul in Kobe urged the
Japanese to establish cotton mills in his country.
Another paper announced that the government of
Brazil was offering subsidies to workmen in other
countries to meet the labor shortage. While this
colonization is primarily meant for the people of
Japan, many in Hawaii and on the Coast have been
considering it. A number of Japanese high-school
boys in Hawaii have been talking about South America.

        Migration from Hawaii to the Mainland. The
young people in Hawaii have a fifth alternative in
that they may migrate to continental United States.[14]
A few years ago a considerable number went, but
disillusionments were reported back to Hawaii and
the number was greatly reduced. Doubtless, the War
and the post-war period with all the propaganda
about democracy, placed a halo about the United
States which led many in Hawaii to expect too much.
Bitter disappointment was in store for many. Some
now go with high expectations and encounter difficulties. Doubtless the anti-plantation attitude
which they carry with them tends to make agricultural work distasteful. They expect something better, but find comparatively few opportunities in
other fields. A number, however, have succeeded and
that has attracted others.

        An Hawaiian-born Japanese dentist has built
up a practice in Chicago where his clientele is
drawn almost exclusively from white people in business and professional life. His charges are said to
be rather high, but he has established such a reputation for himself that he has all the work he can do.
He accepts only those who are referred to him, except
in emergency cases.

This is a good illustration of the "cockroach doctrine"[15] or philosophy of life as enunciated
by a middle-aged Japanese man who had received part
of his education in Hawaii. According to him an
Hawaiian-born youth may be likened to a cockroach in
a bath tub. If he tries to crawl out over the sides,
he will fall back again and again. The wise cockroach will fly up and away instead of trying to
crawl. A young man must have confidence in his own
ability if he is ever to accomplish anything.[16]

The sugar men have told the sons of Orientals that there would be ample opportunity for them
on the plantations if they were willing to start at
the bottom and work up. But the young people have
manifested no great enthusiasm for these promises.
They have seen themselves, like the cockroach, slipping back into the bath tub. They could see no great
security because as individuals they could not bargain on equal terms with the plantations which are
strongly organized through the Hawaiian Sugar Planters' Association. According to some Japanese workers, if a high-school boy should obtain a position
as foreman on a plantation, he would not be secure;
he might be discharged and be placed on a blacklist
which would bar him from employment on any other
plantation. Then, like the cockroach, he would have
to begin at the bottom in some other place. This
outlook has not appealed to the young men of oriental ancestry. There is room at the top for a few
superior persons. The fact that several have made
outstanding successes has been a challenge to a
great many, and perhaps too many have tried to follow these examples.

The Chinese in Hawaii have paid little attention to continental United States. They are
rather well established commercially and have greater opportunities than on the mainland. A Chinese
business man who returned to Honolulu after a trip
to the Coast made this statement:

California has not always given the Chinese the opportunities which are found in Hawaii. Very few Chinese in California have gone ahead on account of their not being given the opportunities which the Chinese in Hawaii enjoy. Consequently they are not found in the professions, in the banking and trust companies, nor in positions of importance. The failure of two large Chinese corporations in California has not given the Chinese a favorable standing at all.[17]

There is perhaps a tendency on the part of the Americans of oriental ancestry to magnify their problems and become impatient because results come slowly. But when compared with the descendants of certain European groups, they may well congratulate themselves on the progress they have already made.

Chapter IX

THE STRUGGLE FOR RECOGNITION AND STATUS

A. Oriental Immigrants and Status

Vocational adjustments are often complicated
when the parents project their ambitions upon the
younger generation. Particularly has this been true
of the Japanese in Hawaii. The majority of them
came to work on the sugar plantations with the intention of accumulating sufficient savings to assure
a comfortable livelihood and a higher social station
in the homeland. Being accustomed to the low wages
of the Orient, the earnings of the plantations seemed
to offer a fair opportunity for acquiring a competence. Many have returned but the majority, in spite
of unremitting toil, have not been able to accumulate
enough to assure a life of comfort in the old country. With their ambitions unrealized, many hoped to
see their dreams come true in and through their children.

The full significance of this situation cannot be understood apart from its oriental background.
Japan is not far removed from a feudal regime in
which distinctions in class and social rank were important. The immigrants lived in their old memories
and planned to return to the homeland to acquire a
superior status in an aristocracy; they were not aiming at the attainment of equality in a democratically
organized society. Many have concluded that it is no
longer possible to return to positions of dignity in
their home communities. They cannot win recognition
and status in America, but there is hope of gaining

110

vicariously through their American-born children what
they had failed to do for themselves. Since certain
limitations are placed upon the younger generation on
account of race, the parents look to education as a
means of betterment.

The projection of ambitions has not ended
with an encouragement toward securing an education;
very often it has been carried over into advice relative to the choice of an occupation. In this connection the tradition of the Orient, particularly of
Japan, becomes evident. The parents are desirous
that their children turn to occupations that will reflect credit upon the family name. If they are not
sufficiently ambitious to rise above the occupations
open to their parents in Hawaii, they are considered
failures and as such bring discredit to the family.[1]

Some parents choose vocations for their sons
and daughters against the better judgment of the
children. A number accept the parental choices as
temporary expedients, but hope to make readjustments
later. Some are torn between duty to their parents
and obligation to themselves. Others rationalize the
situation and endeavor to make the best of the vocational choices made by their parents. A Chinese girl
in Hawaii, who had been projected into the teaching
profession by her mother, found consolation in the
fact that she would have a long summer vacation for
rest and travel. Some gradually become interested
in the parental choices; some even become enthusiastic about their future.

When parents project their ambitions upon the
child, there is no normal development of the child's
own interests and talents. He does not select his
own patterns and work out his own life organization;
his course is directed by fixed ideas of his parents.
With oriental parents, living in memories of the old
country and not understanding their Americanized
children, this parental domination often accentuates
the problems of the young people.[2] Not all parents,
however, make the occupational choices for their

children. Many provide opportunities which arouse
and develop in a normal way the children's own interests and ambitions. While the parents, in project-
ing their ambitions upon the children, are interested
in satisfying their own thwarted wishes, they are
not unmindful of the status of the younger generation. The problem lies in their analysis of the situation from their own point of view and not from that
of the children.

      Differences between the Chinese and Japanese.
The Chinese have been able to entrench themselves
rather firmly in the commercial life of Hawaii. Thus
they have been able to win considerable recognition
for themselves and also to make better provision for
their sons in the preferred occupations. Hence they
have been less eager than the Japanese to project
their ambitions upon their children. The Japanese
have been more sensitive to distinctions in rank and
have been more interested in being recognized by the
white group than have the Chinese. They have been
more concerned about educating their sons so they
might receive recognition. S. Morris Morishita[3] reveals this desire for recognition.

      Race prejudice in California is producing an unusual
phenomenon. It is creating an educated class among the second
generation Japanese the like of which is not duplicated anywhere else in the world. More is required of the Japanese for
their assimilation into American society than is asked of other
racial groups. . . . Consequently, the second generation Japanese in California are studying exceedingly hard to fit themselves for American society. It is the ambition of most of the
Japanese parents to give their sons and daughters even at tremendous sacrifices the highest possible education. They send
their children to the finest colleges and universities in the
states, realizing that only people with wide culture and superi-
or educational attainments, with a command of English such as
that possessed by the second generation Japanese on the mainland will be acceptable in American society where they normally
belong.

The next step, which is most important, many of the qualified second generation Japanese on the mainland have not taken and that is to enlarge the circle of their friendship outside of their own racial group. Sometimes this seems difficult in face of the waves of prejudice which are all too prevalent. However, the waves are not as large as one may suppose on first blush.

Merely becoming highly educated without displaying our inner selves to other racial groups is of no avail in an attempt to be recognized on an equal plane with others.[4]

B. The Younger Generation and Status

The American-born citizens, as well as their immigrant parents, are struggling for recognition and status. Frequently their ideas run counter to those of their elders; but fundamentally the purpose is the same. The idea uppermost in the minds of most second generation Orientals is the acquisition of a status superior to that held by their parents in America. The struggle for status is fundamental in the whole problem of vocational adjustment. It is also closely linked with the problems of education, with church affiliation, and with relationships between various races. The matter of status enters into intermarriage in Hawaii. Some young women marry Anglo-Saxon men,[5] in an attempt to get closer to the dominant group and thus acquire positions of greater dignity in the community.

The students of oriental extraction in the University of Hawaii take a lively interest in military training. This gives a certain amount of recognition. When they wear the military uniforms of the United States, they have proof that they have been accepted to that extent as Americans. When they become officers, they attain a certain status. They have been accustomed to have all orders given by white men, but when they attain positions where they can command others, they have come to be more nearly

on a level with the dominant group. Several of these
students have gone with the University of Hawaii
rifle team to Camp Lewis, Washington, where they have
mingled with white students from mainland universities. That has enhanced their status and has meant
much to them.

Athletic ability has been a valuable asset
in helping a person gain recognition. Japanese high-
school athletes in California have been able to command the respect of the white students to such an
extent that they could participate freely in much of
the social life of the school. White boys will even
elect those of oriental ancestry to captaincies of
athletic teams if they are good players.[6] Furthermore, this recognition has made it possible for several Hawaiian athletes of oriental ancestry to marry
white girls.[7] But even with this recognition, the
star athletes have not been completely lost in the
American group; there has been some discrimination
against them.

The Sugar Industry and Status. Because of
conditions peculiar to Hawaii, the struggle for recognition and status is keener there than on the
Pacific Coast. In the paternalistic system of the
sugar plantations, the workers, mostly Orientals,
have occupied a position which is inferior to that
of all white men, and there has been no competition
between the two groups.[8] A situation in which the
workers are held to be so far inferior to the management tends to develop antagonistic attitudes. On
every hand one could hear the younger generation of
oriental ancestry expressing its resentment against
this imputed status of inferiority. The paternalism,
autocracy, and class distinctions which have been
characteristic of the sugar industry developed in
them a revulsion against anything and everything connected with the plantations. Comparatively few have
been interested in agriculture unless it be of a type
which would afford some opportunity for individual

initiative and for acquiring an honorable status in
the community. When the young people have been in-
oculated with democratic ideas in school, they do
not accept the class distinctions of the plantations
with equanimity.

According to some Anglo-Saxons, the young
people of oriental parentage are lazy and have been
looking for nothing but easy jobs. A casual glance
at the hard work many do in order to go through
school shows how inadequate this conclusion is; it
does not explain why the young people have shunned
the sugar plantations. In Hawaii the sugar industry
has given neither good pay nor respect. The second
has been the more serious. The situation in the Kona
district of Hawaii, an area of independent coffee
producers, has borne this out. Even though the income has been less certain than on the sugar plantations, there has been less drift toward the city.
The coffee growers are entrepreneurs and prefer their
independence, even though their incomes are small.

The following statement from a Caucasian-
Hawaiian college girl reveals the attitude of superiority of the Whites and the status of inferiority
which has been assigned to the workers. It also
brings out her reaction to this imputed inferiority.

My father did not believe in a life of leisure. We
had to do all our own work. It was very unpleasant especially
when the manager's children taunted us and looked down upon us
as being mere workers. Of course I was then too young to understand, but there were some things which penetrated my childish mind and have remained with me ever since. Why look down
upon American-Hawaiian children? Are they not as good as any
nationality? Perhaps they are and I still believe they are but
the white employers who were working on the plantation with my
father did not seem to think so. I suppose you wonder why I
have such an opinion. Like any other child I was fond of playing. Sometimes when I was lonesome I would try to get acquainted with the white children next door. If their mother was not
at home we would have a lovely time but as soon as she would

return she would call her children into the house and send me
home. Her explanation was, "Of course I can't allow my children to associate with those half-white children." Although
I was only six years old I despised the white people who treated me thus. My mother saw how lonely I was so she sent me to
to school with my older sister. As a small child I was very
fond of music. My father once remarked as a joke, that some
day I was going to be a famous singer and then I would live
with white people away in a place called the United States.
Was I happy? No, I secretly brooded and pondered over this
and fretted myself almost ill. One day I couldn't stand the
strain another minute so I asked my mother if I had to be a
singer whether I wanted to be one or not. She said, "Why of
course not. It is up to you what you want to be." I became
happy again. Why worry? I needn't stay among white people.
I was afraid that they were despising me.[9]

> The inferior status of the plantation labor-
ers was recognized even by children and came to be a
line of division between different groups.

We fellows of the village considered ourselves better
than the laborers of the plantation and the boys of the village
used to have gang fights with the plantation boys. We were
outnumbered so that all we could do was to tell them and tease
them about their fathers' and mothers' cane-field jobs.[10]

Occupational Situation Determines Status.
That this inferiority in status is not a racial matter but one that is inherent in the occupational situation becomes evident when we consider the Portuguese. Even though they belong to the Caucasoid
group, they are not included with the other Caucasians in the popular classification of "Haole"[11]
which is used in Hawaii. Because they came to work
on the sugar plantations, they have been accorded a
status of inferiority. The Portuguese resent this
imputation of inferiority. They are trying to throw
off this stigma and to decrease the social distance
between themselves and the Anglo-Saxons. This has a

marked effect upon their behavior; many become loud
and noisy in order to attract attention. They do and
say things to belittle the Orientals in order to appear superior. Many Portuguese call attention very
pointedly to the color differences, using such expressions as "slant-eyed Chink" and "yellow belly."
A Chinese college girl wrote:

> I have often wondered how I would enjoy being a mem-
ber of some other language group, but I have never regretted
the fact that I am Chinese. When I first went to school, I
felt that I was different from persons of other language
groups. Whenever there was a fight, we were sure to hear conversation of this nature: "You old Kanaka!"[12] "I can lick all
the 'Japs' in the world." All this, however, did not make as
much of an impression upon me as did one certain incident. I
was in town when a Portuguese girl unconsciously bumped into a
Chinese girl. Instead of helping her pick up her packages she
walked straight ahead. The Chinese girl said, "The idea!"
"I said, 'Excuse me,' didn't I?" shouted the Portuguese girl
angrily. "Well, say it loud enough so I can hear it next time,"
answered the other. Then the Portuguese girl, with a toss of
her head said, "Shut up you Pake;[13] I'm white!"
>   I cannot see anything <u>white</u> in a person who can say
things so much below her dignity.[14]

Some Portuguese women will not permit their children
to play with Orientals. With many it is a serious
matter; they cannot afford to endanger their status
by permitting such association. The Anglo-Saxons are
in less dnager of losing status by such intermingling.
The Orientals are aware of the situation and
react accordingly.[15] Many of them dislike the dominant Anglo-Saxons but, nevertheless, they envy them
and would gladly exchange positions with them. The
Portuguese, however, are not objects of envy in the
eyes of the Orientals. The behavior of the Anglo-
Saxon is unlike that of the Portuguese: he enjoys a
superior status and does not have to belittle the
Oriental to convince others of his superiority. A

few who find it difficult to compete with the Orientals on the basis of merit, resort to such tactics.

          Status and Solution of Occupational Problems.
The solution of the occupational problems of the
younger generation in Hawaii is not merely a matter
of technical training to make them more efficient in
sugar production. That will not go to the bottom of
things; it is a matter of social status. These
young people will not be satisfied with a classification of inferiors, as men of the lowest social stratum; they will not respond enthusiastically to one
planter's characterization of "human mules."[16] They
must be given an honorable status; they must be
treated as persons of dignity. It will take more
than wages to attract them.[17] Most of the young
people of Hawaii prefer to work in some more dignified occupation, even though the monetary return may
be less than the wage scale on the plantations.[18]
The seriousness of the problem is further enhanced
by the difference in conditions in the Orient and in
America. In the Orient, the person gains standing
in the community as a member of a family; in America
the family name of the Oriental means nothing. The
young person of oriental ancestry must turn to individualistic means of gaining recognition; he must
develop devices to call attention to himself. With
the stigma of inferiority on account of occupation
and with no family name to help him, he has to fight
a double battle. This has had much to do with the
efforts of many Orientals to excel in scholarship,
with their interest in oratorical competitions and
in athletics in order to win recognition. This at
times has led to showy dress or to loud and boisterous conduct in order to attract attention.

          The Chinese and Recognition in Hawaii. The
Chinese in Hawaii have passed through several stages.
The immigrant Chinese cared not a whit what the white
people thought or said about them. Instead of

adopting American practices, they have declared that
their new neighbors should learn from them. The
first Hawaiian-born generation was sensitive to white
opinion and was interested in getting recognition
from the white people. Since affiliation with a
Christian Church gave some recognition, members of
the early second generation became members. As the
American-born group has increased and the entire
Chinese group has become well established in the commercial life of the community, there has developed a
feeling that they were sufficient unto themselves.
They are paying increasingly less attention to white
opinion; they are no longer satisfied with being nobodies in the American group when they may be men of
importance in their own. In the spring of 1927 several newspapers had accounts of some aged Chinese
men who were found in a disreputable alley of Honolulu preparing a stew of dog meat for themselves. The
Social Service Committee of the Hawaii Chinese Civic
Association made an investigation of the conditions
under which these men were living and issued an appeal for funds to provide better institutional care
for them. At first it seemed that the leaders in
the movement looked upon the condition of these aged
men as a reflection upon their group which would
cause them to "lose face" with the white people and
that they were desirous of removing that blemish. A
prominent member of the Chinese community, however,
declared that the young men rendered this service to
these indigents in order to gain recognition from the
Chinese community. This occurred only a few months
after the first Chinese had been elected to political
office. There was a noticeable effort on the part
of several men to gain attention which later might
have political significance.

        The Chinese are creating their own institu-
tions and increasingly their young people are coming
to be satisfied with recognition gained in their own
group. In Honolulu the Chinese have their own University Club which is no mere satellite of the

Anglo-Saxon organization. It is an honor to belong
to this club; they are setting up rigid entrance requirements; they are classifying the colleges and
are planning to admit only graduates from institutions of high standing. Furthermore, members of the
club have begun to consider a matter which may bring
distinction to the entire community. They have asked
why there is no distinguished scholar in the Chinese
community of Hawaii.[19] They have reached the point
where they now consider matters less closely connected with the bread and butter problem. Henceforth they will pay increasing attention to the encouragement of scholarship.

A considerable number of the early American-
born Chinese, after meeting rebuffs and going through
a process of disillusionment, returned to their own
group and became the most enthusiastic protagonists
for their own organizations; they discovered that it
was to their advantage. Many professional men have
found that their clientele comes largely from their
own groups. A number of them have developed a certain amount of bitterness against the Whites and are
called "Haole-haters." This is evidenced by the
"Never-Give-A-Damn-Club" of the Chinese, which is
made up of the disillusioned ones.[20]

Another stage is becoming evident as this attitude of the disillusioned reacts upon the younger
members of the second and third generations. They
pay increasingly less attention to the white group.
They seem to be taking a more rational attitude toward the conditions of life such as they find in
Hawaii and are accommodating themselves more rapidly
than the young Japanese. While a large number of
young Japanese are aiming at things which will arrest
the attention of the white people, the young Chinese
are placing emphasis upon those things which will be
useful and acceptable to their own group.[21]

Chapter X

CITIZENSHIP AND POLITICAL ACTIVITIES

The American-born generation of oriental ancestry inevitably comes into contact with our governmental machinery and institutionalized political
activities. These contacts exercise a profound influence upon their lives and have much to do in
shaping their attitudes.

A. Statistical Data Concerning Citizens of
Oriental Ancestry

Number of Citizens. No adequate figures on
this group are available for continental United
States since the Census does not differentiate between aliens and citizens in the age-distribution
tables. In 1914 there were about 16,000 American-
born Chinese in the United States and all of these
would be old enough to vote in 1935. Some deduc-
tions must be made for deaths and for departures to
China. As a rough estimate we may set the figure
for the Chinese citizens of voting age at 10,000 in
1935.
Various estimates have been made of the number in the Japanese group. A letter from the Consulate General of Japan in San Francisco reported
2,484 American-born Japanese of voting age in California as of October, 1930. On the basis of his
9.7 per cent sampling of the state, Strong placed
his estimate at 3,500 for California in 1930.[1]   The
Japanese American News of September 3, 1934, estimated that there were from 3,600 to 4,000 of voting

age who were born in California, in addition to
which another 1,000 has been added by migration from
Hawaii.[2] This same article estimates that there are
7,000 of voting age in continental United States.

        According to the Census of 1930, there were
in Hawaii 6,998 Chinese citizens of voting age and
13,062 Japanese in the same class.

        Registered Voters on the Pacific Coast. No
adequate data are available relative to the number
that register and vote on the Coast. No attention
is paid to this small minority group in most places.
The Registrar of Voters in San Francisco reported on
August 12, 1934, that 1,250 Chinese and 25 Japanese
were registered. According to T. T. Takimoto,[3]
Secretary of the Japanese Association of America,
there were about 300 registered Japanese voters in
California in 1932. The Japanese papers on the
Coast have urged the eligible voters to register.
At times they have published the names of registrants
as an honor roll in order to stimulate others. With-
in the last few years the Japanese American Citizens
League has been conducting a campaign to bring out
the second-generation vote.

        Registered Voters in Hawaii. In Hawaii the
voters are registered according to ancestral groups.
Table XI gives the total number of citizens for four
groups in 1920 and 1930 and those who registered at
the several elections.

        In Hawaii, both English and racial papers
have urged the citizens of oriental ancestry to register and vote. To this appeal, the Chinese have responded better than the Japanese. The women of
oriental ancestry, however, have not been registering their full strength. Table XII presents the
registration by sex for several ancestral groups in
Hawaii. According to this table only a small number
of the Chinese and Japanese women registered in 1922
but they have registered in increasing numbers and

Table XI

REGISTERED VOTERS BY ANCESTRY AT GENERAL ELECTIONS IN HAWAII
COMPARED WITH THE TOTAL NUMBER OF CITIZENS OF VOTING AGE IN
1920 AND IN 1930

Ancestry	Registered Voters				Total Citizens of Voting Age	
	1902*	1910	1920	1930	1920	1930
Hawaiian	8,680	9,619	14,650	19,858	19,613	21,358
Caucasian**	3,786	4,414	9,886	20,872	21,697	43,642
Chinese	143	396	1,141	4,402	3,305	6,998
Japanese	3	13	658	7,017	2,613	13,062

*In this table the ten-year periods were selected except
for 1902 since the data are not available for 1900.

**"Caucasian" includes American, British, German, Portu-
guese, and others.

Data from Annual Report of the Governor of Hawaii, June 30,
1932, p. 21, and June 30, 1934, p. 10.

have drawn closer to the men at each succeeding
election. The increase in registrants among the
Japanese women has been particularly striking. In
the American-born group the sexes are nearly equal
in number, but oriental tradition, that political
activity is outside woman's sphere, has been a de-
terrent factor. Furthermore, the expense of registration has restrained many. Prior to 1922, officials required documentary evidence of Hawaiian
birth. Some secured birth certificates free of cost
but the majority, and particularly the Japanese, had
to pay about $35 each. The men, in the main, were
willing to pay this, but it was practically prohibi-
tive to the women. A considerable change has come
as the result of agitation by the Chinese and Japanese in the Territory; in 1929 the fee for a birth

Table XII

REGISTERED VOTERS BY RACE AND SEX IN HAWAII, 1922-1932

Race	1922		1924		1926	
	Male	Female	Male	Female	Male	Female
American (White)	6,796	3,138	4,047	3,230	4,761	3,861
Chinese	1,285	214	1,684	332	2,317	589
Hawaiian	9,343	7,474	7,167	5,780	7,338	6,095
Part-Hawaiian	-	-	2,039	1,701	2,322	2,008
Japanese	1,014	121	1,506	205	2,749	343
Portuguese	3,180	1,032	3,622	1,581	4,158	1,957

Race	1928		1930		1932	
	Male	Female	Male	Female	Male	Female
American (White)	4,911	4,053	5,579	4,665	6,478	5,752
Chinese	2,930	1,020	3,174	1,228	3,644	1,712
Hawaiian	8,605	7,374	8,317	7,364	8,754	7,822
Part-Hawaiian	1,590	1,383	2,275	1,902	2,655	2,351
Japanese	3,823	1,016	5,342	1,675	7,774	3,499
Portuguese	4,570	2,487	5,202	2,909	6,041	4,013

Data from the Secretary of Hawaii

certificate was reduced to three dollars.

The Hawaiian-born citizens who migrated to the mainland encountered even greater difficulties in attempting to establish their right to vote. Considerable annoyance was caused for many years because officials in continental United States refused to recognize the Hawaiian birth certificates. A number of the Japanese were compelled to make the long and expensive trip to Hawaii and spend months in going through court procedure. In an effort to remedy this situation, the Territorial Legislature in 1925 sent a commission to Washington. Certain improvements were effected, but even yet conditions are not entirely satisfactory. In recent years, the Secretary of the Territory has been making periodic trips to the Coast when persons of Hawaiian birth might present their evidence to him.

Under such conditions the registration has been light, particularly since no immediate benefit was in view. Election to office of several members of the group, however, has served as a stimulus and there has been a gradual increase in the number of registrants and voters.[4]

B. Political Future of the Second-Generation Citizens

On the Pacific Coast. On the Pacific Coast, those of oriental ancestry constitute a small minority. In most places, their influence will be practically negligible and their participation in politics will be a mere ceremonial, except for certain local matters in some California communities and in the segregated areas of the large cities.

When the anti-Chinese agitation was at its height in California, no politician could hope to win an office unless he attacked the Orientals. A considerable amount of discriminatory legislation was directed against the Chinese, but since they had no votes they were helpless. The politicians on the Coast have also attacked the Japanese, but a decided change has become apparent. Candidates for office makes strong appeals to the voters of oriental ancestry, even where they are comparatively few.[5] An American of Chinese parentage in a Pacific Coast city said:.

The politicians have begun to show an interest in our votes, and several of them have called on me in my dingy office. Since I am the head of the organization of American citizens of Chinese ancestry, they appeal to me to use my

influence in swinging the votes of the group. When R. J._____
was candidating for the office of county attorney, he called
on me and took me out for lunch. When B. W._____ was running
for mayor he came to me for the Chinese vote. I had a statement which he had made at one time that all Chinese were liars.
I handed that to him and asked, "What about that?" He began
to explain that he had been connected with a case where there
had been a number of crooked Chinese and he had come to that
conclusion, but subsequent experiences had led him to revise
his estimate. I told him that because of that the Chinese
would not vote for him.[6]

He was not elected mayor. Even though his
defeat was not primarily due to Chinese opposition,
he, as well as other politicians, will henceforth be
more careful. In one senatorial election, the Chinese in California voted against a man who had been
strongly anti-oriental. It seems that he felt this;
he made reference to it in a subsequent speech. In
the future, candidates will not be overzealous in
attacking Orientals lest they alienate the votes of
these groups, together with those of many white
voters who insist on a square deal for the citizens
of oriental ancestry.
          Furthermore, these small groups of voters
may ally themselves with other minorities and thus
exert considerable influence. As a case in point we
may turn to Fresno, California. This city is divided into two distinct areas by the Southern Pacific
Railway. The East Side is occupied by those of
north-European descent, while the West Side is cosmopolitan in its make-up and has Chinese, Japanese,
Greeks, Negroes, Russians, Italians, etc. A considerable number, particularly the Italians, owned
property on the West Side but they did not get as
many improvements for their tax-money as did the
East-Siders. The Italians presented the facts to
the other residents and "The West-Side Central Committee" was organized, with representatives from the
different groups. This organization has produced

results. Since 1909 Fresno has held an annual
Raisin Festival to which the West-Siders made regular financial contributions, but never did the pa-
rade--one of the prominent features of the festi-
val--cross the railway tracks to the West Side. In
1927 the Committee brought pressure to bear and the
parade crossed the tracks. At one time the West-
Siders circulated a petition to recall a county official. Even though they could not evict him, it
was a real victory. Since then they have received
more consideration from public officials. The politicians, realizing that a young Japanese professional man has exerted no small influence in the affairs
of this Central Committee, have paid considerable
attention to him.[7]

Already some of these voters are receiving
recognition through appointments to committees of
local party organizations. In Seattle an American-
born Japanese woman was appointed to the election
board of one precinct in 1934. A young Japanese attorney in Seattle, undoubtedly, has made the greatest headway politically. After serving on a precinct committee he was named a delegate to the State
Republican convention which met in June, 1934. In
July he filed as a Republican candidate for the
state legislature, and had the support of the Republican Club of his district. He was defeated in
this attempt, but has continued his activities as an
officer of the Young Republican League.

In Hawaii. In Hawaii the situation is far
different; the voters of oriental ancestry are coming to be a real factor. Many Anglo-Saxons fear
that in a few years the voters of oriental parentage
will be in control. Some alarming figures, published in a government report,[8] have been accepted
uncritically and have been circulated widely. According to this bulletin about 47 per cent of the
electorate may be expected to be composed of Japanese voters by 1940. Should the Chinese and Koreans

unite with the Japanese, the voters of oriental ancestry would have a majority. Dr. Romanzo Adams of
the University of Hawaii, after an analysis of the
figures and statistical methods employed in this
government report, has concluded that in all probability the Japanese will not constitute more than
28 per cent of the potential voters in 1941.[9] In
another connection Dr. Adams stated: "The Japanese
did have, in 1930, as nearly as can be determined,
15.3 per cent of the number of persons eligible to
vote and they actually did cast 13.8 per cent of all
votes cast at the general election of 1930."[10]

The sugar interests have not viewed with
equanimity the future strength of the voters of
oriental ancestry,[11] and they have endeavored to
avoid further augmentation of this group. For a
number of years they brought in Filipino laborers
on three-year contracts after which they would be expected to return to the Philippines. The number of
Filipino women is comparatively small. Therefore,
there will be very few children born and educated in
the Islands to become voters.

Citizens of oriental ancestry have been
elected to office in Hawaii. In 1926, two Chinese
were elected, one to the lower house of the territorial legislature and one to the board of supervisors of the City and County of Honolulu. Four
Chinese and one Japanese filed nomination papers for
the 1926 election. Prior to this time participation
in politics had been a mere form. Up to 1924 only
three Orientals, two Chinese and one Japanese, had
run for territorial offices and they were not elected. The success of the two Chinese in 1926 was
hailed with joy. A Japanese wrote: "To have a
citizen of Chinese ancestry enter the chaotic political world as a pioneer oriental politician and
serve the people is a matter of great joy to us
Orientals. Whether the politician is a Chinese or a
Japanese does not matter."[12]

This success encouraged others. In the

spring of 1928 several Japanese were elected delegates to the Territorial Republican Convention in
Honolulu. In the November election of 1928 the two
Chinese elected to office in 1926 were re-elected
while a Chinese on the Island of Maui was elected to
the territorial senate by a heavy vote. A Japanese
in Honolulu was nominated for the legislature but
failed of election by a narrow margin. In the primary of 1930 a Japanese was high-point man on the
Kauai county supervisorial ticket and was thus
elected outright. He has the distinction of being
the first citizen of Japanese parentage to be elected to public office in the Territory. In the election of November, 1930, two Japanese won seats in
the lower house of the territorial legislature. In
the election of 1934, three Japanese were elected
to the legislature and three to county boards of
supervisors.

         A statement from a Japanese college boy in
Hawaii shows how they looked upon politics a few
years ago.

         About this time I had many absurd wishes and ideals,
as most boys of that age have. My greatest wish was to become
a great politician. When I read in history about the great
orators and statesmen of the past, I used to identify myself
with Cicero, Webster, Calhoun or Douglas. I used to imagine
myself in Congress and influencing the heads there. On Satur-
days I used to help father at his work. During the lunch hour
I usually read famous speeches of at least something that had
force behind it, something that would thrill the hearts of the
common people. Sometimes my father used to command me to stop
reading aloud like an insane person, and on such occasions I
did as I was told. Gradually as months went by I began to
realize that it was useless for anyone of my station in life
to try to be a great politician; money was needed and that I
lacked. Whenever I recall such things I always wish I had
been born in a rich family so that I could study as much as I
would wish and could use a part of the fortune in carrying out
my plans and ambitions. Another great thing that clouded my

small mind concerning this ambition of mine was the question
which is common among Orientals, "How much chance will I have
in making good when I am a yellow man? Will I be given the
same privileges as my fellow Americans of the white race?"
After reading and hearing what experienced Orientals had to say
in that line I concluded it was inadvisable to steep myself in
my absurd ambition.[13]

        In the near future, there will be a more
hopeful outlook. This particular boy related how he
studied Cicero and Webster, but in the year 1927-
1928 a Japanese boy at the University of Hawaii began studying the Hawaiian language in preparation
for a political career. For many years Hawaiian
blood was a political asset in Hawaii, for they
would say, "Look at his skin and vote for him." If
a candidate had any Hawaiian blood in his veins, he
would advertise that fact.[14] Perhaps the next to
Hawaiian blood was an Hawaiian wife.[15] In the political campaigns, Hawaiian first and middle names
would blossom out and all political advertisements
would have some Hawaiian words. The aforementioned
Japanese had no Hawaiian blood, but he could learn
the language and that would make an appeal.
        The increase in the number of voters among
the Chinese and Japanese, however, has brought considerable change. According to Dr. A. W. Lind,

    . It is becoming increasingly evident, in fact, that as
the voting population is more evenly divided among several
racial groups the successful candidate must make his personal
appeal to voters on a broad, community-wide interracial basis
rather than exclusively to the Hawaiians or Haoles, who formerly dominated island elections so largely.. There was a time
when a political appeal in the Hawaiian language was most likely to elicit the desired response, but the lingua franca of
present-day political strategy is the English language, in-
telligible to all voters--Hawaiian, Haole (white man), Portuguese, Japanese, and Chinese.[16]

Instead of living in a world of abstraction, these young aspirants to political office are learning the methods of American politicians. Several are becoming quite adept at shaking hands and distributing cigars.

Quality of Citizenship. What kind of citizens will these American-born Chinese and Japanese be? Will they vote simply as American citizens according to their conception of right and duty or will they vote as more or less solid nationalistic groups and on issues of a nationalistic character? Time alone will tell. Mr. Frank C. Atherton of Honolulu stated at the Institute of Pacific Relations, July 28, 1927, that at the last election when a Chinese was elected to the Territorial Legislature the Orientals "plunked" for him, that is, they voted for the Chinese candidate only for an office to which several were to be elected. This method would improve the relative position of the favorite candidate and thus assure his election. The Hawaiians and Anglo-Saxons said later, "You watch the next election; we'll 'plunk' against the Chinese." [17] This practice has been disapproved by party organizations and candidates, in self-defense, have discouraged "plunking" among their supporters.

In the matter of voting as solid racial blocs there need be no anxiety as made evident by experiences in Hawaii. [18] In 1926 Japanese candidates on two of the Islands failed to carry the votes of their own groups. In the primary election of 1928 a Japanese candidate on one of the islands was "knifed" by the voters of Japanese ancestry in his own district. In the campaign of 1928 there developed among the Chinese a strong opposition to the reëlection of Dr. Dai Yen Chang to the board of supervisors of the City and County of Honolulu. In the course of the campaign a Chinese said: "We do not believe in the slogan, 'Right or wrong, he is a Chinese.' We believe when a Chinese is wrong and unfit to represent us, that man must not be elected."[19] Probably the supporters of this first Chinese in office expected the impossible of him. From certain newspaper discussions it would appear that their representative on the Board of Supervisors was all-powerful and should have given them everything they asked. These pioneers in the field of practical politics will make mistakes; election to office does not produce omniscience. Meanwhile this situation brought a division in the Hawaii Chinese Civic Association.

Since the election of 1926, the Chinese and Japanese citizens in Honolulu developed considerable interest in each other as made evident by the union meetings of several of the racial organizations. This get-together spirit has become evident in the San Francisco Bay region also. We quote a statement from an editorial entitled, "It's High Time We Coöperated."

In the past there have been various difficulties in the way of bringing ourselves closer to the Chinese. These difficulties exist no longer. We both understand English and we are both confronted with the same situation, insofar as our relations with the white race are concerned. We need each other's coöperation.[20]

The suggestion evidently fell upon fertile soil; the same paper on November 8, 1927, reported a "goodwill social" in which more than four hundred Chinese and Japanese participated. At a mass meeting of citizens of Japanese ancestry in San Francisco on September 17, 1928, Mr. Clarence T. Arai, a leader of the young Japanese in Seattle, stressed the advisability of coöperating with the Chinese citizens inasmuch as many of the interests of both the Chinese and Japanese groups were identical.

The voters of oriental ancestry are placed in an anomalous situation. If they vote solidly for Caucasian candidates who are endorsed by the dominant white group, even though they be naturalized

Scotchmen, they will be hailed as one-hundred-per cent Americans. On the other hand, should a majority of them vote for a Mongolian of the second or third generation in America, quite probably many would denounce them as dangerous citizens.[21] Nevertheless, they have many ardent supporters. In an address on the Atlantic seaboard in 1927, Governor Farrington of Hawaii was reported to have said:

> So far as the young Japanese natives of Hawaii have come forward and claimed the vote, they have turned out to be good and loyal American citizens, with no predilection for Japan. Some of them are members of the militia; some of them served as American soldiers in the Great War. Even the young Japanese, inscribed as retaining their Japanese citizenship and sent to Japan by their parents to be "Nipponized," generally return to Hawaii, declare that their American education has rendered them unfit or quite indisposed to adopt the rigorous Japanese ways and customs, and settle down to be Americans. Little danger from these American-born Japanese is apprehended by Americans in the islands. Their Americanization would be complete if they received a warmer welcome as citizens by Americans in general.[22]

Dual Citizenship. The dual citizenship of the American-born Japanese has been a subject of discussion for some time. The Japanese government, which has adopted many western practices, has been following the rule of jus sanguinis, the system used by most European governments, according to which she has claimed the citizenship of those born of Japanese parentage on foreign soil.[23] Because Japan has followed the European practice, certain problems have arisen in America where, under the Fourteenth Amendment, all persons born in the United States are citizens thereof. China, less progressive, has not adopted the European system and thus such difficulties have been avoided. According to the law of Japan, a child of a Japanese father was always a Japanese, no matter where he was born. In

accordance with the Law of Nationality promulgated
in 1899, under certain conditions, a person might
voluntarily expatriate himself. This was difficult
unless he had completed active military service or
had been exempted. The law as amended in 1916 made
a slight concession in favor of the American principle of citizenship. The law was further amended in
1924 to give expatriation privileges to Japanese
born abroad, provided that those whose births are
not reported to the Japanese consulates in their localities within two weeks' time automatically lose
their Japanese citizenship. The act also provided
that those who were born in the United States prior
to December 1, 1924, and those who retained their
Japanese citizenship through registration within the
two-week period after birth, may if they are living
in the United States, surrender their Japanese nationality and become American citizens, without restriction as to age or military service.[24]

          The grand total of those who became exclu-
sively American citizens in Hawaii both by expatriation and by failure to report births to the Japanese
Consulate in the period 1916-1928 was 13,784. The
comparatively small number of expatriations under
the law of 1916 was due in considerable measure to
the fact that only those under seventeen or over
thirty-seven years of age were eligible to take advantage of this provision. The law of 1924 removed
the age qualification and immediately there was an
increase. There has been, however, no great rush as
certain propagandists had prophesied. Only a comparatively small percentage of these young people
took any interest in the matter. It is not commonly known that many thousands of children of immigrants from European countries are in a similar situation with reference to dual citizenship. They
simply ignore the claims of the other nation and we
hear nothing about the matter. Like those citizens
of European ancestry, the majority of our citizens
of Japanese parentage have been ignoring the claims

of Japan; by going through the formalities of expatriation they would be recognizing the asserted
rights. More has been heard about the dual citizenship of the Japanese on account of the family system
which plays such an important part in Japan and
which has led to certain formalities of registration. This matter is discussed more thoroughly in
the following pages. The expatriations have also
been retarded because of the difficulties many have
encountered in securing birth certificates and the
policy of the Japanese government has been not to
expatriate her citizens unless they were recognized
by the United States. Furthermore, the proposal
made by some anti-orientalists to amend the United
States Constitution to bar the American-born children of oriental parentage from citizenship made a
number hesitate. In the period 1922-1924 many young
men made inquiries about this matter. Such questions
are rarely asked now, even though an occasional anti-
orientalist revives the idea.

        In spite of the amendment to the Law of Na-
tionality in 1924, a large number of Japanese parents have been recording the births of their children with the consulates. There has been, however,
a rapid falling off in the registrations. A decrease is to be expected, because there is an increasing number of children born of native parentage
or of one American-born parent. According to the
Consulate General of Japan in San Francisco, the
figures as of October 31, 1926, for the Pacific
Coast and Rocky Mountain states were: American citizens of Japanese ancestry, 63,749; those having
only American citizenship, 11,887; those having both
American and Japanese citizenship, 51,862. The Consulate figures for California, Colorado, Nevada,
and Utah for 1930 are: those having American citizenship only 25,442; those having dual citizenship,
24,307.[25]

        Many parents have advised their children to
expatriate themselves.[26] Since they are Americans

and would encounter great difficulties in Japan,
they realize that it is better for them to sever
that connection. Some urge expatriation in the hope
that their children may thereby be enabled to make
better occupational adjustments. Since a considerable number of Japanese parents have continued to
register their children with the consulates, some
Americans have drawn the conclusion that the loyalty
of the Japanese is primarily to Japan and not to
America.[27] Dr. Romanzo Adams[28] analyzed the factors
in the situation and arrived at a different conclusion.

      This registration is primarily a family mat-
ter with political implications because army lists
are made up from the family registers. The Japanese
in Hawaii tried to get family registration apart
from political connections. Since the early immigrants planned to return to the homeland, they were
willing to pay this price in order to have their
children recorded with the family heads in Japan.
A child not properly registered would be deprived of
important rights. Probably the majority of the Japanese will remain in Hawaii. Some plan definitely to
return, while others hope to do so. With all this
uncertainty, there is an advantage in registering
the children with the consulate. "If the family returns to Japan, the child will be able to claim all
his rights and privileges as a member of his family.
If he remains in Hawaii, the child can avoid all obligations to the Japanese government by expatriating
himself by a procedure now made easy."[29]

        Loyalty of Citizens of Oriental Ancestry.
Dual citizenship has been seized upon with avidity
by many politicians for propaganda purposes. The
anti-Japanese agitator has had much to say about divided allegiance. His slogan has been "Once a Japanese, always a Japanese." This situation has placed
the young Japanese in an anomalous position. A
close examination, however, reveals the fact that

the majority have only one country and that is America.[30] A college girl in Hawaii brings this out.

When the Great War came my Japanese ideals were shat-
tered, so to speak. My American teachers stressed American
ideals and loyalty to the United States. They began to shun
the Germans as a nationality, and at the same time taught us
to hate them. We helped in the campaigns for buying thrift
stamps, collecting tinfoil, gathering castor-oil beans, sewing
and knitting for the boys who were fighting for us. We were
loyal to the United States of America. About that time Japanese warships were protecting the islands and the children of
that ancestry were given the opportunity to visit one of them
that anchored in Kahului Bay. The sailors supposed that we
were Japanese--but I was an American.[31]

Most of these young people talk about "our
country" and many of them talk about "we Americans"
and "our forefathers." At times these expressions
bring smiles to the faces of those of old American
stock. In the course of the Oxford-Hawaii debate in
Honolulu in 1926, one of the Japanese members of the
Hawaii team spoke of "the ideals for which we fought
in 1776." No doubt it was a revelation to those
British debaters to learn that their forefathers had
fought against men of Japanese ancestry at Bunker
Hill, Lexington, and Yorktown. Evidently they claim
not only the ideas and rights, but even the traditions and spiritual values of America.[32] At times
white people have objected strenuously when a child
of oriental ancestry has taken any prominent part in
a patriotic activity. In 1924 there was considerable
excitement in Seattle because a seven-year-old American-born Japanese boy had been chosen by the pupils
of his room to play the part of George Washington in
a school program. The Sons of Veterans and Women's
Auxiliary passed resolutions condemning the teacher
of the Japanese boy for what they considered an un-
patriotic act and requested her either to apologize
or resign her position. A white man said, "I do

believe teachers should be instructed to avoid such
incidents; it kind of rubs one the wrong way to
think of a Japanese boy setting himself up as George
Washington." Many have wanted to be good Americans
but have not been permitted to participate in any
real sense as citizens. Many are aware of these
conditions and some actually fear that they may be
forced into positions where they cannot be as patriotic Americans as they should like to be. A Japanese college student wrote:

I wish to say that personally I have not been made to
feel as though I belonged to an inferior race or that I should
dwell in the land of my parents. I firmly believe that I
should have just as many, if not more, rights than a native-
born American for the simple reason that he is a citizen of
the United States because he cannot be a citizen of any other
nation. On the other hand, I had a right to choose between
two countries and I chose the United States. I am a citizen
by choice, but a native-born person is a citizen of the United
States because he cannot help it. I hope that I shall never
live to see the day when I shall say to myself, "Fool, why
did you become a citizen of the United States?" I sincerely
hope to see the day when I shall look back upon the past years
and say, "I have been one of the pioneers to pave the way to
world peace and to the universal recognition of Brotherhood of
Man and the Fatherhood of God."[33]

Many young people in Hawaii tell about participation in flag drills and other patriotic exercises. These have received considerable attention
in the schools because of a desire to show the
doubters in California that our citizens of oriental
ancestry can be real Americans. A college girl
wrote of herself.

Once I played the part of Miss Liberty wrapped in the
Flag, with the audience responding to the strains of the Star
Spangled Banner. I never was so happy and proud in all my
life as I was then. My mother was proud also as I, a Chinese

girl, was chosen to represent Miss Liberty. Soon it was ended
and I was sorry. I wanted to represent America again in many
more entertainments.[34]

    Such activities, however, are largely formal;
much sentiment and emotion are connected with them.
In a flag drill, pupils cannot refuse to go through
the formalities lest they be branded as un-American.
Strong group pressure brings conformity. They do
not reflect about this; in fact, it is not a matter
for reflection. Occasionally, however, one does see
through the formality. In many instances these
empty forms mean very little to the participants; at
times they actually bring confusion. A higher degree of participation in real life activities is
necessary to develop good citizens.
    The loyalty of the Americans of oriental an-
cestry may be measured in some degree by their military record. Early in 1928 a book[35] was published
by the Historical Commission of the Territory of
Hawaii. According to this, the Orientals, both
alien and citizen, old and young, participated in
all the war-time activities.[36]

    The Vote and Race Relationships. What ef-
fect will the vote have upon the relationships between the races of Hawaii and on the Pacific Coast?
The conditions are complex and no single answer can
be given. Without doubt, the vote will improve conditions on the Pacific Coast. Since the politicians
have begun to appeal for votes, they will not attack the young people as they did their non-citizen
parents. Favorable treatment in the political field
is quite likely to carry over into other phases of
life. The American-born citizens have the vote
which they will exchange for certain advantages.
Since competition for votes is keen, probably they
will receive good returns in better treatment for
their political support. Inasmuch as many elections
are won by narrow margins, politicians will be

willing to bid high for their votes. Now that these
young citizens have begun to participate through the
exercise of the suffrage, they have begun to feel
that they have a real share in American life; they
are beginning to look forward with confidence to the
future. [37]

    In Hawaii, the citizens of oriental ancestry
have been treated with courtesy in their political
activities.[38] Because of their large numbers there
is a probability that they will be accorded different treatment from those on the mainland. Several
observers have predicted that race feeling will develop quite noticeably within the next few years.
There are now several Chinese and Japanese in elective offices in the Territory. These office-holders
will exert an influence and will have to dispense
political patronage to their supporters. This will
necessarily reduce the political power and prestige
of the Hawaiians, Portuguese, and Anglo-Saxons. The
influence of these two oriental groups is shown in
some measure by the fact that the Caucasian-Hawaiian
who was elected to the office of city and county attorney in Honolulu in 1928 appointed a Japanese and
a Chinese as deputies in his office. In his campaign for election he made certain promises to the
voters of oriental ancestry for their support.

Chapter XI

THE RÔLE OF INSTITUTIONALIZED RELIGION

The contacts made by the children of oriental parentage with organized religion have conditioned their adjustment to American life. Some have lived in homes and in communities where the old-world religion has been predominant while others have made practically all their contacts with western Christianity.

Children Vary from Parental Religion. The American-born children of oriental immigrants tend to differ markedly from their parents in religion. Under American influences they cannot possibly assume the characteristic parental attitudes. As the children enter school and become acquainted with American pupils, some join Sunday-school classes in Christian churches. Here they are further imbued with the idea that everything American is best. Since the majority of white Americans are nominal Christians at least, Christianity comes to be associated with a superior status; the religion of their parents comes to be part and parcel of a position of inferiority. Consequently to enjoy the good things of life and to be Americans of some consequence, the parental religion is set aside in favor of Christianity--the American religion. To them the Christian religion is an integral part of Americanism; it does not even occur to them that there is an alternative.[1]

Several factors have attracted the children to Christianity. Some have been drawn by the

English language. In the main, they can carry on
the common every-day activities in the parental languages, but do not understand the concepts used in a
discourse on religion. Their ideas are more occidental than oriental. Hence, they have great difficulty in understanding a sermon which is cast in the
thought forms of the Orient. These differences in
language and point of view separate the children
from the religion of their parents. This situation
led some to choose English-speaking churches before
they began to feel conscious of racial differences.
To offset this, a number of oriental churches are
experimenting with English services, but as yet this
has not been entirely successful. The young people
are usually critical of the English used by the
ministers reared in the Orient. White ministers oft-
en talk down to them in what one young man called "a
sort of baby talk"--and this creates a revulsion.
The Buddhists in Hawaii have sensed the situation
more thoroughly than the Christians and have begun
to use the English language with good results. Some
pupils in school have studied Christianity because
they did not wish to confess ignorance if questions
should be asked about the Bible or the Christian religion. Some have turned to Christianity in the hope
that relations with the white group would be more
satisfactory. A number have considered attendance
at American churches advisable because they might become acquainted with the best people of the community
and thus have an opportunity to learn many things of
value.

          Contacts with these various influences have
weaned the younger group from the parental religion.
Some inwardly make light of the old religion, but
remain silent out of regard for their parents. Some
even go through certain ceremonies in order to please
them. Others, who cannot appreciate the point of
view of the older generation, ridicule the religious
practices of their parents. A college boy in Hawaii
relates his experience.

As I grew older and grasped more of the occidental civilization I began to lose my oriental traits. Last summer I attended a Buddhist ceremony back home. I had no intention of going, but just to satisfy my dear mother I went. My two younger sisters, both in high school, were with me. When the ceremony began I could hardly keep myself from laughing, since the priest's chanting sounded so funny. I saw my two sisters giggling with their handkerchiefs against their mouths to avoid any distraction. I had better sense than to laugh, but I laughed within. I couldn't stand it. This shows how much we American-born Japanese are losing the customs of our fore-fathers.[2]

It is not always a matter of holding the parental practices up to ridicule; the young people are at times placed in embarrassing situations. A high school boy in Hawaii reveals his embarrassment.

On one occasion, after I had attended a Christian boarding school for one year, I went to a Japanese temple. Since I was the eldest boy in the family, I was morally obli-gated to attend the ceremony. The first thing I knew the old-er people were on their knees in a meditative mood before the altar illumined with a score of candles and decorated with fruits, candies, and offerings of all kinds. I felt foolish in kneeling down before the altar without knowing what to do, but before I knew it I had gone through the formalities. I felt the icy-cold perspiration streaming down my back. That was probably the most embarrassing situation that I was ever in because my parents' customs and ideas differed from mine.[3]

A college girl in Hawaii gives us further insight.

Unfortunately, to say the least, my mother is still unconverted. We have tried our best to make a Christian of her, but her faith in Confucius is too strong for any one to change her. I have always condemned her worship and offerings. She spends quite a sum of money for these things and sometimes I have made fun of my smaller brothers. She forces them to

bow before the incense and my fifteen-year-old brother has
stopped because, when he was about thirteen years old, I called
him a "heathen Chinese" after he had bowed. I do not know
whether I should be ashamed of myself for not respecting my
parents' religion, but I have been very much embarrassed by it.
We live in a district that has no other Chinese family and
sometimes when it's full moon or some other festival day,
mother pops fire crackers and burns incense. Some of my neighbors have teased me and I do not find it pleasant to have my
friends see the little shrine that she has built in the kitchen.
In this day and age, if your parents are not Christians, they
are not much respected by your friends.[4]

        These experiences tend to develop religious
ideas and attitudes which set the younger generation
off from their parents.

        Effect of Community on Religion. The commun-
ities in which the young people live condition their
attitudes. If a boy grows up in an isolated community where Buddhism is strong, he has no opportunity
to make contacts with Christians. Hence he has no
basis for comparison. Hence he will not think much
about religion but will follow the customs of his
group and will not be embarrassed by their practices.
In such communities, a minority group of Christians
often finds itself at a disadvantage; their children
are practically outcasts. A college boy in Hawaii
presents the situation.

        The children of Christian parents in my home town were
not treated in a friendly manner by the children of Buddhist
parents. They were looked upon as "sissies"; they had to en-
dure being teased and called "Christo" and they were excluded
from participation in many of the children's activities. Some-
how I managed to pass through my childhood years without being
subjected to these discriminating actions. I mixed with the
Buddhist children; I played with them; I talked with them; I
joined their pranks. It seems that I was well liked by them.
I was quite athletic and agile for my size and build and could

do what most of the other children did--in many instances I did
better. I could play ball fairly well, I could run fairly fast,
I was virtually a monkey on a tree. I was about fourth in box-
ing ability among the boys of the town, and in other ways I
could "hold my own" with the boys in most activities. These
factors must have influenced their attitude toward me, I am
sure. Furthermore, I believe that the status of my parents in
the estimation of the townspeople helped me a great deal. My
parents are kind, humble and sympathetic to the people of the
town and vicinity, regardless of religious differences. They
are thus respected by them. [5]

Sometimes a move from one area to another
brings a decided change. In a community that was
predominantly Christian, a boy was afraid to profess
that he was a Buddhist lest he be considered a pagan.
The new environment into which he moved was more favorable to Buddhism and his hesitancy disappeared.[6]

Parental Attitudes and Religion of Children.
A liberal attitude on the part of the Japanese parents has made the situation favorable to the adoption of Christianity by the children.[7] On the whole,
it would appear that the devotees of Shintoism or
Buddhism tend to be more broad-minded than members
of the Christian churches. Some Christians of oriental ancestry are quite bigoted and look askance at
other religions.
     Many Orientals hold to their old-country re-
ligion, but have concluded that this is not suited
to their children who have grown up in America. Some
non-Christian parents encourage their children to attend Christian churches and Sunday schools, and even
to become Christians. A Japanese college boy has
revealed his father's attitude.

My parents came from Japan to Hawaii almost twenty-
five years ago. When they came here, they brought their customs, traditions, and religion with them. They were Buddhists
in Japan and they are still strong Buddhists. Once a year my

parents pay homage to the shrine of their faith. Sometimes the
children accompany them. When I was a child, it was one of the
great events in my life to go out in an automobile and travel
a great distance to visit this temple. This annual event was
kept up until I was fourteen.

When my elder brother was about seven, he was given
the duty of lighting the lanterns of the gods. He continued
to do so, until I became seven. At seven I was instructed to
perform this duty--to light the lanterns every night. I did it
for three years, when my younger brother succeeded me.

One day it happened that a friend of ours took me to
a Christian Sunday school, four miles away from home. My
father raised no objections. I continued to go to that Sunday
school for a year. That was when I was ten. The next year a
Salvation Army officer came to our community and I attended his
meetings. My sister and I were quite regular pupils. At each
meeting we received little cards. We gave the cards to our
mother and she kept them for us. Sometimes, my sister and I
came home a little too late in the night and for that reason we
were punished. Father never objected to our attendance at the
Sunday school.

A strange thing occurred in my life when I was thirteen. I had just completed my seventh grade and was working in
the cane fields for my vacation. One night my father confiden-
tially asked me if I would like to go to Honolulu for my education. I was very pleased to hear this. . . . I had heard a lot
about the Hongwanji Boarding School. I heard that the attendance at Japanese school was compulsory. I hated the Japanese
school and for that reason I asked my father where he wanted me
to stay. When he replied, "You will be in the Christian dormitory," my heart leaped with joy. I was the happiest of all
persons then!

A year passed by and I completed the eighth grade. To
my father I was a good boy for I had made good in the language
school and gotten by in the grammar school. He sent me to
O____'s again. I went to high school a year. I came up to the
expectations of my parents; so I was sent to O_____'s for the
third year. I then finished my sophomore year and went home to
spend the summer.

One night as my father and I were together, he asked

me if I was a baptized Christian, to which I answered in the
negative. He paused for a minute and spoke up as if something
were troubling him. He said, "Why don't you be a good Chris-
tian--be baptized and become a Christian. You are going to
make your living in Hawaii and Christianity is the religion
to follow. Society and the business world call for Christians." This remark struck my innocent mind. I returned to
O_____'s for the fourth time when school opened. On April 1,
1928, I was baptized by Rev. T. O_____ at the Japanese church.

     I have often wondered why my father took such an atti-
tude in regard to my religious affiliation. To say what made
him do so is a difficult story. However, there are two or
three definite things that I could relate which have influenced
him to have such an attitude. First of all, come the books.
He read literature of all sorts, both Christian and Buddhist.
His only recreation after the day's work was reading the Nippu
Jiji [8] and some sort of biography, novel, or essay. Secondly,
his friend Mr. H_____, a Christian, influenced him much. Mr.
H_____ was a product of the O____dormitory and his conduct
among men was a radiant example of higher living. The Reverend
O_____visited my father twice and he, too, influenced my
father. . . . My father met other Christian people who influenced him in the Christian ideas. Thirdly, it was my own self
that made him say that I ought to be a Christian. I had been
much of a rascal at home, but after three years in the dormitory my actions were quite different. My parents both testified
that I was getting better, and my father took the opportunity
to advise me to be a Christian. My father respects Christianity. As I say grace at supper, he pauses and pays reverence.
If I forget to do so, he reminds me. There is no question in
his mind as to the value of Christianity in Hawaii. [9]

     The Chinese in the main, seem to be less
liberal in their attitudes toward Christianity than
the Japanese. A Chinese college graduate presented
the situation as it exists among his people in Hawaii.

     I was baptized in my home town. When I told my father,
he fairly "blew up" and declared that he would cast my bones
outside the ancestral burying ground. When I went away to the

University, however, and made a good record he became more favorably disposed, but in spite of this he was enraged when I
was baptized at the age of eighteen. I have observed that many
Chinese parents do not hesitate in permitting their children to
attend Christian Sunday schools when they are young because
they have control over them and can pull them back at any time.
So long as no positively harmful effects are evident, there is
no hesitation. Since I had been working my way through school,
I have felt rather independent and took the step of being baptized even though I knew my father would object.[10]

Nevertheless there have been many instances of genu-
ine religious toleration among the Chinese where the
children have felt perfectly free to make their own
choices.

Living in an atmosphere of comparative tolerance in religious matters, the children have tended
to develop a tolerant spirit and sometimes an attitude that all religious faiths are equal.

Disillusionment and Christianity. When some,
who have accepted Christianity as part and parcel of
Americanism, meet with rebuffs and discriminations,
they become bitter. They say this "brotherhood
stuff" that Christians talk so much about is all hum-
bug; they will have nothing more to do with it. As
they go through the process of disillusionment, they
gradually give up Christianity and revert to the religion of their parents. They cannot return to it
completely, but they become more sympathetic toward
the whole parental culture system. A Japanese college boy in Hawaii exemplifies the process through
which many go.

My mother was very religious and she had taught me to
worship God, for without his help we would not be able to get
along. As it is the custom of the Japanese people to light
little lamps and burn incense before the shrine and image of
Buddha we lighted our little lamps every morning and every evening. The duty, and privilege perhaps, fell upon me for I was

the eldest son, and I really did have a feeling of worship in
doing this with hands washed and mouth cleansed.

In high school I became interested in Christianity.
Its teachings seemed good to me. I began to reason and doubt
the workability of the gods in the religion of my father and
mother. It began to hurt my conscience to stand before the
image of Buddha or the shrine and light the little lamps of
worship. I had my younger brother about twelve years old do
that thereafter. My mother noticed the change in me and urged
me over and over again to hold to the religion of my ancestors.
She was suspicious of Christianity about which she did not know
a thing other than that Jesus was crucified, and she believed
that Christianity taught one to get rid of all his belongings
and make himself poor. She was afraid that Christianity meant
doing away with all the ceremonies observed for the happiness
and peace of the dead, which was sacrilegious and would surely
bring disaster to the family. However, I firmly believed
Christianity to be the right religion and I consoled her by
telling her that I would do all homage to the memory of any
ancestors even though I should become a Christian. Since then
she made no attempt to hold me to her faith. I was baptized
and after baptism I taught Sunday school and worked diligently
to bring my best friend and my other friends to Christ, which
very happily, with the aid of others, was successfully done. I
was very happy and for a time I wondered if those who were not
Christians were ever as happy, so completely did I lean on the
wonder-working power of Christ and his teachings.

When June came I graduated; I was happy that the days
of schooling were over. I wanted to get a job and have my
father ease up a bit in his work which was getting harder with
the advance in years. I tried to get a job in the office of
one of the big firms in town but without success, therefore I
picked up odd office and selling jobs. My folks were very considerate and did not grumble even when I did not earn any money.
During this year of disappointments I became interested in college. I wanted to be better prepared. It was difficult for me
to ask my father to send me through school. I was afraid to
ask him to let me go to college, let alone his support. I had
thought this way and that way why I should like to go to school.
But after further thought, I made up my mind that it was

unreasonable of me to continue my schooling. I would try harder than ever to get a real job and help my father support the family. I was restful for a while but as I met with further disappointments, the wish to go to college was revived. One day when mother was alone I told her my intention. It was her earnest desire that I be sent to college, but that was not easy since we were poor. Furthermore she wondered if a college education would bring proportional financial returns. I told her that I would work my way through if I could be spared a few years more. My father did not object. He wanted to give me all the education possible. I resolved to make good and repay my parents and the rest of the family for their sacrifice. I registered at the University in the fall of 1922, as a commerce student.

My determination to work my way through school was one thing but doing it was another. I got a job to work a few hours every night but it did not bring enough to support myself. I picked up whatever odd job I could to make good my promise, but I was not altogether successful. But my father and mother were always kind to me and gave me every encouragement to keep on.

Every summer since my graduation from the grammar school I worked for the Hawaiian Pineapple Company. I have come to realize during these years the effect of environment upon the behavior of people. Everybody seemed to have the impression that polite manners are for school or some other uses, but certainly not to be used in the pineapple cannery. At least, I myself have felt free from convention, to some extent, while there. Also a sort of dissatisfaction arose within me. We worked under a contract system that called for the greatest of physical endurance. But because we worked with our hands our bonus was 10 per cent. If we had worked in white shirt and clean collar we might have received 50 per cent or more like the office workers. I became dissatisfied with the distribution of wealth--or rather the discrimination shown--and at the same time I began to get suspicious of the sincerity of the people who preached equality and brotherhood.

In my second year I got a job as assistant playground director which I have kept ever since. Beside helping through school, it played a great part in my change of course from

commerce to education. There were other reasons, too, but I
shall not go into them here.

Strange to say, about this time I began to lose the
faith I had in Christianity. There are other sides to every
story even in religion. There are unbelievable revelations of
the presence of God as taught by the priests of the shrines and
of the temples as well as by the Christian ministers. I have
heard and have seen persons not Christians die with revelations
of heaven before them. Can not all religions be teaching the
same God? I began to see sincerity in the religious worship of
others and it also became unbearable to have any person condemn
as idolatry any worship other than Christianity. I attend
church services regularly, but I fear the constant knocking
down of the religion of my ancestors by the superintendent of
my Sunday school is arousing antagonism within me and drawing
me farther and farther away from Christianity.

The language school question, the Japanese exclusion,
the discrimination in the administration of justice, the widespread use of bribery, catering of the law makers to the rich
at the expense of the needy, are live questions of the time.
I wonder if I am not coming to feel that Mr._____ was right
when he said in his newspaper column that money can buy anything from the legislature to the police court. But this last
year in the University I was living over the experiences of the
high school. I am beginning to move into the circle of wider
association. My outlook on life is a little less pessimistic.
Brotherhood is impossible, but we might learn to understand each
other better.[11]

Effect of Contact with Church People. The
methods employed by many church workers have played
an important rôle in causing a break with Christianity. For some time, Christian work has been carried
on among the oriental groups in America, but the results of Protestant activity, in particular, are open
to question. Church officials, in their annual statistical reports, must show good results for the
money expended. Hence they have adopted methods
which promise the largest immediate returns for the
energy expended, without considering the ultimate

outcome. The method has been to allure individuals
here and there. Children have been most readily won
in this way, but this has pulled them away from their
families. A number of parents, aware of the situation, have become resentful. A certain Japanese in
Hawaii, who had never been strongly opposed to Christianity, offered a number of pertinent criticisms.
On one occasion he quoted the Biblical passage
(Ephesians 5:31) which says that a man must leave his
father and mother, and made the comment that Christianity had pulled children away from their parents
and had broken families. When some of the young
people begin to reflect and begin to develop a more
sympathetic attitude toward the parental cultural
system, they conclude that the Christians have not
played the game fairly, either with themselves or
with their parents.

        In a certain sense, the children have been
"bought" by the Christian group. In the immigrant
homes there was usually a constant struggle to make
ends meet. Hence anything additional from an outside source would be greatly appreciated. Material
rewards of different kinds, such as candies, cards,
free moving pictures, and Christmas gifts have induced many to go to Sunday school and church. The
experience of a Japanese high school boy in Hawaii
is to the point.

        When I was a "kid" I had to go to the Buddhist temple,
but after some time I revolted against that and spent my time
playing baseball with the boys. As we were playing ball one
Sunday morning, a tall, blond Haole missionary came along and
rounded us up telling us he would give us some sticks of candy
if we would come to his Sunday school. We went, and at the end
of the hour we would get each a stick of candy. Usually through
the whole period I would be thinking of the candy. We would
sing the songs very lustily as we hoped to get more candy if we
sang loudly. We sang "Jesus Loves Me This I Know," and I have
never forgotten that song. At times some of the boys in the
gang would get tired before the end of the hour and run out.

They wouldn't, of course, got any candy then. Oftentimes, during the Sunday school hour we would gamble away the sticks of candy we were to get; some of us would then have several sticks and some would have none. At times we would stay for the communion service which lasted about fifteen minutes. We would kneel near the front of the room. For this each would get an extra stick of candy. We would usually get our candy about eleven o'clock. It had a very good taste then, for it was the time we were getting hungry. There were two gospel houses, one on each side of the street, that were competing for us. One held services at ten o'clock and the other at three. On some Sundays we would go to both and get candy at both places. That, however, depended on whether or not we wanted to play baseball or go swimming.[12]

In some instances these methods have brought good results; the children have developed habits which have been valuable to them in later life. In many cases, however, the young people have seen the superficiality and have become disgusted.

Another method is that of making promises to the children; at least they are made by implication, while no attempt is made to correct the impression. Much is said about "brotherhood," "loving one another," "there is no color line in heaven," et cetera, and while the children are young they are accepted by the white group in many churches and Sunday schools. This acceptance makes them feel superior to their parents. This is accentuated by the fact that all too often they are made to feel ashamed of the religion of their parents. When they become self-conscious and the white group fails to cash at face value the implied promises, many revert to the parental group and become more interested in its religion.

Certain zealous religious leaders try to produce results through compulsion. Since it is difficult for students to find suitable boarding places in the cities of Hawaii, they avail themselves of a number of private dormitories. The managers, all too often attempt to force their type of religion upon

the boarders. In some cases it works, but in all too
many instances the results are not gratifying. A
number become rebellious and break off from all religious activities at the earliest opportunity. The
results are much the same be it Buddhist or Christian
dormitory. At times, however, the required attendance upon religious services has worked out satisfactorily. This compulsion has given the initial impulse to an acquaintance with and finally an acceptance of the Christian religion, the outcome of which
has been a wholesome life organization.[13]

        In addition to the revulsion against compul-
sory participation, some young people react strongly
against bigotry and narrowness in religious leaders.
Since they make contacts with several religions and
thus examine them, cursorily at least, they are in a
position to make their own choices. Many see good
in the several religions and when some zealot criti-
cizes another religion too severely there is often a
reaction against this. Oftentimes their studies of
history and science in the schools cast grave doubts
over certain teachings received in church or Sunday
school. After some reflection on the dogmatism of
the religious teachers, their influence is negated,
no matter whether the bigotry be found among Christians or Buddhists.

        In the main, the operation of church machin-
ery in typical American fashion has been not highly
successful in Hawaii so far as the younger group is
concerned. Organizations and methods quite foreign
to those with entirely different backgrounds have
been introduced bodily.[14] No adequate study has
been made of the conditions in order to adapt programs to actual needs. As a consequence, the Christian agencies are not highly efficient in the service
they are rendering in this period of transition and
are unable to elicit the whole-hearted allegiance of
the younger generation.

        Some young people turn against Christianity
on account of unfortunate experiences with church

members, chiefly with those of the Caucasian group.
White people are considered members of the Christian
group and, since Christianity has been highly ex-
tolled, they expect much from them. Under such circumstances the experiences leave a taste which is
all the more bitter. In some instances they conclude
that such are weaknesses common to all humanity and
that all men, whether Buddhists, Christians, Con-
fucianists, or what not, have these failings. Some
are highly sensitive and misconstrue many actions to
be discriminations against themselves on account of
race. They take the position that they are American-
born children of oriental parentage and as such are
entitled to special consideration. Probably they
are unaware of the fact that even Anglo-Saxons often
receive unjust treatment.

Other Contributing Factors. According to a
second generation Chinese, the third generation in
Hawaii is not turning to Christianity in the same
measure as his group did. The second generation
Chinese as youths were sensitive to opinion of the
white group and this had an influence upon their religious affiliations. The third generation is less
sensitive to pressure from this source, because the
Chinese community is now of such importance that
recognition and status gained in this group are sufficient. Hence they evince less interest in the
Christian churches. A number of Hawaiian-born Japanese men, who in their early years and while on the
mainland in college and professional schools considered themselves Christians, have given up all connections with the Christian churches after returning to
practice their professions. These professional men
as yet have to depend largely on their racial groups
for patronage. Since the purse strings are yet
largely controlled by the immigrant Japanese, who in
the main are Buddhists, it is economically profitable
to ally themselves with the adherents of this religion. For many this is not a difficult step to take,

especially after they have gone through a process of
disillusionment with reference to the Christian religion.[15]

   Resultant Syncretistic Religion of the Younger Group. The children of oriental ancestry who come
into contact with a variety of religious beliefs and
practices have no single pattern to follow. In most
localities with any number of Japanese residents,
there is a Buddhist temple or church and also a
Christian church of some denomination. Usually both
conduct Sunday schools and very often parents send
their children to both. Since there is considerable
difference between these religions, perplexity and
confusion often result which at times leads to an in-
difference to both. In some families this results
in a heterogeneity of religious beliefs. A college
boy in Hawaii reported that his father was a Shinto-
ist, his mother a Buddhist, his elder sister a
Christian, his elder brother claimed to be an athe-
ist, while he himself "being in such a situation
never did take religion seriously."
   Almost invariably the religion of the
younger generation of oriental ancestry will differ
markedly from that of others; it will not be a Con-
fucianism of China, a Buddhism of Japan, or a Christianity of America,[16] but in many instances there
will be a syncretism of elements from the several religions with which they have made contacts. A college girl in Hawaii has given an insight into her
religious life.

   In my early days I believed what my parents believed.
My father is a Confucianist while my mother is a pagan. I am
both and more, for I have a touch of Christianity in me. My
religion is of my own making and my God is my own creation. I
was superstitious and I had great faith in the curing and aveng-
ing powers of my mother's pagan gods. I burned incense and
kowtowed to them in submission. As I grew older and came into
contact with more people, I began to see things with a clearer

vision. I realized that these gods did not meet my needs and
all my previous superstitions were unreal, unscientific and of
no value to me. My life has been molded by my religion. I
dared not to do anything that would offend my God. When I am
sick, I always look to my God to cure me. My concentration on
his power of healing is so strong that I usually see favorable
results. Confucius' teachings guide me in my moral actions,
in my relationship between various social groups. Christianity
teaches me to be loving and forgiving. Idols of paganism are
really the policemen of my behavior. I am afraid of them for
I believe that my misfortunes are brought by them as forms of
punishment for my wrong-doings. Then I look upon my own created God to heal me. He is my judge, my savior.[17]

Conclusion. Even though the Christian agencies are inefficient, they have rendered a valuable
service. On the whole, the Christian homes have made
accommodations to American conditions more readily
than the non-Christian ones. As a result, we may
point to several Christian Chinese, past middle age,
in Honolulu who occupy positions of importance in the
community. This gradual adjustment has neutralized
the force of disorganization. Usually in Christian
homes there is a more favorable attitude toward education, and especially toward the education of girls.
In Honolulu the membership of the strongest Christian
church among the Chinese is drawn from the Hakka, and
this group has more students in the University of
Hawaii in proportion to the total number than have
the Punti. There is also a disposition among the
Christians to break with the old system of parentally-
arranged marriages. Many of the young people, particularly the girls, appreciate the changes which
come in their homes through the adoption of Christianity. Because of this, a number of children endeavor to lead their parents to Christianity. Some
become ardent propagandists and do not stop with members of their immediate families, but go outside. A
girl who returned to the plantation after spending
some time in Honolulu started a Christian Sunday

school in her own home. Her Buddhist parents objected at first but soon gave their consent. She then
opened another school in a neighboring plantation
camp. In addition to the personal satisfaction
which comes from an improvement in home conditions,
the desire to give the entire group a higher standing in the eyes of Americans is a factor in the situation.[18]

Chapter XII

THE SCHOOL IN THE ADJUSTMENT PROCESS

The school is of vital importance to any
group that is seeking to adjust itself to a new social environment. Through its instrumentality the
cultural possessions of the dominant group can be
acquired more readily. The greater the differences
in the cultural traditions of the two groups concerned, the more important is education to the more
recent arrivals. Because of the great divergence
between the oriental and occidental cultures, the
young people of oriental ancestry encounter difficulties in making adjustments to American life. Hence
education is of great concern to them.

The educational system in continental United
States which touches the children of oriental ancestry is well known.[1] Since the situation in the
Territory of Hawaii is less familiar, certain salient facts relative thereto will be presented.

A. The Educational System of Hawaii

Type of Schools. The Territory provides instruction from the first grade through the University. In addition to the public schools there.are a
number of private institutions, none of which are of
collegiate rank. All instruction is in the English
language. In McKinley High School of Honolulu, the
largest secondary school in the Territory, the Hawaiian, Chinese, Japanese, and Korean languages are
taught on the same basis as other modern languages.

The Status of Free Education. The Territory
provides free instruction through the University,
but some have opposed this and have recommended tuition in the high schools[2] and University. The sugar
planters in particular have advocated this, and not
without reason. They pay for sending their children
to select private schools and in addition are taxed
to educate the sons and daughters of the plantation
laborers only to turn them away from the soil. The
annual address of the retiring president of the Hawaiian Sugar Planters' Association usually contains
something about the impracticability of the schools
and the burden they are imposing upon the taxpayers.[3]
            During the 1927-1929 biennium a considerable
number of fees were collected for various purposes
in the high schools and junior high schools.[4] Opposition to the fees developed and came into prominence in the political campaign of 1928. The Legislature in 1929 passed a bill under which the Regents
of the University _may_ charge a tuition fee.[5] It was
not made mandatory, but by reducing the appropria-
tion to the University, the administration has been
forced to charge a fee. Governor Farrington, who
has stood strongly for a free school system, vetoed
the measure but it was passed over his veto.

            Schools and the Plantation System. The
sugar men are right in their contention that the
public schools of the Territory are not fitting the
pupils into the plantation system.[6] Because of the
high percentage of Orientals in the population of
the Territory, many, especially the California propagandists, have declared that Hawaii was not and could
not be American, but was thoroughly Asiatic at heart.
The leaders in Hawaii, resentful of this, have determined to remove all cause for such accusation.
Americanization has been stressed very strongly in
the schools of the Territory and it has taken root.
Governor Farrington in an address to a group of ex-
cursionists from the northwest Pacific Coast said
in part:

In our 65,000 school children we have a crop of which
we are extremely proud. This territory spends more money on
its public schools than any other single activity of the government. Our children are being trained to the highest ideals of
American citizenship. Their education is builded on a firm
foundation of American ideals that go back for more than 100
years. Our children are being educated to become loyal, independent men and women, and in this way we are building for the
future.[7]

The American school system infuses democratic ideas into the pupils of oriental ancestry. They
read about democracy in their histories, they hear
their teachers talk about it, and they become enthusiastic about it. They are more interested in
Patrick Henry, Daniel Webster, Abraham Lincoln, and
other outstanding Americans than is the average
white child. When the children of oriental lineage
have been trained in the democratic public schools
of Hawaii where they have won more than their pro-
portionate share of scholastic honors, they hesitate
in accepting an inferior status. The majority of
them, however, are doomed to be disillusioned when,
sooner or later, their democratic ideas come into
conflict with the autocratic industrial system of
the Islands. A Korean boy on the mainland who had
graduated from high school in Hawaii presents in a
letter the anomalous situation in which a person is
placed after leaving the American school to go out
and find his place in the industrial life of Hawaii.

There is no adequate solution to the problem, and the
majority in the category will simply have a beastly time in
life for having been born with yellow skins and educated as if
their skins were white. . . . To ask the sugar-planters to
make conditions so attractive on the plantations that your
graduates will gladly work there. . . . is absurd. In the
first place the planters, despite the Cape Cod missionary
blood in their veins, are hard-headed, tough-minded business
men and as such, more interested in gold than in social

welfare; and in the second place, there is a limit in making
agricultural work attractive. To send a young man through
high school and then to ask him to labor in the fields is,
under the present social system, another absurdity.

B. Orientals and the Schools

Interest of Parents in Education. In the
early days the immigrants from the Orient were not
interested in an American education for their children. The majority planned to return after a comparatively short stay in America. Furthermore, the
treatment accorded them by the Americans did not attract them to our institutions.

The American people in almost every way made the Chinese feel that they were strangers and aliens and that they
were not wanted. Under such conditions, they could not feel
at home, and all they could do was to look forward to the day
when they could return home with their families to the tribal
village of their fathers, where they could spend the rest of
their days in a more congenial atmosphere and where their sons
could take up the task of life after them.
Under such circumstances, the problems of the American-born Chinese were few and simple. Their problems were
identically the same as those of their fathers, for the conditions that confronted them were the same as those that confronted their fathers. To them these conditions were not complicated. They were trained and brought up and prepared to
tackle them without much misgiving. When they returned to
China from California. . . . they were fitted nicely into Chinese environment and society, and in no way differed from the
four hundred millions of their fellows who had never been outside the homeland.
Times have changed radically during the last decade
or two, and so the problems of the young American Chinese have
also changed radically. . . . This condition of affairs was
brought about by American education which has been well absorbed by the younger generation of the Chinese Americans, who

have almost forsaken the ideas and ideals of their fathers. In education, spirit, and temperament they are more American than Chinese, and it seems that the only thing Chinese about them is their complexion. In all other ways they are just as American and, in some ways, they are more so than the second generation of other foreign-born parentage.[8]

In recent years there has been a marked change. Dr. Doremus Scudder wrote[9] that in 1903-1904 he found very few Japanese who planned to remain in Hawaii, and almost all who could do so sent their children to Japan for an education. But a change gradually came and by 1910 the sentiment, "Stay in America and make it your country," had begun to take root and the children were increasingly kept by their parents and educated for American life.[10]

With this change in outlook on the part of the immigrants, they are now giving their children every encouragement to avail themselves of an American education. Some offer rewards for achievements in school. Many, even with the language handicap, make efforts to help the children prepare their lessons. Doubtless their own disappointments in America have accentuated their interest in the education of their children. Many parents attribute their lack of success to their inadequate education. Hence no sacrifice is too great to provide their children with better educational advantages than they themselves enjoyed. A college boy in Hawaii remembers vividly this parental interest.

When I was a tot I was not very fond of books. The lure of the brooks or the valley, where the varieties of tropical fruits grew had greater attraction for me than the weird monotony of the classroom. The occasions when I made myself conspicuous by being absent were not infrequent. Each truancy, however, was rewarded in a warm manner at the hands of my parents. At times the reward was so ample and so hot that I could not stand on my feet or resume my normal sitting

position. I used to resent this sort of treatment and on a
few occasions I actually could not be subdued by them. What
they did was to secure a friend of their's as my private tutor.
He was a stern-looking character, and in his conduct he showed
all the traces of a Samurai training. His method of instruction was far sterner than his superficial sternness. He presented himself night after night at our home to feed my mind
with a sort of morsel which it sorely disliked. A single
fault on my part never failed to evoke a thrashing from the
ruler which he held in his hand. Many a night I cried myself
to sleep because of his severe treatment.

All this sounds very harsh and my parents would appear very cruel. Yet, beneath this harsh treatment, I could
perceive the finer sentiments such as all parents who are fond
of their children have. They wanted to give me a proper training, a proper education in order that I might become a per-
sonage of whom they might well be proud. The fact that any
praise from my tutor was sufficient to win over my parents in
securing me a baseball glove, or a bat, a bicycle, or a musical instrument will amply testify how warm-hearted and how
fond of me they were. These thoughts, however, did not enter
my childish mind and I only regarded their treatment as
harsh and mean. Yet, strangely enough this Spartan training
has inculcated in me a keen fondness for books. As a result,
today I can close myself in a room with a book as my sole companion and remain there until I have read it to its very end.
I proudly attribute my fondness for books to the early influences of my family.[11]

The parents not only encourage their children and help them with their school work, but they
coöperate with the schools in various ways and thus
show their appreciation. Teachers and school officials almost invariably report favorably on the coöperation received from the Chinese and Japanese. A
teacher wrote:

I have never done anything I enjoyed so much as this
work. Every day there are little evidences of appreciation.
One day, while I was working with a small group around me I

heard a little disturbance in the room and looking around I
saw a seventeen-year old boy administering an old-fashioned
spanking to his brother, aged five, whom he had across his
knee. When I took the older boy to task he replied, "But he
won't study. He won't keep his eyes on his book, and mother
told me I must make him do it."[12]

In one school a Japanese boy did something
which was called to the attention of his father.
The father's attitude is revealed in a letter.

Referring to your notice of _____ _____, a pupil
of Spencer School, I have been certainly surprised to learn of
him who was committed a guilty on disgraced act in study hour,
neglecting his class work last Friday. I have been strictly
warned him that if he still acted such a guilty, I myself may
send to a reformatory before Mr. _____ has arranged him for
special school, and I have sentenced him one day confinement
on next Saturday, March 22, and this punishment surely meets
his agonizing experience. I will watch him now he goes on,
and may be not troubled you any further, and your kind advice
of him will be greatly appreciated, and please let me know
again if he has acted any ashamed conduct.[13]

Chinese and Japanese pay more attention to
the education of their children beyond the grammar
school than do several other population groups in
Hawaii. Table XIII shows that the ratio of those
attending high school to the total group of high
school age runs much higher for the Chinese and Japanese than for the Hawaiians and Portuguese.
    The interest in education is also evident in
continental United States. According to Table XIV
the Chinese and Japanese children between seven and
thirteen years of age rank with the children of native white parentage in school attendance and far
surpass the Mexicans and Negroes. In the age-group
between fourteen and twenty years, which is less affected by compulsory attendance laws, the Chinese
and Japanese excel even the native whites. The

results are practically the same if the comparison is made in California where the Orientals are most highly concentrated.[14]

Table XIII

PUPILS OF FOUR ANCESTRIES IN THE ELEMENTARY AND HIGH SCHOOLS OF HAWAII ON DECEMBER 21, 1928, BY NUMBER AND RATIO OF HIGH-SCHOOL PUPILS TO THE TOTAL NUMBER 15-19 YEARS OF AGE IN EACH GROUP

Ancestry	Number in Elementary Schools	Number in High Schools	Total Number 15-19 Years* of Age in 1930	Number in High School for every 1,000 in Age Group, 15-19 Years
Hawaiian	3,187	146	2,198	66.42
Portuguese	5,456	361	3,427	105.34
Chinese	5,187	1,091	2,572	424.18
Japanese	33,152	3,241	13,167	246.15

*The group 15-19 years was selected from the Census of 1930 because in 1928 they were 13-17 years of age. This is the age group which includes the majority of the high-school pupils.

Data from Superintendent of Public Instruction, Territory of Hawaii and United States Bureau of the Census, 1930

There is also considerable interest in education beyond the high school. Many Japanese parents make great sacrifices that their children may graduate from college. Many that have acquired land make no effort to keep their children on the soil. Oftentimes this parental ambition that their sons and daughters shall possess college degrees is somewhat overdone; some are not interested in a college education while others lack the ability to acquire one.[15]

Table XIV

PERCENTAGE OF SCHOOL ATTENDANCE OF THE CHINESE, JAPANESE, MEXICAN, NEGRO, AND NATIVE WHITE OF NATIVE PARENTAGE IN THE UNITED STATES AND CALIFORNIA, BY AGE PERIODS: 1930

Race, Color, Nativity	UNITED STATES				CALIFORNIA	
	PERCENTAGE ATTENDING SCHOOL BY AGE PERIODS				PERCENTAGE ATTENDING SCHOOL BY AGE PERIODS**	
	7-13	14-15	16-17	18-20	7-13	14-20
Japanese	97.2	97.3	88.8	51.8	97.3	80.1
Chinese	96.0	94.9	80.7	44.4	96.8	72.9
Native White Native Parentage*	96.1	90.0	61.0	24.4	97.8	67.2
Negro	87.3	78.1	46.3	13.3	97.1	60.8
Mexican	79.0	68.4	35.3	8.3	95.4	46.8

*This group is selected rather than the Total Population or Total White because of being removed from immigrant conditions it should rank high.
**For the Chinese, Japanese, and Mexicans, the data is available only for the 7-13 and 14-20 age periods.

Data from U. S. Bureau of the Census, 1930. Report on Population, Vol. 11, Chap. 12, pp. 1095, 1100, 1132

In some instances, emphasis upon education
is due to a desire to break from the galling tyranny
of the class distinctions transplanted from Japan.
For the immigrants themselves there is little chance,
but they hope to compensate their own thwarted wishes through the successes of their children.

Because of this failure of the Eta to be accepted in
Florin, Rosalind's father, a tiny cricketlike creature with
alert peering eyes, has worked himself to the bone to send his
two sons not only to college but to the universities as well.
For if there is no escape for an Eta farmer in the Pacific
villages, there may still be an escape for a professional man
in the coast cities. [16]

The immigrants have seen a number of their
children make successes in professional life or in
other preferred occupations and this tends to buoy
up their hopes. Furthermore, the attitude of superiority assumed by the dominant white group is a
challenge to the Orientals to show that they are in
no way inferior. The immigrants know that they cannot compete with the Americans on equal terms, but
spare no effort in urging their American-born children to win honors in their stead. The fact that
the white people have made use of the additional educational opportunities is an additional spur.

Parental Interest in Education of Girls.
The increase of girls in high school is a most significant index of parental interest in education.
Certain figures from Hawaii indicate that the traditional idea relative to the education of women is
changing. Table XV presents the percentages of the
Chinese and Japanese girls in the high schools of
the Territory as compared with the Portuguese.
According to the data in Table XV, the
greatest increase in high-school attendance has been
among the Japanese girls with the Chinese next in
order. The figures for the Japanese stand out even

Table XV

ENROLLMENT OF CHINESE AND JAPANESE IN THE PUBLIC HIGH
SCHOOLS OF HAWAII WITH PERCENTAGE OF THE TOTAL
ATTENDANCE FOR THE GIRLS IN EACH GROUP AS
COMPARED WITH THE PORTUGUESE, 1913,
1920, 1927

	Chinese			Japanese			Portuguese[tt]		
Year	Total	Girls	Per Cent	Total	Girls	Per Cent	Total	Girls	Per Cent
1913*	83	24	28.9	103	14	13.5	64	25	46.2
1920[t]	339	113	33.3	602	150	24.8	94	63	69.1
1927**	820	399	48.7	1995	718	36.0	232	163	70.0

*Hilo and McKinley High Schools. The only two high
schools for which the data are available.

[t]Hilo, Kauai, McKinley, and Maui Senior High Schools.
Race and sex distribution of pupils not available for the
other high schools.

**All Senior Public High Schools in the Territory.

[tt]The Portuguese group is selected for comparative purposes because in most respects it is the most nearly normally
distributed of any group in Hawaii.

Data from Records in Office of the Territorial Superintendent
of Public Instruction.

more strikingly when we consider that in 1920 [17] in
the age group from fourteen to seventeen years there
were 129 males to 100 females, and among the Chinese
there were 110 males to 100 females, while in the
Portuguese group the females outnumbered the males.
The parents have had more hope of realizing their
ambitions in and through their sons. The boys,
therefore, have received the major attention. It
has been a common practice for all members of the
family to work and sacrifice in order to send the
boys through high school and college, but

increasingly they are giving these educational advantages to their daughters. Even though many mothers hold to the tradition of the Orient that girls
do not need an education, it is evident that many
women are more fully aware of the handicaps from
lack of schooling than are the men. At times, they
help the children against the opposition of the male
heads of the households who hold tenaciously to the
old idea.

It is more difficult to secure data relative
to the Americans of oriental ancestry in the schools
of continental America. There is no segregation in
the statistical reports, except in a few instances.
Figures from Seattle, Washington, show that the Japanese girls increased from 11.1 per cent of the
total Japanese in high school in 1914-1915 to 40.0
per cent in 1926-1927 while the Chinese girls increased from 15.0 per cent to 30.2 per cent in the
same period.

Attitude of the Children toward Education.
The children of oriental parentage manifest great
interest in school work as reflected in their attendance records. Truancy is not a problem in this
group. Some of these children, nevertheless, break
the school regulations since they are often placed
in situations where there is considerable temptation
to play truant or to misbehave in other ways. When
notices concerning pupils are sent to parents in
English, many cannot read them; the children may interpret them as being advertisements for new can
openers or bargain sales.

Many, particularly among the Japanese in Hawaii, have come from plantation homes where the parents have been unable to assist them financially.
This has not deterred them; they have worked and
struggled in order to go to school, not only through
the grades but also through college. The pineapple
canning season is at its height during the summer
season and many make the most of this opportunity.[18]

A boy in Hawaii discloses the struggle through which
he passed.

Never a night passed by without my asking God to give
me an opportunity to go to school again. Sometimes my fishermen friends thought that I was insane because I prayed. It was
a good thing that they didn't understand a word I said, for if
they knew they would never have given me a position on their
boat. The only thing I wanted to do was to work; I needed
money to go to school. The bright month of August approached
slowly. I had saved a fair sum of money within several months.
I purchased clothes and bought other necessities. I never
forgot and I will never forget the day, August 15, when I
bought my school clothes. I had read in the papers that the
Normal School was to be opened on August 27th. I had waited a
year for this day to come. At last my prayers were answered.
My father permitted me to go to school under one condition,
that I try to support myself the best I could. What does work
mean to me? What does education mean to me? How much does it
mean to me if I am able to be a leader, a teacher? I couldn't
afford to lose the opportunity to go to school, so I took advantage of the one condition offered me.[19]

Even though many have to struggle for an education, their names frequently appear on the honor
rolls. In the colleges and universities a number
have won Phi Beta Kappa and Phi Kappa Phi honors, as
well as election to scholarship societies of different departments. Many receive honors;[20] others fall
by the wayside. There are repeaters in the schools,
but several causal factors account for this. Some
are of inferior ability, but in many instances lack
of proper guidance is evident. Parents are unable
to assist them; some teachers are unsympathetic and
prejudiced, while others are in no position to give
the needed counsel. The financial condition of the
homes, necessitating outside work, is also a prime
element. The language factor is important in school
retardation. Dr. Marvin L. Darsie of the University
of California, after studying 700 Japanese school
children in different areas of California, wrote:

In comparing the grade location of Japanese children
with those of Americans of corresponding ages, it was found
that on the average the Japanese child is about one-half grade
behind his American brother. On the other hand, in Los
Angeles and San Francisco there is no Japanese retardation,
Japanese children, in fact, being slightly ahead of Americans
of the same age. . . . In the tests measuring achievement in
school subjects, the Japanese children were found to be far
behind Americans in reading and the language subjects generally. They equalled American children in arithmetic, and surpassed them in spelling and handwriting. . . . The San Francisco Japanese were definitely superior to Americans in knowledge of American history and literature![21]

American superiority is largely limited to the specifically linguistic tests. . . . There is a very definite
tendency for the Japanese to equal or exceed American norms as
they pass from the linguistic to the non-linguistic tests.[22]

C. Effect of the School

Doubtless the public school is the outstanding instrumentality in the Americanization of the
children of immigrants. The school not only touches
the children directly but it touches them indirectly
through its influence on the parents. The children
introduce into their homes occidental ideas which
bring changes in parental practices. A girl in one
of the collegiate institutions of Hawaii reported
the changes which the school brought into her home.

There was very little furniture since Japanese do not
sit on chairs or sleep on beds, but at present my brothers and
sisters do not sleep on the floor. We have tables and chairs
in the parlor and a bureau in one of the bedrooms. We do not
sit on the floor and eat on low tables as most Japanese do,
but sit at a table as the Americans do. Of course we use bowls
and chopsticks but my brother favors forks and knives. I feel
very happy when the whole family sit around a large, round
table for the meal, every one with a smiling face. We eat two

types of food, namely American and Japanese. My father favors his old style but the rest favor the American style. This did not come until my eldest sister learned to cook at the grammar school.[23]

Oftentimes these changes in material culture produce modifications in non-material customs, ideas, and attitudes which bring the parents into closer harmony with the school. Under such conditions the children profit more from the school and are enabled to make more wholesome adjustments. On the other hand, the school has tended to develop a chasm between the children and their parents. The school brings them in touch with a new world which is largely beyond the experience of their elders. The children make contacts and acquire ideas which tend to set them off from the parental group. They become saturated with ideas which the parents do not appreciate, while no attempt is made to have the children understand their parents. In the great haste to Americanize the children of immigrants, and particularly the multi-colored children of Hawaii, America and everything American have been glorified, while many elements in the culture of the parents have been held up to scorn. As a result, many children have come to feel ashamed of their parents and of everything pertaining to the parental culture. The democratic spirit of the school develops attitudes which clash with the more autocratic and formalistic tradition of the parents.[24] This often produces disorganization and the young people become vacillating and uncertain, because the old system of control has been largely broken down while they have not fully become a part of the American group. This has actually reduced the efficiency of the school, for it cannot do its best without the coöperation of the home. Assuredly the most favorable condition is not found where the child has been taught to disrespect his parents. The school may

actually defeat its own purpose by applying so much
of this pressure that the group will become disorganized. To avoid this disorganization many parents,
aware of the resultant estrangement between the two
generations, have sent their children to the Orient
to be educated.

Chapter XIII

THE LANGUAGE SITUATION

In the adjustment of any group to a new environmental situation, language is a most important consideration. Unless there is a common medium of communication, serious obstacles are encountered in the development of an understanding between the two groups. The new arrivals can take over but little of the culture of the resident group unless the language is mastered. Newcomers may observe and endeavor to imitate some of the primary economic processes and may learn to do their work as others do it. In the main, however, this will be very superficial and will result in strange behavior, because they do not appreciate the meaning of the forms they have copied. When the immigrants learn the language, they acquire a tool which facilitates the acquisition of the new culture. While each group or generation has to discover its own wisdom through its own experience, language tends to shorten the process of coming into possession of a social inheritance.

The home is very important in connection with the acquisition of a language. The child of immigrant parents has a far more difficult task in mastering the English language than one in an American home. The child of oriental ancestry has a more difficult undertaking than one of European ancestry because the mother tongue is farther removed from the English language. Furthermore, the immigrants from the Orient, isolated because of racial and cultural differences, have had meager opportunities to learn English. Hence the home has been a hindrance in the linguistic development of the child.

     <u>Language Situation in Hawaii</u>. Because of
conditions peculiar to Hawaii, it has been a big
problem to secure a medium of communication between
the many-tongued people resident there. There are
several nationality groups and within each group
there are usually several dialects which at times
are widely divergent. Out of this situation has developed pidgin,[1] or pidgin-English, a curious but
serviceable jargon which is a mixture of several
languages.[2] It may be heard anywhere and everywhere
in Honolulu. Even some white persons, who have
grown up in the Territory, use pidgin as if it were
the real mother tongue. Many residents of Honolulu
transact a considerable share of their daily business by means of this jargon. It is useful anywhere
in Hawaii. An American preacher addressed a group
of Japanese in one of the plantation camps. He began to tell the story of "The Prodigal Son," but
soon realized that his audience did not understand
his presentation in English. An Hawaiian school
teacher who had lived in the community for many
years offered her services to translate the story
into pidgin. We quote a portion.

     Long time before, ah ray, one man, two musko gotchi.
Ah ray, number two boy, opiopio (younger) no too muchee guru
look see (meaning handsome). Number two boy papa talk talk,
"Me dala (money) likee, any kind you pololei makana (help) me.
This time makana, me another place likee go." Papa house too
muchee guru kaukau, too muchee guru, any kind too muchee guru.
Ah, number two boy too muchee dala likee no. Papa he give
dala (money) number two boy wiki-wiki horse maluna go. Nother
place go. Number two boy bime by Honolulu place all same go
(city). He too muchee milumilu (see) any kind guru look see.
Bime by, guru musume (girl) guru wahine look see, guru clothes,
guru any kind look see. Dala too muchee wiki-wiki hemo (lose)
no. Bime by too muchee aikane (friend) come doh. Guru kaukau
all time kaukau. Guru clothes all time put on. Too muchee

hokana hana hana. Bime by, hula-hula house go, all dala wiki-
wiki hemo no. Bime by he no more dala pocket stop.[3]

The Japanese men in Hawaii used the Japanese
language in their homes, but pidgin when dealing
with the foremen and other non-Japanese on the plantations. The women, who made fewer outside contacts, learned less of the pidgin and stayed more
closely by their own language. Since the Japanese
came in large numbers to the plantations, they have
been able to maintain their language in considerable
measure. Practically everywhere a Japanese went in
Hawaii he would find some of his countrymen and could
thus use his mother tongue. The children learned
Japanese at home (although it was very simple in
many instances) and gradually some pidgin as they
made contacts with non-Japanese. Many plantation
children never heard English spoken, except for the
corrupted English words in pidgin, before entering
school. To be sure, this gradually changed; the
younger children could learn English from their older brothers and sisters, who had been in school, and
from other children in the neighborhood.

While pidgin is a great problem with the
Japanese in Hawaii, some of the Chinese in rural
places have suffered even more from it. In these
areas the Chinese have been a minority element in
the population since 1900, too few to maintain the
purity of their mother tongue as they have been isolated among non-Chinese where pidgin has been in
common usage. In certain homes the children could
not speak Chinese while the parents could not speak
English; consequently pidgin was the only language
used.

A number of the young people of oriental ancestry, realizing their handicap, apply themselves
with such diligence that they learn to use better
English than many of their white classmates in the
schools.[5] But the conditions prevent the majority
from acquiring a pure English. A business executive

in Honolulu stated he had received a large number of
applications for positions from young Americans of
oriental ancestry and not one of these letters was
without some error in English.

Some distinction should be made between the
Chinese and the Japanese with reference to the language situation. On the whole the young Chinese in
Hawaii have the better command of English. The Chinese have been in the Islands longer and the majority have been residents of Honolulu for a considerable period. In the capital city they have had better opportunities for acquiring good English. The
majority of the Japanese have until quite recently
lived on the plantations where it has been customary
to segregate the workers in different camps according to language. In this way the Japanese children
virtually grew up in Japanese communities. When
they made contacts outside their own group, it was
usually with Portuguese, Hawaiians, and Chinese
whose English was almost invariably of the pidgin
variety.

Language Situation on the Pacific Coast.
The Americans of oriental ancestry on the Pacific
Coast, in the main, have a better command of the
English language. Pidgin is not a problem on the
Coast. While some immigrant Orientals use it,[6] the
children's speech is not corrupted because in most
places they are almost completely immersed in an
English-speaking population; they are actually
forced to discard the language of their parents.
There are many in California whose English cannot be
distinguished from that of any cultured Anglo-Saxon.

In California, some white people have asserted that a heavy burden was thrown on the school
because the Japanese children could not speak English when first enrolled. They protested that busy
work was given to the white pupils while the teachers spent their time in teaching English to the Japanese. Certain Japanese in California, being aware

of this condition, have employed American kinder-
garten teachers to instruct their children in English before they entered the public schools.

Language and the Schools. The schools in
Hawaii have been struggling with the language problem. Where conditions have been favorable, they
have succeeded remarkably well, but in many instances they only could increase the English content of the pidgin and secure a pronunciation and
accent with a skew toward English.

Investigations. . . . disclose the fact that when
children of the islands enter school at six or seven years of
age, not more than two or three per cent can speak the English
language. The teachers, therefore, from the very first,. . . .
must establish a working vocabulary to serve as a medium of
communication between teacher and child. In many instances
it is weeks before the teacher can make herself understood.
Furthermore, many of those who do come with some knowledge of
English would better not have any at all, for it is the jargon
of the plantations and the pidgin English of the streets. . . .
The teacher. . . . is further handicapped. . . . by the fact
that there are virtually no children from English-speaking
homes to mingle with the children of the various races in
their sports and games, thereby serving as powerful allies in
popularizing the English tongue. Enrolled in the schools of
the islands, public and private, there are only about 2,400
children with whom the English language is native; 1,500 of
these are in private schools and 900 children scattered among
36,000 will exercise no appreciable influence; rather the danger is that they themselves will be overwhelmed by sheer numbers and their own language corrupted.[7]

Some maintain that the study of Chinese and
Japanese in America has been a hindrance to the acquisition of good English. In Hawaii it is not the
Chinese and Japanese languages, but pidgin that is
the real obstacle. In school the pupils may try to
use good English in the classroom but in the free

atmosphere of the playground they revert to the
pidgin. In fact, many pupils make sport of the one
who tries to carry his classroom English outside.
Under such pressure there is a tendency to use pidgin rather than "school" English.

Language and the Two Generations. The great
difference between the oriental immigrants and their
children is, in large measure, a function of language. As the children acquire the concepts which
are current in the American group, they are given
entrée into a world which is almost entirely sealed
against their parents. On the other hand, the young
people are not mastering the mother tongue and do
not have full access to the world of their parents.
As the children progress in school, their gain in
vocabulary is in English and their intellectual
growth is in that language. Many of the young people speak the best of English and betray not the
slightest foreign accent; they can use the latest
slang and can make humorous plays upon words, which
indicates that they have mastered the language.[8] The
parental language is gradually crowded into the
background; it even becomes corrupted through the
influence of the pidgin. The young people usually
learn enough of the mother tongue for the ordinary
routine of daily life, but do not have sufficient
vocabulary for the maintenance of an adequate communication between the generations. They lack the
vocabulary and the concepts in which the ancestral
traditions and higher things of life are transmitted.[9] Many of them are unable to understand figures of speech or appreciate humor in the mother
tongue. Some know so little of the parental language that at times they find themselves in embarrassing situations.[10] When there is no adequate
medium of communication between the young and old,
misunderstandings result. The children cannot share
with their parents the occidental ideas acquired in
the school. Hence conflicts often arise. Since the

children cannot discuss their difficulties with
their parents, they are left to solve their own
problems by their own devices.

In some instances parents have tried to
force their children to use the mother tongue. This,
however, has not prevented them from learning and using English. Oftentimes parents are forced to use
English, broken though it may be, in order to con-
verse with their children. On the other hand, many
parents give their children every encouragement in
the learning of English and do not insist on an acquisition of the mother tongue.

Various influences are conspiring to place
barriers between the two generations. The books and
newspapers which the young people read are almost
entirely in English. In Honolulu there are several
Chinese and Japanese newspapers with English sections. The two American dailies in Honolulu are beginning to cater to the younger generation of Oriental ancestry. There are also several Japanese
papers on the Coast which have English departments.
On January 1, 1928, The Japanese-American Courier
began publication in Seattle, Washington, as the
first all-English newspaper of the second generation. It has increased considerably in size since
the first issue [11] English is increasingly coming to
be the only language of the younger group.

Interest in the Mother Tongue. Because of
the conditions peculiar to Hawaii there has developed some interest in the mother tongues of the
different groups. Since the Japanese constitute the
largest group in the Territory, they find more use
for this language and are in a position to appreciate its value more fully. During the past few years
there has been a growing interest in the Chinese
language in Hawaii. The Mun Lun Chinese School in
Honolulu had about one hundred pupils in 1902 while
in 1926 there were over nine hundred.[12] The growth
of Chinese nationalism, the agitation and litigation

relative to the language schools in Hawaii, the interest in the Mass Education Movement in China, and
the fact that some have begun to see greater economic opportunities in China than in America have
been factors in stimulating the study of Chinese.

But even though these languages may be given
considerable attention, there are comparatively few
who learn to speak them fluently. Many simply waste
their time in the language schools, often to their
regret in later life.[13] The young woman who wrote
the following paragraph began to study Chinese seriously after she had graduated from a mainland college and had spent some time in postgraduate study.

I attended a Chinese school when I was too young to
get any benefit from such an education. As father was one of
the trustees of the school, we children took advantage of that
and instead of studying we spent our time fighting and playing. The teachers, being afraid of us, did not dare punish
us. Though we did not take examinations, we were always promoted and, as a result, we did not learn much. We were sent
to school merely to make a good impression so that other parents would send their children to the same school. . . . My
parents are indifferent about sending the other members of the
family to Chinese school now that they have seen how fruitless
it was when they sent my sisters and me.[14]

In continental United States, the aversion
to the mother tongue is accentuated by the fact that
many young people of oriental ancestry have acquired
the typical American attitude that the English language is all sufficient and superior to· all other
languages. Furthermore, since the users of English
are superior in economic status, many take a more or
less contemptuous attitude toward their elders and
their language. Then, why learn the parental language? Learning one of the oriental languages--in
itself a difficult task--is made doubly distasteful
because many can see no value in it. Moreover, some
do not want it to be known that they can speak one

of these languages--they are Americans and why
should they speak a language that might classify
them with the "Chinks" or the "Japs"?

Language Schools and the Second Generation.
The conditions in the oriental communities in Hawaii and on the Pacific Coast have been favorable to
the development of the foreign language schools.[15]
Because of the barrier that was growing up between
the parents and their children, the language schools
were established to teach the younger generation the
mother tongue that they might communicate with their
parents. There has been much opposition to the language schools, both on the Pacific Coast and in Hawaii. Former Governor Farrington of Hawaii stood
against this institution.

Many language schools have developed a nationalistic
character that raised a serious question in the public mind as
to their influence on children who are accepted as American
citizens. . . . It is the opinion of many Japanese and Americans that the recommendations of the Federal schools survey
commission, published in 1920 (Bulletin No. 16 of the United
States Bureau of Education) to eliminate these schools, should
be made effective. Wherever these schools have shown a nationalistic tendency, it comes in striking contrast to the
progressive policy adopted by the native Hawaiian people. The
Hawaiians, recognizing the desirability that their children be
trained in the English language, voluntarily abolished Hawaiian and insisted upon English as the language of instruction in the elementary schools. . . . The Hawaiian people, as
a whole, are Americans in speech and thought and the advantages to the Hawaiian children are obvious. It is to be hoped
that in the not far distant future the same may be said of all
alien elements in the Territory.[16]

An examination of the delinquency statistics
makes one hesitate before accepting this conclusion.
The report tells of the Americanization of the Hawaiians. But together with this dropping of the

language we find a high ratio of juvenile delinquency. The Japanese language schools have been
criticized more than any others, but at the same
time the young Japanese have the most favorable delinquency ratio in the Territory. Even some young
Americans of oriental ancestry are antagonistic to
the language schools. This is usually found in the
early years when everything moves along smoothly and
they look upon everything American as being superior.
When disillusionments come, this attitude of antagonism tends to be replaced by an appreciation of the
mother tongue and the parental culture. Some, however, more considerate of the feelings of their parents, make an earnest endeavor to bridge the gap between the generations. They see the value of the
mother tongue and study it diligently that they may
be able to keep in closer touch with their parents,
both while living at home and while away.

    The Chinese and Japanese language schools
have performed, and for a time will continue to perform, a most useful service in bringing the two
generations closer together. When all factors are
considered, it is remarkable that there has not been
more disorganization and demoralization of the youth.
Much credit is due to the language schools for their
stabilizing influence in this period of transition.
As the immigrant group gradually passes from the
scene, there will be less and less need for these
schools and they will disappear without suppressive
legislative enactments. The attempts to drive the
language schools out of existence have in reality
served as boomerangs; they have actually prolonged
the life of the schools. These attacks have been an
integral part of prejudices and discriminations
against the Orientals. According to Dr. A. W. Palmer,

    While ordinarily these schools would tend to be un-
popular with children and gradually to disappear, their continued life and vitality are largely due to that uncertainty

of status produced by racial discrimination and the denial of
economic opportunity to the young American-born Japanese.
These young people discover that they are most likely to find
employment in situations where their knowledge of Japanese is
an asset, or they and their parents wonder if, denied economic
opportunity in America, it may not be necessary ultimately for
them to return to Japan, in which case they would need to know
the Japanese language. Hence the prejudices and economic barriers set up by the American community itself keep the language schools alive and popular.[17]

Chapter XIV

DISCRIMINATIONS AND RACIAL CONSCIOUSNESS

In their early years, children of diverse racial inheritance mingle freely. If left to themselves, children know no race distinctions; that is, they do not know them as a basis for social discrimination. Blond Nordic children play happily with children of oriental ancestry, no matter whether it be in San Francisco or in Laupahoehoe. Some children of oriental parentage become so completely fused into the white group that they are not even conscious of any differences. A Japanese college girl presents this fact.

One day my sister, who is nine years old, came home from school and said to me: "There are too many 'Japs' coming into our school." When I asked her to name them she did so, but did not include any members of our own family who were in the school. We have lived in a community where there are very few Japanese and because we have mingled so freely with Americans, she evidently does not consider us Japanese.[1]

There have been many instances where children of north-European and oriental ancestry have formed close friendships. A white high-school boy in Hawaii had become so friendly toward the Orientals that he was lonesome for them when on a visit to the mainland. He was happy only when he visited a city which had a cosmopolitan population that reminded him of Honolulu.

Gradually, however, changes have come. Many persons of oriental ancestry have unfortunate experiences; bars are raised against them.

Furthermore, they observe the treatment others receive. They become sensitive and often magnify trifles. When a person is ignored because of his own individual peculiarities, it is often construed to be a racial matter. Thus the rift between the two groups is widened. A statement by a Japanese high-school boy in Hawaii is typical not only of a large number in his own group, but of the Chinese, Hawaiians, Filipinos, Porto Ricans, and Portuguese as well.

I began to realize that I was different from other races when I really awoke to this world. I would like to cite some examples. A judge would let off a Haole with an easy term, but is it so with an Oriental? A policeman would be very easy with a Haole, but is it so with an Oriental? One day I was standing on the corner of King and Fort Streets, waiting for my car. A Haole lady, one of the many passers-by, suddenly shoved me with one of her large arms and said, "Get out of my way." It is a fact that many Japanese are ignorant and greedy for money which is earned in a crooked way. I, too, hate those people. I wish they were back in Japan, but there is no reason why some people should loathe all the Japanese people.[2]

After mingling freely with white children in their childhood years, many in their early teens have come to a realization that they were no longer to be accepted. In many instances this awakening has come as a rude shock bringing heartaches and bitter feelings. A Japanese girl wrote:

I have been with this Philathea class so much that I am one of them. I go to their homes, eat with them, sleep with them, and take part freely in all their activities. In fact, this close association with these girls caused me a great disappointment at one time. Our Philathea class went to Monterey Beach where we planned to have a good time in the plunge. We lined up at the ticket office and when I came to the window the girl said she wouldn't sell me a ticket. When

I asked why, she snapped out that she had orders not to sell
any tickets to "Japs." That made me indignant. I told the
girls to go into the plunge for a good time while I stood by
and watched them. I felt this keenly, but concluded it was
best to say nothing and act in a courteous manner. . . . I
didn't have the slightest idea that I would be treated in this
manner; I was perfectly innocent; I was with the girls and
never even gave a thought to any such possibilities.[3]

  The Schools and Race Relationships. The
schools have much to do with the development of
friendliness or prejudice. Where teachers are partial, a division readily develops among the pupils
and this may ripen into hatred. Realization of race
differences may come out of class discussions into
which white pupils inject ideas acquired from the
newspapers or from their homes. Frequently white
pupils make disparaging remarks about the "Jap."
  Race distinctions are rare in the primary
grades in school. The pupils mingle freely and happily together and even though they notice physical
differences no distinctions are made. As they advance in school, pupils of oriental ancestry gradually discover that these physical differences are
important factors affecting their social relations.[4]
Marked changes often come when pupils enter high
school. In the larger cities in particular it usually means a change to another school where new
friendships are formed. Under the departmentalized
system in the high schools, where the pupils go from
group to group, there is little opportunity to be-.
come well acquainted.[5] The selection of friends becomes largely a matter of conscious choice and differences are more likely to receive attention.
Adults make comments which are noticed. Oftentimes
when white children have accepted those of oriental
ancestry, parents or other white adults have stirred
up difficulties.[6] Furthermore, it is the period
when the two sexes develop an interest in each other.
It is the time when they are twitted about

sweethearts, and they are becoming conscious of and responsive to considerations of class status. They prefer friends of recognized standing and begin to avoid those whose friendship may create embarrassments.

<u>In Continental United States</u>. The following documents reveal the condition in a junior high school in California.

Creating one of the most delicate situations with which Hollywood and Los Angeles school authorities have ever had to deal, a Japanese pupil has been elected president of the student body at the _____ Junior High School. Surface activities at the school today indicated a determined movement to have the young Oriental removed from office, although he was elected by a reported majority of 600 votes. Indignation of parents of pupils in the school is said to be rising, and there is talk of a formal protest to the board of education. . . . The Japanese was regularly elected by the students. His election was in the nature of a landslide. . . . First reports of dissatisfaction over the election came from parents who termed the selection of the Japanese an "outrage." . . . Movement for the recall of the Japanese president started in earnest at the school today. . . . One of the leaders among the opposition in the student body, announced his intention to circulate a petition demanding the removal of the president. "We don't want a Japanese boy for President. . . , even if he was regularly elected." . . . "The girls voted for him," declared one of the leaders among the boys. The general sentiment among the boys is said to be that the Oriental may be a fine fellow and a good politician, but it would be setting a bad example and serious precedent to allow him to maintain the office of president of the student body. . . . One report was that students of Hollywood High School are preparing to make a formal protest. . . . against the election of the Japanese.[7]
Spurred by an increasing determination to remove John Aiso, a Japanese boy, recently elected commissioner of boys' welfare. . . . students of the ninth grade were circulating a petition this morning demanding that the Oriental be

removed from the office. In solid opposition to their efforts
is the stand taken by the faculty, the teachers maintaining
that the Japanese boy has not yet proved himself incapable and
there is no reason for his recall. Regardless of the interpretation placed upon the significance of his office, students
assert that in this position the officer has power to direct
policies and activities of other commissioners, thus making
him actually, if not in name, president of the student
body. . . . An unsuccessful attempt was made this morning to
get the ninth grade to strike, but lack of organization was
apparently the reason for its failure.[8]

The following petition was circulated among
the students for the purpose of removing the Japanese boy from office.

This is a protest in opposition to the newly-elected
Japanese president of the student body of the Junior High
School. We students want an American president over the student body and consider it a serious matter, and a bad example
for any American boy or girl to submit passively and take no
part in the opposition to remove the boy from the presidency
of the student body of our school. We stand for America and
want no other but an American as our student-body president.
The reasons for a recall are based upon those principles of
freedom for which American patriots sacrificed their lives and
fortunes. I therefore believe it is the duty of all our American students to support our country, our schools by placing
an American boy in the office of president of our student
body. I am in the B-9 grade of the Junior High School and for
nearly all of my school days I have repeated the "American
Creed" in class: "I believe in the United States of America,
as a government of the people, by the people, for the people."--It has taken root in my heart and soul and I protest
against an Oriental taking the place of president of our student body. Give us an American boy![9]

The central figure in this drama gave his
version in an interview, together with other high
school experiences.

When the Junior High School opened I entered and when
the time for the election of student officers came I was nominated by a group of my friends, and was elected by a vote of
about three to one. Immediately after the election some of
the rougher boys began to talk against me and soon there was
considerable excitement created because some of the parents
began to take part, and the newspapers also had articles about
the matter. The newspapers published several articles which
were not fair until the Los Angeles Times and the Los Angeles
Record came to me for my side of the case. I felt hurt about
the matter, but it did not seem so bad to me when I learned
that the boys who headed this movement were those who did poor
work in school, who smoked and played truant at times. The
better pupils treated me well and our relations were pleasant
all through the year. I did not feel any hatred toward any
of the pupils who were responsible for this. In the grammar
school my sister, brother and I were the only Japanese; my
best friends were Americans.

In the Junior High School we had an oratorical contest, in which another boy and I were tied for first place.
He won on delivery and I on my composition. This was not satisfactory and so I suggested that the other boy be given first
place that our school might be represented. This they did,
but when the other boy would not accept this arrangement it
was decided that our school should not be represented.

I am now in the high school, where I am pretty much
of a book worm. I entered my name to try out for cheer leader,
but our principal advised me to withdraw in order to avoid any
difficulties which might arise and create unpleasantness for
me. I am fond of athletics but since I am too light for any
of the regular school teams I am planning to try for one of
the 110-pound teams. I am also planning to try out in debating. Ever since I was quite small I have attended one of the
American churches where I am now president of the Intermediate
Christian Endeavor. I have always enjoyed my associations
there.[10]

While this boy was in the Senior High School,
he entered the national oratorical contest on the
Constitution of the United States where he won first

place in his school but, when it came to the final
contest for the area, the white boy who won second
place represented the school, won first honors, and
was sent as district representative to the national
contest in Washington, D. C., where he was the winner. The newspaper reason for substituting the
white boy was that the Japanese boy had failed in
health and was therefore unable to enter the final
contest. In a speech in Tokyo this boy said of the
contest: "Immediately my own school asked me to resign, on the ground that a Japanese in the contest
would upset the peace of the different schools in
the city."[11] The high school students raised a fund
to pay the traveling expenses of the Japanese boy so
that he accompanied their representative to Washington.[12]

There has, however, been considerable change
since 1922 when this occurred; a considerable number
of honors have come to students of oriental ancestry
in the schools on the Coast in the last few years.
In four high schools in Seattle, Japanese graduates
appeared as speakers on the commencement programs in
the spring of 1934. During the year 1933-1934 a
Japanese boy was president of the sophomore class in
a high school of Seattle. In the spring he was
elected to the Boy's Advisory Board of the school
for the coming year. This Board is usually composed
of seniors, but because of exceptional ability he
was chosen to serve while a junior.[13]

In the universities on the Pacific Coast,
there has been noticeable uneasiness among oriental
students and they have been reticent about partici-
pating in class discussions. Frequently these students compensate for their reticence in the classroom by handing in superior written products which
have been prepared where they were not embarrassed
by the presence of white students. In activities
outside the classroom, they have been hesitant in
taking part. When they do participate, they often
appear ill at ease.[14] Since they form a small and

powerless minority in the larger institutions, they
are usually ignored and no issues arise to create
tensions. In the smaller colleges they are usually
accepted by the group. In several institutions,
students of oriental lineage have been elected to
societies and fraternities based on scholarship,
but even in such organizations the color line has
been in evidence. The Alpha Kappa Delta, national
honor society in sociology, is purported to be based
on scholarship, but it was several years before any
non-white person was admitted into the original chapter which is on the Coast. The social fraternities
draw the line sharply and very rarely is a person
of oriental ancestry admitted.

   In the institutions of the Middle West and
East there is more liberality than on the Coast, but
even in the eastern states persons of oriental ancestry are not able to lose themselves completely.[15]
An American-born Chinese related his experience.

   When I was in college on the mainland, I had some experiences which have had considerable influence over me. In
college I was taken into a fraternity. In my second year I
took part in the initiation of the new men. We had them lined
up and were paddling them with some boards and staves. Several of the fellows had paddled them and then my turn came.
After I had given one of the fellows a swat he turned around
and said, "You damned Chink! What business do you have to hit
me?" That was a big shock to me. Why should he pick on me?
I said nothing and when it came to the election I voted that
he be received. After some time we became the best of friends.
   During my medical course I was doing some work in the
hospital. Once I gave a pill to a woman and she grew worse.
Then I was accused of drugging her. She became worse; I was
Chinese; we were near the Canadian border; and Chinese had
been accused of smuggling drugs across. That was the chain of
reasoning. I was called into the dean's office and was
shocked to think that he believed that. Soon after that I
went to the army for two years and that absence helped me to
get revenge on the dean. During my absence I was elected to

the Greek letter society to which the dean belonged so that
when I returned I met him there. This seemed to be a blow to
the dean, but he gradually adjusted himself to it and began to
treat me better.[16]

   (2) In Hawaii. Members of the oriental
groups are permitted to participate more fully in
the life of the community in the Hawaiian Islands.
This is plainly evident in many of the schools. In
the classroom they usually participate freely, but
without going to extremes. Extra-curricular activities, such as dramatic productions, glee clubs,
choruses, bands, orchestras, and other voluntary activities are cosmopolitan in their personnel. Many
young people of oriental ancestry are not aware of
racial discriminations to any appreciable extent until after they have entered college or, if they had
felt any distinction previously, it was greatly accentuated in this later period.
   The situation inside the University of Hawaii differs markedly from that on the outside. In
the industrial life of the Islands there is a considerable gulf between the Occidentals and Orientals;
there is little direct competition between them.
The University, however, is a public institution,
with a democratic atmosphere, and all races, colors,
and creeds are on an equal footing. This brings all
into direct competition and, in the main, the Orientals hold their own. For many years the majority of
the sons and daughters of the sugar planters were
sent to universities on'the mainland and comparatively few white students attended college in Hawaii.
In recent years the white students have increased.
In this group have been a number who could not meet
the requirements of the eastern universities, together with some who were financially unable to
enter mainland schools. A considerable number from
both groups feel a certain loss of status in being
thrown into direct competition with the oriental
students. This often results in strained

relationships as the white students endeavor to
maintain a position of superiority. A Japanese college graduate in Hawaii reveals the situation.

My brother Kazuo ran against Frank Harvey, renowned
football star, for the presidency of the student body. I shall
never forget the bitterness of that election. George Wells
was third nominee. Just before election time he dropped off
the ballot and attached his votes to Harvey in a Haole bloc.
Call it what you will. To me it was unmistakable dislike on
the part of the Haole students of having an Oriental as president. Let the Orientals keep minor positions but hold the
presidency of the student body sacred--open only to non-Orien-
tals. A number of Haole votes probably went to Kazuo, but it
was quite evident that Harvey's campaign managers had done a
thorough job. Harvey won by a close margin.[17]

In Hawaii, students of oriental ancestry are
in the majority in practically all public schools.
Because of this, many white people send their children to private schools where the line can be drawn
against non-Caucasians. This, however, is an added
expense and some have favored the reservation of
certain public schools for white children only. In
1920 a movement was inaugurated for an English
Standard School in which pupils would be selected on
the basis of proficiency in English. Some advocated
openly that it be made a "white" school. This, however, aroused considerable opposition. When a public high school was opened on one island, the white
group attempted to restrict it to their own children.
When a number of Japanese pupils enrolled, the white
people objected. The principal maintained that a
school supported by public funds was open to all.
The white people, nevertheless, continued their objections until the principal was transferred to another island. Pupils of all races, however, are
still admitted. A high school was built in a rural
district of another island a considerable distance
from the population centers. The underlying idea

was that the white pupils would commute on the railway line, while the Japanese would be debarred by
the added expense. This, however, was not a sufficient barrier. On December 21, 1928, there was a
total registration of 411 of which number 237 were
Japanese and only twenty-eight were of north-European ancestry.

      <u>Scholarship and Race Prejudice</u>. It is usu-
ally found that white students with strong prejudices are weak in scholarship. Superior students
can compete successfully in the scholastic field and
may associate freely with other races without en-
dangering their status; the weak ones draw the race
line and defend themselves behind a wall of prejudice.[18] A white girl in one of the high schools of
Hawaii, who did not rank high in scholarship, found
refuge in an all-white club.

      If I had the choice of any one club in the High School,
I would join the Totem Club. The other clubs may be just as
fine as the Totem Club, but in every one of them there are
more than half a dozen Orientals and I don't care to mix with
them. Not that I am any better than they, but after all every
one has a caste. The Totem Club consists only of the Haoles
and here no Oriental can get the best of you--they are ahead
of us in many ways, but here the Haole has a chance. It is a
funny thing that most of the Haoles don't care or don't like
the idea of an Oriental ruling over them; for instance, the
president of a club may be an Oriental and I for one wouldn't
want to obey his commands. Therefore, I would join the Totem
Club where I would be amongst my own kind. I have no ill-
feeling towards the Orientals, though; it's just the idea of
mixing with them.[19]

      In the University of Hawaii, the men have an
organization, "The Hui Lokahi,"--to all intents and
purposes a social fraternity--which is avowedly
white and anti-oriental. One Japanese, however, has
been admitted, but he was said to be rather

thoroughly "Haolified" and associated more with
Haoles than with those of his own race. In the
spring of 1928, a Chinese-Hawaiian (one-fourth Chinese) was elected to membership.

    Industry and Race Attitudes. Labor Unions
and other organizations usually have drawn the line
against Orientals and their American-born descendants, but a more favorable attitude is in process of
development. This became evident when organized
labor in California, in 1928, passed a resolution
which extended an invitation to all American citizens of oriental ancestry to join the several unions.[20] This action could mean much; if they were
accepted by the unions, rigid lines could not well
be drawn against them.

    In 1927 the carpenter's union of Hawaii in-
vited them in. Not all labor unions in Hawaii have
let down the bars. The plasterers' union of Honolulu does not admit them and does not take any ap-
prentices from the group. In October, 1928, the
Y.M.C.A. school in Honolulu made plans for conducting a class in plastering to which those of oriental
ancestry would be admitted but they encountered
strong opposition on the part of the union. A white
instructor had been engaged for the course but before actual instruction had begun he informed the
administration that he would be unable to conduct
the class.

    Discriminations in the occupational field
have been far-reaching. In civil service positions,
on the mainland in particular, Chinese and Japanese
have not been accepted on an equal footing with
white men. Not even in the army during the World
War, when so much was said about democracy, were
they accepted on an equality with others.

    Many white people object to side-by-side
working relations with those of oriental lineage.
Consequently many employers cannot hire them because
of the other workers. In California, if the

Oriental occupies a status of inferiority, there is
usually no serious objection to him. It seems that
certain employers, even in Hawaii, are intent on
maintaining a distinction which implies inferiority.
Assignment to a lower stratum by the dominant group
was a bitter disappointment to this Chinese boy.

      Life so far had only shown me its bright side and not
until I worked for the principal of the school did it become
ugly. Heretofore I had lived under the assumption that all
people were good, particularly the white people, and especially the educated among them. However, it did not take me long
to discover the contrary. In reply to the following advertisement on the school bulletin board I landed a job: "Boy wanted
after school hours, room and board with twelve to fifteen dollars a month." In the course of a few days I was cook, waiter,
boot-black, yard boy, garage man, errand runner, housemaid,
and governess. Knowing my lot I consented to take more than I
really could afford to execute. Each morning I was up at six
o'clock attending to the odds and ends. Lunch was prepared in
advance and kept warm with the aid of a fireless cooker. To
facilitate a speedy luncheon service I was obliged to miss the
daily assembly to get back in time to set the table. Finding
me so accommodating my employer now asked me to drop my morning class in biology to stay home to watch over his boy until
he went to school. His wish was complied with and I was to
take a final examination at the end of the year for my credits.
Evidently it never occurred to my educated employer that he
was enjoying more service than was really due him and at the
end of the first month he paid me with a characteristic com-
pliment: "George, ten dollars is all I can afford to pay you.
If I hired a Japanese girl she would be here all day." The
blood rushed to my face. For the moment I was tongue-tied as
I held the check. I had a notion to politely advise him to
hire his Japanese girl to do all that I was doing. But I did
not dare to offend him. He was the principal of the only high
school I could afford to attend. What if he should flunk me?
With all considerations for myself I swallowed the irony.
      To yield an inch was to yield a foot. To me the
"villain" grew daily bolder and more cold blooded. But my

employer was not to know my discontent. My oriental patience
and meekness blinded his selfish eyes. Upon my drying the
much-needed clothes on the porch instead of in the yard during
a rainy season he laid aside the rôle of a gentleman and said,
"I tell you what is the matter with you! Your head is too big
for you!" He meant I was lazy and tried to put off the job.
Again my emotions did not permit me to deal with him as diplo-
matically as I had wished. So with equal Anglo-Saxon aggres-
siveness I informed him that Pluvius wept again after he had
given me the orders to put the clothes on the line. I had
come to delight in experiencing an occasional display of narrowness. Before the year was over I was treated to three more
eruptions of his master mind. One came when he asked for some
lamb stew. The previous meal he and his son had devoured a
large portion of the dish and I in the kitchen had consumed
the remainder of it. When told that there was no more left of
the stew, he flung this sharp retort at me: "What became of
the rest of the stew? Did you feed it to the dogs?" My reply
was equally direct but more laconic, "Then we must have been
the dogs!"

     The second occurred on a night when we were to have a
class social. Our kind class advisor, knowing my circumstances, advised me to ask for permission from Mr. Blank to
attend the affair as he,being the principal, was invited,
which meant that I was obliged to remain at home to keep watch
over his weak-minded son who on several previous occasions had
nearly set the house on fire by playing volcano with matches,
newspapers, koa tables and cracker tins. I already had on my
blue serge coat and linen trousers and met Mr. Blank in the
kitchen. "May I go to the social tonight, Mr. Blank?" I
asked. My employer gave a start. "You can beat the Dutch.
Are you hiring me or am I hiring you?" he brayed. I did not
say a word. I thought he could have refused me a bit more
kindly. My teacher knew why I was not at the social. She
asked Mr. Blank to let me go to the social after he returned
home. He consented and told me that I could go. I went; I
couldn't have spurned the consideration my teacher had for me.
Upon my arrival she brought me the cake and ice cream she had
reserved. But I was too dejected to eat.

     The last was most stinging. I did not think that

Mr. Blank, a minister in Alabama before he became principal, could have had so little religion. His son had come into my room and asked me to read him a story. As I commenced the boy complained of the poor light in my room and led me into the parlor to read to him. Before I had started Mr. Blank came in. "Don't you come into the parlor until I invite you!" he said. For the moment I was overwhelmed with shame and retreated to my dingy apartment. It was a puzzle. I could enter the parlor with the broom and dustpan but not to read to his son. Then I understood--he was master, I was servant. I became conscious of my humble position.[22]

There are considerable differences in the industrial conditions in different areas of the Hawaiian Islands and these diversities result in variant attitudes. In the coffee belt of Kona, where Japanese farmers operate their own leaseholds, there is no anti-plantation or anti-Haole attitude; prejudice is at a minimum and the young men of that district can go to other places and associate more naturally and normally with white people.[23] In striking contrast, on the Hamakua Coast of the same island, which is jocularly called the "Scottish Coast," the lines are sharply drawn. This is in the cane belt. On the sugar plantations a small group of north-European lineage is in a position of dominance and directs the enterprise. Immigrants have been brought from several regions to do the manual labor on the plantations and these laborers, no matter what their origin, are always accorded a status of inferiority. Even the Portuguese are given a status much inferior to the Anglo-Saxons and only a little above the Orientals. Between the management and the workers there is an all but unbridgeable chasm.

The tourist traffic, now rated as the third industry of the Territory next to sugar and pineapples, is a factor of some significance. Since large numbers of visitors come from the Coast they bring their prejudices with them. This is reacting in particular upon those who depend largely on the tourist business for their livelihood.

Restrictions on Residence. Members of the
oriental groups in the cities of the Pacific Coast
have encountered difficulties in finding suitable
places to live outside the congested districts. A
Japanese reported his experience in Los Angeles.

I had great difficulty in finding a room or house.
Several owners refused to rent to me because I was Japanese.
Finally one lady allowed me to take an apartment, if I would
tell everybody in the house that I was not a Japanese, but a
Filipino or a member of some other European race. An old lady
in the house asked me one day if I was Italian to which I replied, "Yes." Three months later the lady told me that I
would have to move out because the owner found out that I was
Japanese and the lady who had leased the place had agreed to
take in no Japanese.[24]

In the spring of 1923 the Hollywood Protective Association began to operate and brought pressure to bear on property owners in an effort to prevent them from renting to Japanese. Threats of different kinds were used to induce Japanese to give up
houses they had rented. A prominent member of the
Anti-Asiatic Association, a clerk in the County Re-
corder's office, would report promptly any real
estate transfer to which a Japanese was a party.
Then they would act with vigor. Due to activities of
this organization, the City Council of Los Angeles
passed an ordinance authorizing the establishment of
a park through the condemnation of ten lots which
were owned and occupied by Japanese for residential
purposes. The Japanese carried the matter into court
but lost the case. The Judge, however, set such a
high price on the property that the Japanese were
willing to vacate. Then the people in the district,
against whom this cost would be assessed, objected
and requested the city council to abandon the proceedings. The council acceded, but compelled the
signers of the petition for condemnation to pay the
expenses incurred both by the city and by the

Japanese in fighting the case. This amounted to almost $10,000. Since this case was decided, the Jap-
anese have not been disturbed and they have encountered less difficulty in finding more suitable
houses.

            Recent years brought considerable change on
the Coast. A real estate slump left many houses
vacant in Los Angeles, and white men rented less
grudgingly to those of yellow race. A reaction
against the extremists discounted popular race dog-
mas. Furthermore, passage of the Exclusion Law in
1924, which allayed fears and gradually released tensions, was responsible in part for the improvement.

            According to Professor J. F. Steiner of the
University of Washington,

        During the past twenty years there has been an ex-
    traordinary movement out of the Japanese ghetto to areas of
    second settlement. . . . Unfortunately the extent of this dis-
    persion of Japanese families cannot be accurately measured,
    but there is no doubt that this movement is proceeding with
    great rapidity. A recent study of the distribution of the
    Japanese in Seattle showed that only a small minority of the
    families were residing within a distinct racial community.[25]

A careful study would probably reveal a greater dis-
persion in Seattle than in San Francisco or Los
Angeles because California took the lead in the
anti-oriental agitation and raised more barriers
against the Orientals.

            In Honolulu several areas are almost exclu-
sively white. Several Orientals tried to buy homes
in one of these areas but without success. They are
excluded by a "Gentlemen's Agreement" among the real
estate men. Furthermore, it would be considered un-
neighborly to sell to an Oriental. There are two
Japanese families in the area who secured their
property because the white owners wanted to "get
even" with their neighbors. One of the Anglo-Saxon
men had a "white"[26] Portuguese wife to whom the

neighbors objected. He retaliated by selling to a
Japanese.

     Institutional Discrimination. Persons of
oriental lineage are restricted in their access to
many organizations in America, such as clubs, the
Y.M.C.A., and many churches.[27] According to Professor Eliot G. Mears,[28] the Elks, the Exchange Club,
and the Native Sons of the Golden West have actual
rulings against the admission of members of oriental
race. The Knights of Columbus admit a few. The
Masons on the Coast have admitted a few. Rotary International draws no color line in its constitution
but since each local club selects its own members
very few men of oriental lineage will be elected to
membership in the Pacific Coast clubs for some time.
On the Atlantic Coast, Rotary has Chinese members.
Kiwanis International likewise makes no distinction
in its constitution. The Lions Club specifically
debarred Orientals until a provisionally organized
Club in Hawaii petitioned the national convention
to delete the word "white" from the constitution.
The Honolulu Lions Den has had in its membership Hawaiians, Part-Hawaiians, Chinese, Japanese, Koreans,
Filipinos, Portuguese, a Negro, and Anglo-Saxons.
     For many years it was taken for granted that
the Central Y.M.C.A. of Honolulu, organized in 1869,
was a Haole organization. No others were included.
An application from the Japanese Vice-Consul raised
an issue. At first it was refused. The President
and Treasurer of the Board, fearing that the application represented an official test by Japan of the
Christian institutions of America, went personally
to deliver the membership card to the Vice-Consul.
He was never known, however, to make use of his
membership privileges. In 1918 a branch was opened
for Orientals, but since the equipment was meager
they continued to make application at the Central
Department. Meanwhile the Anglo-Saxons began to object to the presence of so many Orientals. In 1920,

after a study of the situation, a rule was adopted
limiting the Orientals in the Central Department to
a maximum of ten per cent of the total membership.
This rule was responsible for no small amount of resentment. The secretaries have not always applied
the regulation stringently. In 1927 considerable
feeling again developed among the Anglo-Saxons.
After a new study of the problems involved, the ten-
per cent rule was repealed in May, 1929, and the
Central Y.M.C.A. was thrown wide open. When an outstanding Japanese applied for membership in the University Club of Honolulu, a furore was raised but he
was admitted. It is reported that he paid his dues
for sixteen years but never set foot inside the club
house. The Outrigger Canoe Club of Honolulu does not
admit Orientals, even though this organization developed out of the Pan-Pacific movement which has
branches in the Orient and has much to say about interracial friendship.

Many other bars have also been raised
against the Orientals, a considerable number of
which are applicable to their children as well. On
September 17, 1920, the City Council of Los Angeles
passed an ordinance[29] greatly restricting the Orientals in their use of recreational facilities. While
it did not specifically bar the American-born group,
they were not at all welcome. A public swimming
pool in a coast city was open to non-white people
only one day each week and that just before the
water was changed. The Sutro Baths in San Francisco
had been rather exclusive and did not admit Orientals, but a change in policy became apparent soon
after the opening of a pool which was under city control and free to the public.

The Military Group and Discriminations. The
military group in Hawaii, a garrison of some 16,000
men, is a factor of considerable importance in connection with race prejudice. The military men talk
much about an inevitable war with Japan and

discriminate against the Japanese, be they alien or
citizen. A secretary of the Y.M.C.A. in Honolulu,
who went to the Pearl Harbor Naval Station on a matter of business, had with him his assistant, an
American-born Japanese who had served in the army
during the World War. The marine at the gate informed them that he had orders from the commandant
to exclude all "Japs" from the reservation. When
the United States fleet visited Hawaii in April,
1928, the writer went aboard the U.S.S. California
at the dock in Honolulu. After walking about the
ship for some time, he asked a sailor for permission
to go to a lower deck when he received the reply:
"No! there are too many 'Japs' around and we can't
permit them to go below, so we have to refuse everybody." The Intelligence Department of the Army
keeps a careful check on anything that is said or
written about the Japanese. The military group,
however, is rather inconsistent, for many officers
have Japanese servants within the military reserva-
tions. An advertisement in a Honolulu paper in 1928
read as follows: "Wanted--Two first-class car wash-
ers. Japanese preferred. No others need apply. The
Post Exchange Service Station, Schofield Barracks."
        Late in 1931 and early 1932, considerable
feeling was aroused in Honolulu in connection with
an assault and a murder in which a naval officer and
his wife were the central figures. According to one
writer in Honolulu,

        Feeling locally is that the actions and statements of
high-ranking officials, for example those of Admiral Pratt,
have tended to create a real breach. With rare exceptions the
military-naval group do not remain long in the Islands. They
exhibit very often typical military psychology toward non-
white people. For the most part they show no interest in
identifying themselves with the life of the resident community.
Thus a separate caste, self-contained, conscious of superiority, tends to be maintained.
        From time to time groups of sailors or soldiers have

tilts with hoodlums, but these have not been alarming in fre-
quency or violence.   There is a certain undercurrent of resentment against soldiers and sailors on the part of some people in which men of the service are involved. Hawaiian girls
seen in association with soldiers or sailors fall under sus-
picion in most cases.   Some service men have married local
girls, but this seems not to be resented so much as irregular
relations.[30]

   Restrictions on Service to Orientals.   In
many eating places on the Coast, members of the
oriental group will not be served, be they alien or
citizen.   Salesmen in stores have even refused to
wait on Orientals.   Many barber shops on the Coast
discriminate against them.   A Japanese college girl
related her experience.

   I have been with American young people more than with
Japanese. I went to school with American children and I was
among American girls in college. I never felt any prejudice.
I was always accepted as one of them and had many friends.
There have been times when I have felt a little like a fish
out of water. While I was in college, one day I went for a
marcel. When I came to pay for it, they charged me two dollars. On the way back to college I asked my friend who was
with me what they charged her and she said a dollar. So the
next time I wanted a marcel I telephoned for an appointment
telling them I was a Japanese and asked if there would be an
extra charge. The woman said it would be an extra quarter.
"It will be a dollar and quarter then?" I said and she replied that it would. I knew the lady who has charge of the
social work there and I thought if there were any difficulty
about it, I would go and talk to her. ' They were very nice to
me and did the work well but, when I went to pay, it was two
dollars again. Well, I felt so hurt and I didn't like to say
anything, so I just paid it. But when we left and I told my
friend who said, "I wouldn't stand for it. I would go back
and make a fuss about it." The next time I asked about it.
They were very apologetic. They said there had been a big
Chinese wedding a short time ago and a great many Chinese

girls had come in to have their hair done and some of the customers objected; so they had been putting on the extra charge
to discourage their coming. They said they were very sorry
it had happened; they didn't know whether I was a college girl
or not. I just wanted to know why they charged me two dollars
when they said it would be a dollar and a quarter.[31] They
were very nice then but I soon found a lady barber who would
do my hair, and she was nearer the college, so I went to her.[32]

  Discriminations in Social Life. Discriminations in social life are marked; they are in evidence even in Hawaii. Those of oriental ancestry
may mingle rather freely in the ordinary daily activities and in much of their work,[33] but in social
relationships the lines tend to be drawn. The distance maintained socially often influences the occupational situation. A promotion in the vocational
field usually implies an advancement in social relationships, but since that is not acceptable to the
dominant white group an efficient Chinese or Japanese must often stand still while inferior white men
are moved ahead of him. On one plantation a white
man was reprimanded by the management for mingling
too freely with the Orientals; he was told to leave
unless he amended his ways. The school administration of the Territory has difficulty in placing
teachers, particularly Japanese, in certain communities. They will be "frozen out" socially.
  Doubtless, the line is drawn in social affairs because a mingling on the basis of equality
would carry with it the inference, at least by implication, that intermarriage is acceptable; as yet
there is no readiness to accept that as a practice.
The extremes to which some Californians go in keeping boys of oriental ancestry away from white girls
are indicated by the following item.

    Charged with contributing to the delinquency of a
19-year-old "dancing instructress," Roy Lim Sing, Willie Wong
and Jimmie Wong, Chinese patrons of a dance hall on West Third

Street, were held to answer yesterday by Judge _____ of the
Juvenile Court. The girl, who was called as a witness by
Deputy District Attorney,____ declared that the Chinese were
guilty of no offense against her and at all times had sought
to act as her protectors until they could locate her friends
or relatives. When they finally learned she had an uncle residing in the city, she testified, the oriental youths immediately took steps to get in touch with him.

It developed that the Chinese had met the girl at the
dance hall where she had been employed as an "instructress"
to dance with male patrons of the place. . . .

The girl told juvenile investigators she left the
dance hall and joined the Chinese to escape some other youths,
who were seeking to get her into their automobile.

The case was filed by the District-Attorney's office
as the first step in a program of city and county authorities
to take regulative measures against dance halls in which it is
said white girls are permitted to dance with Chinese and
others not members of the Caucasian race.[34]

There are great differences in the way those
of oriental ancestry are accepted. In some instances, the situation has not been completely defined. The colored porter, in the following document, did not quite know how to treat the Japanese
passenger; he was less certain about enforcing the
"Jim Crow" law than he would have been with a
Negro.[35] We quote a portion of the story of this Japanese boy who had been born and reared in Hawaii and
had gone to continental United States to enter college.

From St. Louis, I proceeded south to New Orleans,
through Memphis and Vicksburg. On my way to New Orleans, on
the Panama Limited, I experienced a most unusual incident.
Perhaps it is not unusual to the Southerners and others who
are well acquainted with the "Jim Crow Law," but it was new to
me. The incident occurred as soon as the train left Memphis.
I went from my Pullman to the observation car when a porter
informed me that I was not allowed there. I thought, perhaps,

that I was intruding on some other people so I asked him
whether or not I was encroaching on other people's liberty.
He answered "No," but hesitated to tell me the rest. Finally
he told me that there was a law prevailing in the Southern
States which restricted the colored people to the "Jim Crow"
car and that none but the colored people were allowed in that
coach. People who refused to heed this were subject to a fine.
This statement came to me like the blow of a hammer. I did
not know what to say, whether I should apologize to him or
have compassion for him. Well, I did both. Indeed this was
the first lesson in race prejudice shown openly.[36]

This same boy wrote of his experiences in
being invited into white homes in two different
places. In some instances persons are able to break
over into the white man's world in considerable
measure, but in most cases the parting of the ways
comes sooner or later.

Skin Color and Discrimination. We do not
have adequate data at present on which to base a
conclusion, but it seems that skin color is of considerable significance in connection with race relations. While pigmentation is of comparatively
slight value as a criterion of race, it is very important sociologically. Men tend to react more
readily and more violently to color than to any
other mark of race. When linked with the facial
features it is a badge which classifies the American-born with the immigrant group, with the result
that there seems to be comparatively little difference in the treatment accorded the first and second
generations. Business establishments that do not
employ alien Orientals usually do not offer positions to their American-born sons and daughters.
Ability to speak English, to be sure, is a determinative factor in certain instances.

Without doubt the physical differences, particularly skin color and facial features, are noticed by white people. In the everyday parlance of

California the rather common use of certain expressions such as "yellow," "yellow-belly," "little
brown men," "slant-eyed Chink," "skibee," etc.,
would bear this out. Whether or not the white people react to skin color, many of the younger generation believe that this is one of the prime reasons
for discrimination. Many wish that it were possible
to change their color.

        Immigrants from Europe can lose themselves
in America more readily than those from the Orient.
When the children grow up in America and learn to
speak English fluently they can break into the American group quite readily since they have no racial
marks to hold them in check. At times their names
hold them back. It is a comparatively easy matter,
however, to Anglicize a name or even to take an entirely new one; but this will be of slight assistance to a pure-blooded Chinese or Japanese.

        An Hawaiian-born Japanese maintains that
biological amalgamation which will obliterate racial
marks will be a distinct aid in the assimilation of
the children of oriental ancestry.[37] A certain
amount of evidence is available to support this position. In Hawaii it has been observed that many
part-Chinese have enjoyed privileges and advantages
denied those of pure race while on the Coast several
persons of mixed blood have been accepted in larger
measure than those of pure stock.[38]

Chapter XV

DISORGANIZATION AND REORGANIZATION

A. <u>Disorganization</u>

To have an organized and well-integrated
life, a person must have membership in a group that
has a well-defined scheme of behavior which impinges
upon the conduct of the individual members. The
young Americans of oriental ancestry do not have any
well-defined behavior patterns to follow. They have
been reared in homes where old-world heritages have
dominated. But when the immigrant parents sought to
adjust themselves to a new culture, new demands were
made upon their habits, and the old-world behavior
patterns failed to function efficiently. Confusion
in their standards and codes was inevitable. Because
of this breakdown in the socially systematized rules,
the immigrants have been unable to set up well-defined behavior patterns for their children. Old-
world codes were frequently imposed, but the westernized youth rebelled against them. While the old controls have not functioned adequately in directing the
behavior of the youth, the young people have not yet
become completely organized with reference to the
American group and its standards of conduct. They
have made contacts with American life at many points,
and these very contacts have exerted a disorganizing
influence.[1] The person must be able to understand
and appreciate the socially regulatory devices of a
group if he is to be controlled by them. But since
the young people of oriental ancestry do not fully
understand either the parental group or the Americans,

Table XVI

JUVENILE DELINQUENCY BY SEX IN RELATION TO ANCESTRY IN HONOLULU

Ancestry	Number of Children 10-17 Years of age in Honolulu in 1920			Juveniles Found Delinquent, 1914-1926*			Annual (Average) Number of Convictions to 100,000 Children 10-17 Years of Age			Percentage of Each Group 10-17 Years Residing in Honolulu in 1920
	Male	Female	Total	Male	Female	Total	Male	Female	Both Sexes	
Hawaiian and Part Hawaiian	1,577	1,512	2,889	1,817	588	2,405	10,151	2,991	6,404	39.5
Porto Rican	65	102	167	82	52	114	9,704	2,413	5,251	13.7
Spanish	69	79	148	17	10	27	1,895	974	1,403	27.7
Portuguese and "Other Caucasian"	1,435	1,497	2,932	903	160	1,065	4,840	822	2,789	41.4
Chinese	1,072	951	2,023	568	65	633	4,793	526	2,415	64.2
Japanese	1,522	1,352	2,874	423	67	490	2,158	404	1,312	21.5
Korean	57	78	135	65	9	74	8,772	888	4,216	39.1
Filipino	48	49	97	52	22	54	5,129	5,454	4,282	11.8

*Figures are for the First Circuit which includes the island of Oahu. According to the chief probation officer, the number of delinquents outside of Honolulu is so small that it is practically negligible in any computation.

Data from Reports of the Chief Justice of the Supreme Court of the Territory of Hawaii and the Fourteenth Census of the United States, 1920

their behavior is frequently non-descript and puzzling; some behave in ways that are contrary to all socially prescribed modes of conduct.

Juvenile Delinquency and Disorganization.
Since juvenile delinquency is one of the indices of disorganization, both social[2] and personal,[3] we shall introduce some figures relative to this problem.

(1) In Hawaii. The statistical data relative to juvenile delinquency in Hawaii are comparatively adequate. The Chief Justice of the Supreme Court of the Territory publishes a report for all the islands in which the cases are segregated by ancestry.

Table XVI presents the juvenile court cases by ancestry for the city of Honolulu. A study of the situation in the largest city is of greater significance than that for the entire Territory. City conditions are more conducive to delinquency than those of the country. Consequently this is a better index to the actual situation.

The ratios, or the annual average number of convictions to 100,000 children in each group, give the Japanese the most favorable position with the Chinese ranking third. The Koreans occupy fifth place.[4]

Of the three oriental groups, the Chinese have been longest resident in Hawaii. They are also most completely urbanized. This has given the children greater opportunities for making contacts, for becoming Americanized, and for setting aside the parental traditions. Since the Japanese system of control is more flexible and adaptable, the children have been controlled better.[5] Some predict that the Japanese delinquency rate will rise as the children become more Americanized and emancipate themselves from the old system of control.

The delinquency ratio for the Korean group (Table XVI) is much higher than that of the Japanese or Chinese. The mere fact of numbers is important.

Since the Korean group is small, the young people
necessarily make many outside contacts. Usually
when a boy goes to work, he meets few Koreans and is
thus removed in considerable measure from Korean influences. The mother tongue is of little use to him;
he must turn to another medium, English. This condition tends to Americanize the young people rapidly.
Hence the children break away from parental control
and become delinquent more readily.

A study of the different ancestral groups by
sex reveals additional elements. Table XVI, presenting the data for Honolulu, gives the Japanese girls
the most favorable position while the Chinese girls
follow in second place.

When compared with other groups[6] (Table XVI)
the Chinese and Japanese girls are evidently well
controlled.

(a) Family Disorganization and Delinquency. Family disorganization as disclosed by the divorce statistics of Hawaii throws light on the delinquency situation. Table XVII presents the status
of divorce by ancestral groups.

According to Table XVII the Chinese and
Japanese have the lowest divorce rates. They also
have the most favorable delinquency ratios as revealed by Table XVI. We must, however, proceed with
caution in drawing conclusions from these figures because the court records give the ancestry of the
plaintiff only. Certain groups have married those
of other races in considerable numbers. The percentage of Spanish outmarriages runs high. Since the
percentage among the Japanese is low, their figures
may be taken as more nearly representing the actual
situation than those of any other group.[7]

(b) Neighborhood Conditions and Delinquency. Dr. Andrew W. Lind of the department of sociology, University of Hawaii, has shown the influence of neighborhood conditions upon the delinquency

Table XVII

AVERAGE NUMBER OF DIVORCES PER YEAR TO 100,000
MARRIED WOMEN BY ANCESTRAL GROUPS IN THE
TERRITORY OF HAWAII, 1914-1926

Ancestry of Plaintiff	Average Number of Divorces Per Year to 100,000 Married Women, 1914-1926
Chinese	750.63
Filipino	1,000.84
Hawaiian and Part Hawaiian	1,253.11
Japanese	870.74
Korean	1,423.92
Porto Rican	928.35
Portuguese and "Other Caucasian"	1,477.38
Spanish	1,091.37

Data from Bureau of Vital Statistics, Territory of Hawaii,
Compiled by Dr. Romanzo Adams and Mr. Shih Po of the University of Hawaii

of Japanese in Honolulu.

  Almost by accident our attention was directed to a
rather striking set of facts in the area of disorganization,
just back of the city proper. It was discovered that in this
section the cases of Japanese delinquency came from neighbor-
hoods where the Japanese population was not highly concen-
trated--where in fact the Japanese were mixed rather indiscriminately with the rest of the population. To be more specific, in the area A. . . . our map showed a very high and
almost exclusive concentration of Japanese population and
likewise a complete absence of juvenile delinquency. Just
across_____Street, our map indicated a rather non-
descript neighborhood, B, where a few Japanese youngsters and
a few children of every other racial and cultural group

represented in the Islands--Hawaiian, Part-Hawaiian, Portuguese, Porto-Rican, Koreans, Chinese, Filipino, and others--
were thrown together. From among fifteen Japanese school children, three were brought before the Juvenile Court during the
year. A house-to-house canvass of these two sections recently
revealed in neighborhood A a concentrated Japanese population
of 342 as against 36 of other races. In neighborhood B, our
canvass indicated 140 Japanese mixed indiscriminately among 58
Koreans, 187 Chinese, 30 Filipinos, 28 Hawaiians, and 20 Porto-
Ricans. . . . _____ Lane and _____ Alley are characterized not so much by the absence of moral codes and restraints,
as by the conflict of a number of distinctly different cultures and values--no one of which is taken very seriously by
the second generation.

Americanization, in the sense of the breakdown of the
traditional primary-group controls and the "individualization"
of behavior, proceeds at an unusually rapid pace in such areas.
One sees in the flesh-colored silk stockings hanging out to
dry in front of the family shrine, evidence of a rapid assimilation of certain aspects of American civilization, but one
seldom finds in such sections any evidence of a vital substitute for the type of social control which is thus flaunted.[8]

(c) Parasitic Occupations and Disorganization. The reports of the Chief Justice of the
Supreme Court of the Territory of Hawaii reveal the
fact that very few of the citizen Chinese turn to
parasitic occupations. In Hawaii 57 per cent of the
Chinese were resident in Honolulu in 1920. Since
they have been able to make rather satisfactory occupational adjustments for the young people, it has
not been necessary to turn to the questionable employments. The relative absence of race prejudice
permits them to participate more fully in the life
of the American community. Since they receive greater social recognition, they are held up to higher
moral standards than the Orientals in the ghettos of
the Coast cities. The situation in Hawaii makes the
young Chinese more responsive to public opinion of
the white group.

There is probably a graver danger that the citizen Japanese in Hawaii will turn to questionable employments than the citizen Chinese, for the simple reason that the Japanese group is not so well established economically and cannot make adequate provision for all the young people. In Hawaii the Japanese have been the chief offenders against the liquor laws. According to the federal prohibition administrator in the period from May, 1928, to February, 1929, of 304 Japanese arrested for violations of the prohibition law, 8 per cent were Hawaiian-born.[9] If this continues to be profitable for the older generation, probably more of the younger generation will turn to it to increase their incomes.

(2) On the Pacific Coast. No adequate statistical measure of delinquency among the second generation of oriental ancestry in continental United States is available. Letters from several probation officers on the Coast[10] indicate that the problem is a small one as measured by contacts with the juvenile courts.[11]

Factors in Disorganization. A number of factors contribute to the disorganization of the younger group.

(a) Traditional Systems of Control. The Chinese system of control is rigid and does not adapt itself readily to changed conditions. Several girls on the Pacific Coast have considered leaving home to break away from their old-fashioned parents. Girls in particular are restricted. For a girl to join the Girl Reserves and talk about hiking is incomprehensible to those who retain the old traditions.[12] The rigid system of the Chinese, which all too often refuses to bend, must finally break. Then some of the young people, left to their own devices after a long period of repression, go to extremes.

Many young Chinese have emancipated themselves from
the old system in considerable measure. But herein
lies a danger because many Chinese girls are attractive to white men. Being seriously limited in their
vocational opportunities, a number on the Pacific
Coast accept employment as waitresses in cafes and
tearooms which cater to the after-theatre patronage.
At times these waitresses go on automobile rides
with white men after the tearooms close at two
o'clock in the morning.

        The Japanese on the Pacific Coast have shown
themselves more responsive to the new environment
and have, on the whole, made more successful accommodations than the Chinese. The Japanese have
been sensitive to the feelings of the American community and have endeavored to adjust themselves in
such ways as to arouse the least possible resentment. [13] Outside the grosser crimes, the affairs of
the Japanese seldom come before the public eye, because of the unofficial system of regulation within
the group. The secretaries of the Japanese Associations have settled many difficulties between members
of their own group and those of other races and thus
have avoided unfavorable publicity. The Japanese
are solicitous in counselling their children to com-
mit no act which might tarnish the family name or
disgrace their racial group in the eyes of the Americans.

        (b) Abnormal Life of Orientals in Ameri-
ca. The more or less abnormal life of the Orientals
in America has been a significant factor in the delinquency of juveniles. The case record of a Chinese boy on the Coast who had made several appearances in juvenile court for running away from home,
for incorrigibility and burglary was easily understood when it was learned that the boy had no wholesome home life--his mother lived in China while his
father and uncle conducted a gambling house in
Chinatown.

        (c) City Life and Disorganization. The
Orientals in America have, in the main, been a law-
abiding group until many have been forced into situations where the conditions have been unwholesome.
The Anti-Chinese agitation which began in the early
days of California and which was repeated at a later
date in Oregon and Washington resulted in an exodus
of a large number of Chinese from the Coast. Furthermore, those who remained on the Coast crowded
into the cities. The Japanese have also been con-
gregating in the cities since the passage of the
alien land laws, and this shift to an urban environ-
men has exerted an unwholesome influence.

        There was a not' :eable increase of parasitic indus-
tries among these people. Gambling houses which had heretofore been in the hands of the Chinese were now taken over by
the Japanese. Several large new gambling places were opened
and soon became prosperous. Bootlegging and other remunera-
tive but questionable enterprises were undertaken so the younger generation is constantly thrown into the dangerous atmosphere,[14] and the temptations to take the easy way to earn a
living are hard to resist.[15]. . . So far as th econd generation is concerned this moral problem is a possibility rather
than a present fact.[16]

        In the opinion of a white professional man
in the northwest the young Japanese will not continue to go to the salmon canneries of Alaska for
seasonal work when there is an opportunity to make
more money in the parasitic occupations; they will
follow the lead of the Chinese unless there is a
change for the better in the occupational situation.
        In the case of the Chinese, who are an older
group on the Coast, this is not a future contingency
but a present condition. Many immigrant Chinese
have engaged in parasitic industries, but a considerable number of the American-born generation have also turned to these activities.[17] Many old men traf-
ficked in opium, but the younger men use and sell

other drugs as well.[18] Gambling has been common, particularly among the immigrant Chinese, but it has
also attracted some of the younger group. A native-
born Chinese girl who had been educated in our
schools was selling lottery tickets in one of the
northwest cities. She could make eighty dollars a
week in this activity while anything of a legitimate
nature open to her would bring only a small fraction
of that amount.[19]

        So long as there is nothing open but unin-
teresting manual toil at an inadequate wage, many of
the young Chinese will continue to turn to the more
interesting and thrilling occupations such as bootlegging, prostitution, gambling, and drug vending
where the returns are larger. Congestion in undesirable city quarters is favorable for plying these
trades. Here the young people make contacts not
only with the undesirable elements in their own
group but also with white persons who resort to
these areas to ply their pernicious activities. Purchased police protection, which decreases hazards,
is also very common.[20] Hence the situation in the
cities is most favorable for carrying on the parasitic occupations.

B. Reorganization

        The situation as presented thus far is only
a part of the picture. As the young people of
oriental ancestry have made contacts with the various phases of American life, new attitudes have developed, resulting in behavior not in accord with
the sanctioned schemes of the immigrant group. Furthermore, this behavior has not conformed to the
patterns recognized by the American group. Since
they have had no single pattern to follow, behavior
has been uncertain and more or less disorganized.
But a reorganization is in process. They are redefining the situation. New schemes of behavior and

new institutions which are better adapted to the social situation in which they find themselves are
gradually evolving. While these new schemes usually
depart radically from those of the parental group,
they are not fully occidental. They are, however,
more in accord with the new attitudes and make more
satisfactory provision for their expression in action. These new schemes provide certain foci to
which the individuals may attach their loyalties and
thus they become instrumentalities for bringing the
group closer together. This process of reconstruction will necessarily be slow and there will have to
be much experimentation.

A word of caution may be necessary. Some of
the young people whose behavior does not follow any
standardized pattern are not to be considered disorganized but rather as unorganized. The home conditions have been such that their lives have not
been organized in accordance with oriental patterns.
Hence they have had nothing from which they could
break away. They have not made any particular moral
code their own and accordingly they are amoral rather
than immoral. With them it is a matter of organization and construction rather than reorganization and
reconstruction.

Development of Organizations. On account of
the disorganization in the various oriental communities in America, many organizations of different
types have been developed in an attempt to make the
necessary adjustments.[21] When a group is held at a
distance and is not permitted to participate freely
in the life of the American community, a large number of organizations develop. It is apparent that
organizations spring up quite readily whenever there
is a need, or alleged need. In the main, the organizations have followed American models, but some give
evidence of oriental influence. Some of the American-born Chinese, with but little western education,
cling to the oriental type of village organization.

The more progressive tend to break over these bounda-
ries. A good case in point is the Hawaiian Chinese
Civic Association of Honolulu which draws its membership from all classes, without reference to family or district in China. Organizations developed by
the immigrant groups do not meet the needs of the
younger generation. The tong is gradually dying out
because it, as a first-generation organization, does
not meet the needs of the second-generation Chinese.
Likewise the Japanese Associations on the Coast belong to the past and are in process of dying out.
Some of the associations are attempting to survive
by taking on new functions.[22] These new organizations and institutions are gradually bringing order
out of more or less chaotic conditions as they are
bringing the young people together into a number of
coöperative ventures.

        Differences in Organizations of the Two
Generations. In this process of organization,
marked differences between the native-born and immigrant generations become evident. Many of the organizations of the immigrants were brought into being for defensive purposes because of the antagonism
of the white Americans.[23] On the whole it may be
said that the immigrants were culturally passive as
they did not plan to make any contributions to American life. The organizations of the American-born,
however, are not primarily for defense; they are demanding their rights as citizens.[24] They are not
passive, but are preparing to enter actively into
politics and into other community activities where
they desire to make their contribution.

        The Leader and Organization. In this proc-
ess of organization, the leader will play an important rôle and he will have to be more inventive
than one in a stable group where tradition has defined his course of action.

Whereas, in social reconstruction his task is to discover and understand the new attitudes which demand an outlet,
to invent schemes of behavior which would best correspond to
these attitudes, and to make the group accept these schemes as
social rules or institutions. More than this, he must usually
develop the new attitudes in certain parts of society which
have been evolving more slowly and are not yet ready for the
reform; and often he has to struggle against obstinate de-
fenders of the traditional system.[25]

According to Thomas and Znaniecki,[26] there
are three types: leadership by hope or fear, by
prestige, and by efficiency. Among the Orientals in
America, hope and fear do not play any significant
part. In this group there are not many who hold
power or have much which they can give or withhold,
thereby enhancing their own positions through making
others dependent on them.[27]

In the Orient many have prestige by virtue
of membership in a prominent family, but that does
not avail much in America because the majority of
the immigrants came from the peasant class and not
from outstanding families. Furthermore, class distinctions and family names which had prestige in
the Orient do not have the same significance in
America.[28]

In keeping with oriental tradition, certain
men acquire prestige by virtue of attachment to some
profession. Professional men in America usually occupy positions of honor and dignity in their communities.

Efficiency, or at least a popular belief in
a person's efficiency, is a big factor. The person
who does something of benefit to the group is highly
honored. The newspapers of Honolulu--English, Chinese and Japanese--gave much space in December, 1927,
and January, 1928, to Dr. Fred K. Lam of Honolulu,
who went on a mission to Washington, D. C., and was
instrumental in bringing a change in the ruling on
"liver fluke." Because of this disease many Chinese

had been refused readmission to the United States.
After Dr. Lam's return from Washington, banquet
after banquet was given in his honor. Prominent
members of the white community also participated.
Prior to this Dr. Lam had not been very well known
but at once he rose into prominence. On the day before his return to Honolulu he was elected to the
presidency of the Chinese University Club. Dr. Lam
was honored by Chinese in all parts of America. A
second-generation Chinese doctor in Honolulu became
well known and attained a position of leadership because he had done a considerable amount of medical
work for poor Chinese. He was also a good mixer and
had been active in several of their organizations.
A Chinese-American professional man in Honolulu acquired a position of prominence because of his anti-
Haole attitude--he was all for the Chinese. Some of
the Chinese intellectuals assert that certain men
attain their positions of leadership not on account
of merit or service rendered to their group but
rather because they are liberal with cigars and the
glad hand; they are good mixers and good advertisers.

(a) Leadership among the Japanese. The
American-born Japanese, up to the present, have been
largely under the domination of immigrant leadership.
This has not been the most satisfactory arrangement,
due to the fact that there is such a wide divergence
between the points of view of the two generations.
The immigrants are vitally interested in the problems
of the American-born generation, but they do not
understand the young people. The younger generation
is beginning to feel the need of an adequate leadership. This must needs develop out of their own
ranks. Both in Hawaii and on the Pacific Coast American-born Chinese and Japanese are beginning to
stand out as real leaders and are exerting considerable influence. In the choice of their leaders,
there is evident a marked departure from oriental
traditions, for a girl was unanimously elected to

the presidency of the Japanese-American Citizens'
Club of Stockton, California.[29] In one California
town an American-born Japanese girl of the Eta [30]
class was elected to the presidency of the Japanese-
American Loyalty League, an organization of American
citizens. At one time, when she tried to withdraw
from this office and from the organization, the boys
told her: "If you won't be president, we'll just
give up having a society."[31] In the Orient, girls
would not be elected to such positions of leadership.

Education in the Process of Organization.
In certain groups, when any consideration is given
to reconstruction, a movement toward popular education is the first and indispensable step; there are
many who cannot read. A condition such as this necessarily retards progress. This, however, is no
problem so far as the second generation of oriental
ancestry is concerned. In the Orient learning and
scholarship are highly regarded. With this tradition and because of an eagerness to improve the
status of their children, the immigrant parents have
given every encouragement to their children in their
school work.[32] This general interest in education
has been an important factor in preparing the group
for social reconstruction. It has not been necessary to spend time on rudiments. Consequently we
may expect the process of organization to move forward rapidly.

The Press and Organization. In this process
of organization, the press is an important instrumentality. Several Chinese and Japanese newspapers
on the Coast and in Hawaii have English sections
edited by members of the American-born group.[33]
These papers afford media of expression for the
American citizens of oriental ancestry, and they are
speaking pointedly on many vital issues. A number
of organizations, particularly student groups, both

in Hawaii and on the mainland have published annuals
which have given some opportunity for expression.

Through the press the leaders are speaking
to a wider community than their own local constitu-
encies. They are thus tending to develop standards
which will influence all the citizens of oriental
ancestry. Through editorials, articles, and news
items the press is endeavoring to present certain
ideas to the entire group and thus create a nation-
wide social opinion. In this way wholesome schemes
of life organization will gradually evolve and the
behavior of the group will become standardized and
stabilized.

Chapter XVI

THE SECOND GENERATION AND THE FAMILY

The American-born children of oriental ancestry have made contacts with several types of
family life. There has been no standardized oriental pattern to follow. In some homes the oriental
pattern has been followed with slight variations,
but in most instances there has been considerable
disorganization and a certain amount of reorganization to fit the new conditions. The young people
have made contacts with the oriental type of family
life as it has been going through this process of
change; they have also made contacts with the occidental family system. As they have tried to steer
their course through this uncharted sea, they have
broken with many of the oriental practices.

A. Breaks in the Oriental Family System

Opposition to Autocratic Family Control.
The young people, who have become imbued with democratic ideas, object to the old-fashioned, autocratic family control. The native-born girls, who
observe the freedom of American women, are doing
much to break down the idea of male domination.[1]
They consider themselves Americans and are unwilling
to acquiesce in an arrangement which would reduce
them to a perpetual minority. Many oppose their
parents and argue against their ideas. Some girls
are not even satisfied with a status of equality.
They state in no uncertain terms that they desire
to be the dominating heads of their households. This

is not mere idle talk, for some of the women are carrying their ideas into practice. This is made evident by an immigrant Japanese.

> You know, my wife, she used to help me all the time;
> bye an' bye she catchum baby, then she not help me so much.
> Bye an' bye she catchum 'nother baby, then she say to me, "I
> no help you no more." I say, "Yes, you will." She say, "No,
> I won't; I American citizen." This afternoon, my wife, she
> telephone me, "You come home." I say, "I no can come, truck
> gone, I no can come." She say, "You come home!" I go home.
> Truck gone, I walk home.[2]

Many boys advocate greater freedom for the women but
they are unwilling to go as far as the girls; they
are not ready to surrender completely the idea of
male superiority.

The girls of oriental ancestry are not willing to submit to a system under which the mother-in-
law dominates the young wife;[3] they do not want to
live with mothers-in-law or other relatives according to oriental custom. Wherever possible the young
people move out of the crowded tenement sections.[4]
The rapidity of the movement, however, is determined
in considerable measure by the economic situation.
While the young people prefer to live under their
own roofs, oftentimes the economic circumstances
will not permit.[5]

Opposition to Parentally-Arranged Marriages.
Many of the young people are outspoken against the
idea of parentally-arranged marriages.[6] Many refuse
to accept the arrangements made by their parents.
Financial independence, particularly among the Chinese of Hawaii, has been an important causal factor.
Many Chinese women feel free and independent now
that they are wage-earners. Some go to extremes in
order to make the emancipation complete; they marry
men distasteful to their parents just to parade their
freedom. Some have left their homes to avoid

marriage with men selected by their parents. Some
have declared that they would do as they pleased--
but when the time for marriage arrived, the parents
took matters in hand and settled all. The parents
may adopt American dress quite readily, but the attitudes relative to family matters are deep-rooted
and change less easily.

It has been a common practice, particularly
among the Chinese where the ratio of women was low,
to marry off their daughters to middle-aged men who
were well established financially. This practice
has been followed more closely by those in the Chinatowns; those outside the ghettos, mainly the Chris-
tianized ones, have given more freedom to their children. Oftentimes the distance between the two was
so great as to make life intolerable for the young
Americanized bride.

On July 11, 1928, southern California was
startled by the murder of a young Chinese woman. On
March 24, 1927, this California-born Chinese girl,
sixteen years of age, was married to a wealthy Chinese jeweler, forty-eight years old, who paid the
father a handsome sum for her. After a few months
the young wife grew tired of the custom-bound practices of her husband's household and told him that
she wished to return to her American standard of living and earn her own way. He offered her wages to
work in his jewelry store, but she declined. He
then assisted her in opening an ice-cream parlor,
called "The Sugar Bowl," which soon became the
rendezvous of the younger generation in Chinatown.
This business served to widen the breach between the
two, since the young wife became friendly with many
of the younger Chinese and joined them in their
parties and automobile rides. The husband sought
the aid of his father-in-law to bring about a re-
conciliation, but all to no avail. The young wife
told her father that she could not live with her
husband. He advised her to return to her husband,
saying that in married life quarreling and

difficulties were inevitable. Love letters found
after her murder showed that she had turned to a
youthful sweetheart. The letters revealed her un-
happiness with her middle-aged husband and her determination not to return to him "as long as I got a
little breath in me." According to the father, she,
with her occidental upbringing and education, would
naturally shrink from a marriage according to Chinese custom and might in desperation break all
oriental traditions and engage in an illicit love
affair.[7]

The young people have seen parentally-arranged marriages go on the rocks and this has conditioned them against the system. A young woman related her own story.

At thirteen years of age my father married me off to
a wealthy middle-aged man who seemed like a father to me.
Naturally, I was taken from school, which I regretted very
much. At every opportunity I read my books and always watched
the other children going to and from school with envy. I
always felt as though I belonged to them. I did not dare to
tell this to my parents, not even to my mother, as it is
against our religion to entertain even a thought of dis-
obedience to one's husband. This feeling, however, became
very intense within me and at last, after three years, I decided to leave him. There was much anger and consternation,
but I was determined. I had read of American wives acting in
this manner under such circumstances and I still feel it is
right. I defied anyone to interfere any further with my actions. Some time later I met a student at the night school
which I attended regularly. On further acquaintance we found
our view of life very similar and decided to marry.[8]

In Japan, when a person desires to make a
strong protest against anything, he commits suicide--
that is a language well understood by the Japanese.
As the young people in America speak in this language, the parents will pause and consider. Items
like the following appear from time to time--and
doubtless they will produce results.

Because the father of the girl with whom he was pas-
sionately in love absolutely refused to give his permission to
marry her, Kenji Yamamoto. . . . threw himself under a speed-
ing train at Wahiawa Sunday night and was mangled almost beyond recognition. . . .

About two weeks ago, the deceased became so in-
fatuated with the girl that he simply could not resist, and
went to his sweetheart's father for permission to marry her.
Taking a dislike for Yamamoto, he declared that he would not
let his daughter marry him under any circumstances. Terribly
broken-hearted, the deceased tried to end it all by jumping
into the reservoir at Wahiawa but on second thought he determined to try again and swam ashore.

Again he approached the girl's father and once again
he was denied permission. Last Sunday night he suddenly disappeared and fearing that he had met some sort of foul play a
search was undertaken. The search was short lived for a
short distance from the town along the O. R. & L. tracks lay
the headless body of the youth. . . . in mute testimony of
the suicide.[9]

Many young women set high standards for
their future husbands. If such are not found they
will not marry. This is quite revolutionary when we
consider that bachelors and spinsters have no place
in the oriental scheme of life. A considerable number of young women are not marrying, or, at least,
they are postponing marriage. They are not remain-
ing single because of inability to marry. According to one writer, "The American-oriental flapper is
the most courted woman in the world, for she is
wooed not only by the 'sheiks' of her own age but
by the tens of thousands of oriental bachelors on
the Coast, who can no longer import wives from their
home country."[10]

Tenacity of Familial Sentiments. Although
many have broken with the old traditions there is,
nevertheless, a marked family solidarity. The
familial sentiments of many young people are strong.

Because of this many deny themselves rather than
disappoint their elders. Many make definite plans
to care for their parents in old age. The parents
have sacrificed to give them a start in life. In
return they bend all their energies toward making
their elders happy. Some save in order to build
comfortable homes for them. Some, desirous of preparing for professional life, give this up and turn
to vocations with a more immediate income. Even
where home relationships have not been happy, there
are young people who care for their elders and make
sacrifices for them.

        Family solidarity of a high order is found
among the Japanese in the rural districts of Hawaii.
Many plantation families have worked together to assist one of the girls through the Normal School.
Then, when she began to receive a regular teacher's
salary, she was expected to assist the family. Usually this took the form of aiding another sister
through the Normal School. When these two girls
were on regular salaries, they made it possible for
the younger children to attend school. Meanwhile
the father and mother continued to work on the plantation. After the two teachers had served an ap-
prenticeship in isolated places, they were transferred to one of the cities. When they had become
well established in the new location, the other members of the family followed them to the city. At
first the father would work as yard boy for a white
family. Little by little he would become acquainted
with city life and with the assistance of the children who were earning, would open a small neighborhood store. Then by all working together, the boys
who were youngest in the family were sent to college
and professional schools. After completing their
courses, they returned to practice in the city. The
Japanese call this the "hand-vine method." [11] They
liken the process to a grape-vine which sends out
tendrils that fasten themselves to some object and
then draw the vine in their direction. The two

Japanese girls who became teachers were the tendrils and they gradually pulled the whole family away from the plantation into the city where they acquired a higher status.

B. Attempts to Follow American Family Patterns

Perplexities Due to Unfamiliarity with American Customs. The young people are setting the occidental family before themselves as an ideal to be followed. Many indicate a decided preference for western practices; some even go to extremes in carrying them out. In the discussion of love affairs, there is a great difference between Orientals and Occidentals. Orientals do not have love affairs; hence they are often shocked by the freedom with which Americans discuss such matters. Many of the young people have begun to treat these subjects in characteristic occidental fashion. The following poem, written by a Japanese boy in a junior high school in Hawaii, is not oriental.

SWEETHEART

I wonder--wonder--do you know;
And how I love you! Love you so,
Makes my head and senses reel,
With the longing pain I feel,
Thinking, dreaming, feeling gay,
Oh! I want you here today.
I want your tender teasing ways,
Want your smiles--that always pays;
And I want the thrills divine,
Your warm lips close to mine,
Oh! I really think you may
Come to me for just today.[12]

The lines relative to kissing are indicative of the great change that is taking place. The shock which

the new arrivals from the Orient receive at the
first sight of kissing in America brings out the
contrast quite strikingly.[13] Some, however, are opposed to this freedom; it is too extreme and actually scandalizes them.

Very few of the young people have had sufficient contact with American family life to pattern
after it, but they are eager to learn from every
available source. Books, magazines, and Dorothy
Dix's column in the newspaper are read with avidity.
Some have learned by working in American homes. Many
of their ideas are acquired in the moving-picture
theaters. Many of the patterns, however, have not
been of the best. Because of their relative unfamiliarity with occidental life, the young people
have not been able to choose with discrimination
from the things pictured on the silver screen or
portrayed in the latest novel. Consequently, certain romances which have followed the sensuous and
daring patterns have ended in disappointment.[14]

Uncertainty Concerning Courtship. Many
young people are in a difficult situation. They
have not learned the technique of American courtship
which differs greatly from the oriental practice
where the go-between, or match-maker, plays such an
important rôle. When they try to adopt Western
methods they find no adequate guide-posts to direct
them, and in this period of transition many suffer
heartaches.[15] But even if they had made the occidental mode of courtship their own, they would
still encounter difficulties. Most houses of the
Orientals are not of such size and character that
the daughters could conveniently and with appropriate dignity entertain young men friends. More important, however, are the parental attitudes which
are encountered. If a boy calls on a girl, the parents consider it a serious matter and that marriage
is almost certain to follow. According to many of
the older Chinese in the United States, disaster

lurks in the automobile rides of young American couples. The young people hear these ideas expressed in their homes. Since many of them do not fully understand American customs, standards, and ideals, an automobile ride not infrequently leads to a forced marriage.

In this period of transition, there will be some experimentation. Doubtless a number will follow the plan of a Japanese in Hawaii who would endeavor to find a wife for himself, but failing in this, would ask his parents to select a girl for him. Many young people are very considerate, and even though they plan to choose their own mates, will seek parental approval. A teacher in Honolulu shows how this idea is operating in actual practice.

A Japanese came and asked me to correct the English in a letter. It was a marriage proposal. When I asked him about it, he said: "My father called me in and said that since I was now twenty-one years it was time for me to marry. He said that in Japan the parents would make all arrangements, but since we were living in America I had better choose a girl and bring her home for their approval." Some time later I met the young man and asked about the outcome of the proposal. He replied that he had taken her to his home, but after his parents had looked up her family history they decided that she would not be a suitable daughter-in-law.[16] He found another girl who was acceptable to his parents and they were married.[17]

C. Results of Following American Patterns

Mingling of the Sexes. Changes in the method of choosing mates run athwart the old ideas relative to the mingling of the sexes. This greater freedom in social intercourse very often offends the moral sensibilities of the older generation, and, as a consequence, the younger generation is subjected to much odious criticism. The experiences of a college girl are illuminating.

The greatest change in my life came soon after I went
to the high school. Early in April, a young man, an Imperial
University graduate, came from Japan to be the principal of
the high school department of the Japanese school. . . . Within a very short while, he took a liking to me and took me
along on his after-supper walks. My heart was overjoyed to go
out with this university man, and I thought it was a great
privilege. The first high school vacation came and went. Our
friendship grew stronger with an elapse of three months. An
unpleasant rumor started concerning us two (young girl and
young man going out for a walk after dark) so we abandoned our
usual walk for a while, but as soon as the rumor died we started out again. Everything went on smoothly and we enjoyed each
other's companionship very much. Rumor started again. For
everything we did, we were criticized. This time, it was severe and unbearable. The principal of the elementary school
did not approve of us being together so often from the Japanese ethical point of view. Besides he thought that Mr._____
was doing something below his dignity and position to get too
well acquainted with his pupil (a girl, too, imagine!). He
wanted to separate us before anything serious happened between Mr._____ and myself. But this man could do nothing, so
he went to the school directors and asked them to advise
Mr. _____ not to get too well acquainted with one girl for the
public was watching them with critical eyes. The directors
took it for granted that there was something drastically wrong
between us. They appointed a spokesman to advise Mr._____
what he should do and what not to do. Before the spokesman
finished his mission, Mr._____ sent in his resignation,
packed up his belongings and left the school. He was working
at one of the local papers as editor-in-chief so the next day
he wrote a whole front page article concerning his resignation.
There were two other local papers in town and one of them
sided with the school and directors. A few days later the
three large Honolulu papers had a write-up concerning us two,
and we both had quite an undesirable publicity.[18]

Crossing of Race Lines in Marriage. The
change in method of choosing mates is leading some
to cross race lines, particularly in Hawaii. Under

the old system, especially where considerable attention was paid to family histories, outside marriage
was precluded. As the young people of various ancestries become a culturally homogeneous group,
doubtless there will be an increasing number of outmarriages. A number have already crossed race lines
in spite of parental opposition. The following document typifies the attitude of a considerable number
of the younger generation in Hawaii.

My parents do not believe in intermarriage, but I
have no objection. I have several cousins who married Ha-
waiian-Whites and Hawaiian-Chinese. Many of my friends of
oriental birth marry other nationalities. My cousins are
happy. My friends, too, with the exception of a very few, are
very happy. Why shouldn't a boy marry the girl he loves, even
if she be white, brown, or red, especially if both of them
are educated, broad-minded, and love one another?[19]

In the choice of mates, it is not the racial
but the cultural factor which is most important. In
the main, they would select mates of their own race,
but many prefer American-born persons of other races
to foreign-born ones of their own. Unhappy unions
with foreign-born mates are matters of observation.
There have been cases of divorce and even suicide
where American-reared girls have married immigrants
much older than themselves. An American-born Japanese girl, after divorcing her Japan-born husband,
said to a friend, "Those 'Japs' don't know how to
treat their wives."

Family Disorganization. This attempt to
follow American patterns has led to a certain amount
of family disorganization in the younger generation. [20] This disorganization would doubtless be
greater if the younger generation were completely
accepted by the white people. Since the white group
raises barriers against them, they are not able to
move far away from the parental group and break

completely from its control. The American-born
youth may mingle freely with the white children in
their youthful years, but at the age when they become interested in selecting life mates the bars are
raised against them. These rebuffs tend to make
them more appreciative of their own group and they
accept its control more gracefully. But the more or
less chaotic conditions in the family life of the
oriental immigrants have exercised a disorganizing
influence upon the American-born group.

D. Conclusion

        Such is the setting in which the American-
born children of oriental ancestry find themselves.
It is not typically oriental, but it is far from being occidental. But whatever the condition, the
family plays a most important rôle--either positively or negatively--and may in reality be termed the
matrix in which attitudes are formed. In the pre-
school age, the children have been largely under the
domination of homes with an oriental atmosphere. At
times, to be sure, the influence has been a negative
or repellant one, for some persons have reacted
against the system of home control which has been
transplanted from the Orient. [21] But it is mainly because of this home environment that members of the
second generation cannot become fully westernized;
they develop a marginal culture in which elements
both from the East and the West unite.

Chapter XVII

CULTURAL HYBRIDISM

Because of the barriers raised against the oriental group, the young Americans of oriental lineage are not given full entrée into the white man's world. They have, nevertheless, taken over much of the occidental culture--customs, habits, ideas, ideals, and, in some measure, attitudes. In this way they differ markedly from their parents, but in spite of the differences between the generations, the younger group has not been able to eliminate all influences of the Orient. They have acquired many cultural elements from this source. In a measure, the American-born group is developing a culture of its own which is a syncretism of the Orient and the Occident. This cultural hybridism is exemplified in the marriage ceremonies in which there is oftentimes a mixture of oriental and occidental elements. It is not unusual to read in a Honolulu newspaper an account of the marriage of a young Chinese couple as follows:

Last Friday cakes were distributed by the bride-to-be to all relatives and friends, which is in accordance with the Chinese custom of announcing one's marriage. Tonight the bride-to-be will spend her last evening as a miss in the company of a few of her intimate friends, which is also in conformity with the Chinese custom. Tomorrow night, at eight o'clock, the marriage ceremony will take place at the Chinese Christian Church.

The younger Japanese generation has also introduced western elements into the marriage ceremony,

239

in spite of the fact that the parental group has
clung quite tenaciously to the old-country practice
and has tried to impose it upon their American-
reared children.

> The fact that. . . . there was solemnized at the
> Hongwanji Buddhist mission at Kealekekua, Kona, the first
> American style wedding ever held there is more than of usual
> significance. . . . The American wedding is an indication that
> the younger generation is accepting American customs. . . .
> The customs of their fatherland were carried out by the bride's
> family, however, who entertained at an all-night celebration
> in honor of their future son-in-law the night before the wed-
> ding.
> This combination of customs is common with weddings
> solemnized in the Hongwanji Buddhist temple in Honolulu. These
> weddings are frequently very elaborate and are often attended
> by guests of a half dozen races. The burning of incense and
> the striking of gongs lend an oriental atmosphere to the cere-
> mony, but it is the old favorite, the march from Lohengrin,
> that heralds the approach of the bride and her party.[1]

The cultural hybridism is revealed not only
in such externalities as marriage ceremonies, but in
deeper ideas, attitudes, and outlook upon life. This
is illustrated by the writing of poetry. Miss Kimi
Gengo, an Hawaiian-born Japanese girl, has recently
issued a book of verse. A reviewer commented that
her verses are unique, a blend of two cultures.[2]
Many of the younger generation are in sympathy neither with their ancestral group nor with
the Americans. They are no longer oriental; neither
are they completely occidental. A Japanese social
worker reveals this cultural hybridism.

> I wanted to know about proper relationships with
> girls, but my friends knew very little about it. I hated to
> tell my parents about my feelings relative to girls or even
> ask their opinion of my going with a girl. Yet I wanted to be
> friendly with girls, but ignorance did not help me to become a

good associate with them. Social gatherings began to appeal
to me and I attended several, but the inability to make myself
feel at home gave me little chance to know or learn much. The
inconsistencies of American conduct when compared with that
set forth in books began to raise questions in my mind. I
feared to break away from my parents' religion, still I was a
regular attendant at a Christian church. I questioned my
standing in a Japanese home as well as in the American society.
I considered myself an American citizen but at the same time I
retained some Japanese characteristics, such as loyalty to my
parents, obedience, etc.[3]

     Many of the younger group live in two
worlds[4]--in their oriental homes and in the American
school and community. At times this clash of cultures has resolved itself into a conflict of loyalties. To which group shall they give their allegiance? There is confusion, for they do not fully
understand the culture of either group. Furthermore,
they are understood neither by Occidentals nor by
Orientals. This often results in grave inner conflicts. A college girl in Hawaii presents the situation.

     At the end of my second school year I went home for a
vacation and there I met the problem of my life--the racial
problem. I am afraid I will be called a hypocrite, but when
you finish reading this you will understand. I am proud of
what I am, but there is a constant conflict within me that I
can't control. I am an American of Chinese parentage and I
have been educated in American schools, lived with the Americans, and worked with them in social groups. Consequently I
am Americanized. How much of the Chinese custom could I follow when I didn't even know enough of it to make myself soci-
able? I was lost in a crowd of Chinese-speaking people. I
couldn't understand their ideas of customs. I could not speak
Chinese except baby talk; every time I started to say something I was laughed at. The Chinese friends of my parents
thought that my brother deserved an education more than I, in
spite of what I was sacrificing to obtain it. Because I was

unable to explain my point of view in Chinese, these people
would take advantage of me by jeering at me in the presence of
my brother. Many quarrels had taken place between us simply
because of the perpetual talking of those old-customed Chinese. Oh, I hated Chinese then. I wished I was something
other than a Chinese. I thought that I could never live with
a Chinese unless he were thoroughly Americanized, although I
admired them in their moral aspects. I loved to hear the tales
and stories of the great men of China, but I never had the notion of calling China my own and of being loyal to her. I had
played Miss Liberty for America, but I couldn't play that for
China--not that I wanted to be a hypocrite but merely because
the training in the schools had developed and strengthened
American ideas in me.[5]

Evidences of Occidental Influence.
(1) Misfits in the Orient. In the main the
younger generation is more occidental than oriental.
This becomes evident when they go to the Orient.
Many who go there feel lost because everything is so
confusingly different. They cannot realize that
their own grandparents and other relatives are in
any way related to themselves.

Those who go to the Orient to visit accept
most of the experiences as interesting diversions
and have a stock of humorous incidents to relate on
their return. But many are taken to the Orient by
parents who intend to remain there;[6] to them it is a
serious matter. An American social worker in Hawaii
made a visit to China where he met several unhappy
Chinese girls from Honolulu. One of them threw her
arms around him and said, "Daddy Brown, take me back
to Hawaii." Letters written by many of these ma-
rooned persons to friends in America reveal a dissatisfaction with the Orient and a longing for America and things American. When an American-born Japanese girl writes from Japan that "their ideals,
their customs, their conceptions of right and wrong
are as different from mine as night from day," it is
small wonder that she says of her life there that

"it almost engulfed me with bitterness and despair."
An American missionary to Japan gives an insight into the situation.

One day, as I was waiting for a train in Tokyo, a
young Japanese, who spoke excellent English, stepped up to me
and said: "Gee, I'm glad to see you!" We entered into a conversation when he told me that he had come to Japan with his
parents and had just returned from visiting some relatives in
a rural district. He spoke of the poverty and other conditions in Japan and said that he did not like to live there.
When he learned that I had spent several years in Japan as a
missionary, he made this significant remark: "How in hell can
you stand it here?" Conditions are so different from those in
America that an American-born Japanese finds it difficult to
make adjustments, and many of them are very unhappy.[7]

Some make earnest efforts to adjust themselves to the Orient, but fail. On account of a
disillusionment an American-born Chinese girl developed an interest in China, began to read about
this land of promise, and study the Chinese language for the purpose of going there for her life
work. When she left for a visit to China, she was
happy and enthusiastic. She returned heartbroken;
she found that she was a misfit. She wrote:

I gave up trying to be a Chinese; for as soon as the
people in China learned that I was an oversea Chinese, they
remarked, "Oh, you are a foreigner." Some asked, "Where did
you learn to speak Chinese?" Some thought it remarkable that
I spoke Chinese at all. So you see I was quite foreign to
China. I wore Chinese clothes and tried to pass as a Chinese,
but I could not so I gave up and admitted my foreign birth
and education. I lack very much a Chinese background, Chinese culture, and Chinese manners and customs; I have neither
their understanding nor their viewpoint nor their patience.
Sometimes I was homesick for America. Where I had friends, I
felt better. I got more or less adjusted to some things—one
of them was the rickshaw. But most of the time, I had very

mixed feelings. I find that unconsciously now I try to avoid
the subject of China; I try to put it out of my mind and attention; I don't want to think or feel about China. . . .
America is really my country and my home.[8]

Many people in the Orient are surprised and
shocked by these anomalous visitors masquerading in
oriental disguises. They comment on their dress,
their manners, but most of all on their speech. A
white American may go to the Orient and cause no
commotion because of his behavior; he is readily ex-
cused if he makes errors in his speech. When a person with a Chinese or Japanese face cannot speak the
language and is American in dress and manner, it is
a far different matter. The Chinese and Japanese
are disgusted with an Oriental who is not an Oriental. Oftentimes these visitors from America do
things which annoy their relatives in the Orient
where form and etiquette mean so much. They are set
down as being indecent and almost obscene because of
their brusqueness and candor in manner and speech.
A Japanese minister, born in Hawaii and educated on
the mainland, made a trip to Japan and on his return
related an experience.

One day in Yokohama I caught a street car which was
soon jammed to its capacity. Since I was one of the first to
board the car I naturally had a seat. However, I did not feel
exactly comfortable in occupying my seat while among those
standing were a number of women. I stood up to offer my seat
to one of the ladies, but just as soon as I made a move toward
her, a man who stood near took my seat without as much as saying, "Thank you." I was so dumb-founded by this incident that
I narrated it to one of my friends who told me that I should
never have done that. By offering my seat to the inferior sex,
I had humiliated myself in the eyes of the passengers. With
me, however, the offering of the seat was merely a matter of
common courtesy, and any Japanese reared and educated in Hawaii would have done the same thing.[9]

(2) <u>Reactions to New Immigrants</u>. The extent
to which the younger generation has become Americanized is also shown by reactions to new immigrants
from the Orient. They have no difficulty in dis-
tinguishing the "green" arrivals and often make
sport of them. A Chinese school boy did not enjoy
the unconventional dress of his relatives.

In the year 1921 my older brother, born of the first
mother in China, came to the United States. Oh, the curiosity
he did arouse in me! I looked at him for a whole day scruti-
nizing his clothing--pants reached about to the middle of his
leg; coat sleeves about one-fourth up his arm; shirts about to
show above his belt; and the curious shoes he had! I had lots
and lots of fun seeing him and looking at him and his things.
One time, about 1921, a cousin of mine went out on the street.
He had been in America for a long time but he seldom went out;
he would always send a boy to buy his necessaries. He came
out on the street this time in the costume of 1909 and with
his queue on. How I wished I had a rotten egg or a pair of
long scissors! These men disgrace our civilized nation, our
modernized race.[10]

It is not merely a matter of holding the new arrivals up to ridicule; the young Americans are frequently embarrassed and humiliated by the practices
of the immigrant group. A Japanese school boy does
not like to walk with his mother if she wears a
kimono and wooden shoes. Many do not like to be
present when older persons are speaking loudly in
the mother tongue.

(3) <u>Adoption of American Sports</u>. The younger group has taken over American sports and athletics
in a thoroughgoing manner. On the Coast there are
several organizations with baseball, basketball, and
football teams. Both the Chinese and Japanese have
athletic teams of their own and they also have representatives on various other teams. In Hawaii,
they have made a good record in athletics. In 1912,

the Chinese of Hawaii sent a baseball team to the
mainland, which played from coast to coast. In the
spring of 1928 "Buck" Lai Tin, a Chinese from Hawaii, was given a trial with the New York Giants.
The Japanese came later but took baseball so seriously that they have surpassed the Chinese. These
young Americans have not been prominent in football.
Doubtless, this is due to their lighter weight.
There are, nevertheless, certain stellar performers
among them.[11] The lineup of the baseball team of the
University of Hawaii in 1927-1928, with slight variation, could have represented Osaka, Tokyo, or Yokohama. In 1923, Tin Luke Wongwai, a Chinese from
Honolulu, went to the University of Kansas and made
a record as a sprinter. Even the girls have taken
to athletics.

        The Japanese in Hawaii have a monthly sports
magazine, The Hawaii Undo-Kai, which is published in
both Japanese and English. The Chinese and Japanese
newspapers in Hawaii and on the Coast devote considerable space to athletics.[12] The Japanese American News of San Francisco, January 24, 1928, carried
an editorial with the heading, "Too Much Athletics,"
which set forth the idea that athletic activities
were being stressed entirely too much and that all
else was being sacrificed.

        (4) Interest in Moving Pictures. The moving
picture houses are patronized liberally by the young
Orientals. Many are eager to learn about occidental
life but, since they have little contact with real
Americans, they substitute the actors on the screen
for the actuality. The pictures which appeal to
them show that they are more occidental than oriental.

        (5) Adoption of American Music. The younger
group has turned from oriental music to American
jazz. The following item is interesting because of
the incongruity--American jazz in a Japanese Buddhist Church.

On Friday night, May 27, the quiet neighborhood of
Channing Way in Berkeley was startled into insomnia by a weird
hash of harmony issuing from the staid, old Buddhist Church....
But all joking aside, the "syncopatin' sirens" of the Berkeley
Buddhist Church have organized a "synco-symphony" orchestra
with four saxophones and clarinets, and a "baby-grand." However, with a couple more trombonists, violinists, cornetists,
banjoists, and drummers, they hope to turn out a "jazz band"
that will make Rube Wolf drink castor oil.[13]

(6) <u>Adoption of the American Dance</u>. The
young people have learned to dance in occidental
fashion, and in this respect they have departed far
from their oriental heritage. The free intermingling of the sexes would not have been tolerated in
the days when their parents were young. Many encounter strenuous parental opposition. But the young
people view the dance as an innocent and enjoyable
form of recreation and tell their parents that their
ideas are old-fashioned, absurd, and ridiculous.

(7) <u>Adoption of American Names</u>. Many young
people exercise every endeavor to fuse themselves
into the American group. They are desirous of acquiring status in this group and of being accepted
fully as Americans. Many feel that such recognition
will be more probable if they separate themselves
from their racial group, and many things are done to
bring this about. Many detach themselves from the
Orient by adopting American names.[14] School officials in Hawaii encounter numerous difficulties from
this change of names with the opening of each school
year.

David Akana of the Territorial Birth Registration
Bureau says that upon entering the 'teens Chinese and Japa-
nese children give themselves English names. According to
Akana, the name must change when the native costume does, and
Oriental flappers and sheiks search for names that will be
better suited to the dash of American sport clothing.

Consequently, the names of Yoshi, Yuki, and Haru become rein-
carnated into Elsie, Daisy, and Rose. Girls are more fickle
than boys in the matter of changing their names.[15]

The practice of changing names is not restricted to
Hawaii. A teacher in one of the Chinatowns of California reported a day of "wholesale re-christening"
when the whole school took American names. From
this ceremony Mow Meng emerged as Margaret and Hung
Wai as Robert.[16]

　　　　Younger Generation Eager to Become American.
There is ample evidence that these young people are
eager to learn American ways. A class, conducted
for Chinese boys at the Y.M.C.A. in Honolulu to discuss etiquette, had a perfect attendance. In one
high school library a book entitled Manners and Conduct was in great demand. When one girl made a trip
to the mainland, it was the only book she carried
with her. Some young people work as domestics in
American homes in order to learn American ways and
etiquette. In some instances it hurts their pride,
as well as the pride of their parents, but they are
eager to get rid of any awkwardness so they may be
able to go anywhere and mingle freely with Americans
without making breaches in social usage. An American-born Chinese professional man in Hawaii expressed himself thus:

　　　　　　A lot of the stuff handed out around here along the
line of Americanization is just pure buncombe. In our schools
we are taught Americanization from books; we are taught to
salute the flag and all that, but this is quite shallow. When
I was in Peoria, Illinois, at one time, the United States flag
was carried through the street at the head of a procession.
I took off my hat as the flag passed by, and I was shocked
when others kept their hats on. That began to raise questions
in my mind. Others from Hawaii who have been on the mainland
have had like experiences. These bookish forms of Americanization do not go very far. It would mean a lot more if

American homes would be opened to some of the youth of oriental
parentage so that they could see what the interior of a home
looks like, for many do not have the slightest idea. If they
could see how things are arranged in the house, it would be of
great help to them in arranging their own homes. Many young
people, who have homes of their own, have never been in an
American home. They fix them up according to the pictures
they see in books, but often the fittings or furnishings do
not go well together--they want things to be different, but
have no chance to see good models. Very few Chinese are in
homes where they use knives and forks. Many who go to the
mainland have their first experiences in the use of these
utensils, because they have the good fortune to be invited into some middle-class home. One time in the East I was invited to a home for dinner and, even though the hosts were
dressed in evening clothes while I had ordinary street clothes,
I was made to feel comfortable. When the maid came to serve,
she had a tray on which there were several dishes of vegetables. She seemed to be nervous and the tray shook a little.
I thought that it would be perfectly proper for me to hold the
tray and steady it as I was helping myself to the vegetables.
They told me that she would hold it safely. I had made a mistake, but they told me in such a way that I did not feel embarrassed. That meant very much to me.[17]

The young people are sensitive and eager to
avoid anything which might attract attention to
themselves and make them appear queer in any way.
They are responsive to American public opinion and
desire to live up to the standards set by the white
people. The first Chinese member of the territorial
legislature in Hawaii introduced a bill in the 1927
session to repeal the law forbidding foot-binding
among the Chinese. The law had been a dead letter
for many years and was of no importance, but the
mere fact that it was on the statute book was a
stigma. The idea that such a law was needed to control the Chinese in this respect could no longer be
tolerated.

Conclusion. The children of oriental parentage, in the main, are eager to become throughgo-
ing Americans, but this is not entirely possible because of the homes in which they live.[18] The culture
systems of the parental groups inevitably leave
their impressions.[19] On the other hand, because of
skin color Americans classify them with their immigrant parents. So far as outward appearances are
concerned that is correct. This judgment, however,
is superficial. An older Japanese in California
said to one of the younger group, "You look like a
Japanese, but you are not one; you do not think as
we do." They are oriental in appearance, but not in
reality. It is more accurate to say that they belong to both groups and yet to neither; they are
neither fully oriental nor yet fully occidental.[20]
A Japanese college girl wrote:

We belong to two groups, the Japanese and the American. In ancestry and in physical appearance we are Japanese,
while in birth, in education, in ideals, and in ways of thinking, we are Americans. Nevertheless, the older Japanese will
not accept us into their group because, as they see us, we are
too independent, too pert, and too self-confident, and the
Americans bar us from their group because we retain the yellow
skin and flat nose of the Oriental. Thus we stand on the
border line that separates the Orient from the Occident.
Though on each side of us flow the streams of two great civili-
zations--the old Japanese culture with its formal traditions
and customs and the newer American civilization with its freedom and individualism--the chance to perceive and to imbibe
the best things from each has been withheld from us.[21]

Chapter XVIII

SECOND GENERATION PERSONALITY TYPES

As our citizens of oriental ancestry are gradually unfolding their lives in America, the majority of them are coming to be markedly different from their parents; still they are not like white Americans. In view of the practical circumstances of their lives, they cannot be like either group. In the Orient, stability has been the dominant idea for many centuries and, except for the innovations which have come in the large centers through modern industrial developments, change has been under strict taboo. Because of this stability and uniformity in the external conditions, there have been only a limited number of influences which could act upon an individual. Furthermore, the individual had to fit into a predetermined scheme of activities. He knew in advance that he would not be permitted to remain an old bachelor; his marriage would be arranged for him; his career was very largely determined in keeping with the standing of his family in the community; his education was arranged for him in accordance with a fixed pattern; and there was no question as to his religious affiliation. The laws and the moral standards of the community prescribed certain forms of behavior and prohibited others.

The more thoroughly schematized the whole round of life is, the less can be the variation in the individuals, because they come under the same standardized influences. In China and Japan the social framework has been very rigid. Hence, in certain areas and in certain classes of the population there has been a relatively high degree of

uniformity as between the individuals in these
groups. As the immigrants from the Orient have come
into an American environment, disorganization of the
old schemes of life has been inevitable. With the
great preponderance of men over women, it was impossible for all men to marry and rear sons to perpetuate the family name; they could not choose occupations along traditional lines; and they could
not carry on their religious activities in the usual
way. With their old system disorganized they could
not direct their children to follow any one single
pattern in their life activities. Furthermore, the
children made contacts with American life at certain
points and that stimulated forms of behavior not in
keeping with the traditional standards of the Orient.
These outside contacts are favorable to individual
self-expression which brings variation from the norm.

      Because of this condition the younger gen-
eration is going through a struggle. The parental
group, in considerable measure, is endeavoring to
make the young people conform to their standards
while the dominant white group is bringing pressure
to bear to make of them thoroughgoing Americans as
rapidly as possible. The organization of activities
on the plantations in Hawaii tends to mould the employees into a rather uniform type--provided, of
course, that they submit.[1] Many young people oppose
both of these forces and seek to express themselves,
while some oppose one of the forces and yield, in
large measure, to the other. These forces play upon
them in a variety of ways under the different environmental conditions. As the young people face
the various situations and struggle for self-expression their personalities gradually evolve. Whereas
they are not subjected to the same scheme of influences which played upon their parents, they develop personalities which are markedly different and,
since the plan of this behavior organization is less
uniform and steady than that to which their parents
were subjected, a greater range of personality types
will be developed.

A consideration of the various personality
types is of importance. They are indices "of assimilation of the members of a social group to one
another, and represent, therefore, various stages in
the assimilative process. These types may also be
conceived of as the effect of mobility upon personal
behavior. They express the range of contacts of the
individuals with other cultures." [2] They also reveal
something of the kind of contacts made.

Personality Types

Several social types of personality patterns
are distinguishable as we consider the American-born
generation of oriental ancestry. There are no hard
and fast lines of demarcation between these different types; there is much overlapping. There is no
person who can be classified under any single type,
for in some aspects of his life he shows tendencies
which would place him in another class. For instance, a certain Japanese girl in Hawaii rebelled
against the traditional system and threw off everything she could of the parental culture, but remained a staunch Buddhist. Since personalities are
not static but gradually evolving, a person may at
one time be classified as of one type, but due to
certain experiences may change so markedly as to
come under a different classification. A person may
be bitter and rebellious at one time but gradually
develop a philosophical attitude toward the whole
situation.

1. The Conformist Type. In the first place
we may note the conformist type. Some tend to accept in toto the traditions of their group and do
not vary from them. There is considerable variation
as between the conformists and we may further classify them under several sub-heads.

(a) The Old-Fashioned Type. There is
the old-fashioned type. These are the so-called
"China Jacks," the "Typs.,"[3] et cetera. These persons hold to the ideas and customs of their parents
and appear to be perfectly happy in such a life.
They are as completely Chinese or Japanese as their
old-fashioned parents can keep them. An Anglo-Saxon
man said of two American-born Chinese men in Honolulu that they were in reality more old-fashioned
than their immigrant father who was more than eighty
years old. Conformity often reveals itself in connection with matrimonial matters; the young people
accept without question the traditional practice
where the parents arrange for the marriages. Furthermore, the young man wants a wife who has in no
way been spoiled by American notions while the young
woman offers no objection to accepting a position of
inferiority.

(b) The Submissive Type. Certain ones
submit to the control of the parental group and conform to the old customs, but are unhappy in this arrangement. While they are unhappy in their situation they see no other way out. A Chinese high
school boy in Hawaii said that he did not like the
traditional custom of arranged marriages, but what
could he do when his parents had made all the arrangements and would request him to marry? Many
white people are amazed at the number of Americans
of oriental ancestry who accept the parentally arranged marriages. An analysis of the situation
makes it evident that early home influences have
made a deep impression and that group pressure is
strong. A Japanese high school girl in Hawaii appeared to be unhappy; she kept herself aloof from
the other pupils. It was learned that a sister had
married a so-called "four-fingered" Japanese, or one
who belonged to a lower class. This had disgraced
the entire family and as a result suitable marriages for the other sisters were practically

precluded. Since the Japanese have not yet become
sufficiently westernized that the "old maid" has
been entirely accepted by them, the time-worn tradition relative to marriage still exercises a strong
influence; it tends to give the family a strong control over the young people.

(c) The Conventionalized American Type.
Persons of this type have adopted American conven-
tionalities and are ashamed of their race or of anything that bears any semblance to the parental culture. They are diligent students of the books of
etiquette. They are, however, thoroughgoing Phi-
listines;[4] they are not rational in their behavior;
they imitate blindly and conform only to avoid dis-
comfort.

In this conventionalized American group some,
who have accepted Christianity because it is the
predominating religion of America, may be designated
as a Puritanical type. They accept a Christianity
of the more traditional and literalistic kind,
rather than the progressive and dynamic type which
seeks to adapt itself to the changing modern conditions. Their ethical system is a rigid one which
must be followed to the letter.

2. The Marginal Type. The second main group
may be called the marginal type. Some are torn between two worlds; they do not find any real satisfaction in either; they do not fit either one. Some
try to live as Orientals in their own homes and as
Americans outside. A number of this type have tried
to break away from the parental group, but have
learned to their sorrow that they will not be accepted by the white people; hence they have returned
to their own group.[5] This is revealed in some measure by the young people who are turning to a study
of the mother tongue after spurning this in their
early school days. Some, in trying to break away
from their own group, have met with rebuffs and have

become bitter. They try not to show it; they pretend to laugh about the whole matter. According to
a Chinese professional man there is an organization
of Chinese in Honolulu called the "Never-Give-A-Damn-
Club," made up of young and middle-aged men, many of
whom are of high standing in the community. They
have become disillusioned and attempt to be face-
tious, just as if they did not care. But underneath
it all is a bitterness. They are practically saying
to some people whose behavior has not kept pace with
their professions, "We see through you and all your fine
talk about brotherhood and other kindred subjects."
A Chinese college girl in Hawaii reported that a
number of the younger set also had a club by the
same name.

        3. The Rebellious Type. A number react vio-
lently against the old system, but have not necessarily worked out any consistent schemes of behavior.
Emancipation from the old seems to be of greater importance than the development of any new scheme of
life organization. A statement from a Japanese college boy in Hawaii gives an introduction to the
group.

        Categorically, No! I shall never accept any one as a
wife but my own choice, even if it means the severance of parental relations. I cannot afford to sacrifice my happiness at
the expense of upholding traditional customs. Departing from
the conventions of my parents may be sacrilegious, but I hold
my liberty, my independence, more sacred than all the conven-
tionalities combined. If my parents should regret my behavior,
they may well blame themselves for it. For if they had willingly let me have gone back to Japan to enlist in the military
school, I might not have been imbued with American ideals, especially, in matters pertaining to self-independence and freedom of activity and would have behaved in a manner which would
have been well suited to their ideas.[6]

        A number rebel against the restrictions

placed upon them by the white group and set out to
demand their rights. Even though many have to con-
tend against great handicaps, they are not crushed
down. In 1925, after a study of several Chinatowns
on the Pacific Coast, Winifred Raushenbush stated
that the young Chinese were bitter, but still they
were unquenchably hopeful. The Hawaiian Club of San
Francisco had an article in one of their bulletins
on "The Rights of Japanese-American Citizens in
California." The old idea among the Japanese immigrants has been to say nothing and suffer injustices,
but some of the younger people are beginning to demand their rights. Some are even beginning to carry
chips on their shoulders and daring anyone to touch
them. The Chinese, particularly in Hawaii, have begun to speak out, as was made evident in the fight
on the English-Standard School of some years ago.
The Hawaiian Chinese Civic Association is not typically oriental. In 1927 an Hawaiian-born Chinese
was detained in the immigration station of Honolulu
on his return from China and shortly thereafter
the Association invited the Director of the Immigration Service to address the Association. In February of 1927 the students of a school, the majority
of whom were of oriental ancestry, sent a letter to
a local newspaper demanding an apology for something
the paper had published which was derogatory to the
institution. The letter was published in the paper.

4. The Emancipated Type. Certain ones have
almost completely broken away from the oriental culture. Some of them have not necessarily completed
the process of acquiring the western culture, nor
have they been accepted completely by the white
group, but they do not understand or appreciate the
culture of the parental group--in fact, some of them
hold it up to ridicule. An American writer has
shown how completely a certain Chinese girl on the
mainland has broken away from the traditions of her
group.

Ming Toy, daughter of a chop suey palace proprietor, is a beautiful and brazen child. Her shoulders are, so the California artists say, incomparable, and her sulky pomegranate mouth has been deemed worthy of attention and of praise, not only by the susceptible Pacific Coast poets, but by more ordinary men as well. The sons of Japanese samurai, the nephews of Korean intellectuals, tennis-playing American university instructors, and the whole tribe of native sons from Chinatown's suavest sheik to its earnest betortoise-shelled medical students, cluster about Ming Toy's doorstep as iron filings cluster about a magnet.

Ming Toy is very beautiful and she is very brazen. She has refused to honor her ancestors, she has ridden through Chinatown Alley on horseback, she has traveled alone in a sleeper, she has walked upstairs at three o'clock in the morning and called out "Hello, folks!"--while her little Chinese-American girl friends were paddling upstairs in stocking feet so as not to be heard. She has written stories about Chinatown society that almost precipitated a tong war. In fact, Ming Toy has so thoroughly shocked the older generation of Chinatown by her attempts to behave like an American flapper that various men offered to pay for the eastern university education that they knew Ming Toy had set her heart on. "Any string to the offer?" said Ming Toy in her hard-boiled way, and did not accept.

When the disapproval of Chinatown's older generation became too hot for Ming Toy, she left for the East to get a university education for herself. Ming Toy has never seen China, and has no desire to see China. Ming Toy was born in Chinatown, but she has no desire to live in Chinatown. Ming Toy is an American.[7]

This same girl has given us a further insight as she wrote of herself.

I was born here in Chinatown and attended the city schools and graduated from the high school and have had two years in the State College.

When I was a little girl, I grew to dislike the conventionality and rules of Chinese life. The superstitions and

customs seemed ridiculous to me. My parents have wanted me to
grow up a good Chinese girl, but I am an American and I can't
accept all the old Chinese ways and ideas. A few years ago
when my mother took me to worship at the shrine of my ancestor
and offered a plate of food, I decided it was time to stop
this foolish custom. So I got up and slammed the rice in
front of the idol and said, "So long Old Top, I don't believe
in you anyway." My mother didn't like it a little bit.

As I grew older I came to see that American life is
also full of conventionality and foolish customs and it became
a fad of mine to study things and to write about them. I long
for unconventionality and freedom from all these customs and
ideals that make people do such ridiculous and insincere
things.

I have written a good deal in local papers about Chinese life. Much of this has displeased the Chinese people.
My article on "The Sheiks of Chinatown" (a description of the
young sports of China alley) was a take-off on certain well-
known native-born Chinese. It made a terrible fuss in Chinatown. I have had three blackmailing letters sent to me for
writing so openly about Chinese life. One of the Chinese students from North China became very angry at my article on the
Sheiks and wrote me a very long, fat letter attacking me and
picking to pieces everything I had said. He thought that I
was trying to disgrace China, which I distinctly was not, but
only trying to have a little fun with my Chinese friends. All
Chinatown got very excited and two of the boys, one from North
China and the other from South China, fought a kind of duel
over it. North boy said that I had disgraced China. South
boy said, "No. We should be too proud to let a little dust
like this hurt us!" A delegation of Chinese students met me
in college and I challenged them to show what I had said that
disgraced anybody or anything. They put on their spectacles
and after ten minutes could not find anything. I said, "Ta,
Ta, Kiddos, when you find any disgrace you just put me wise.
I can't wait all day."[8]

5. The Defeated Type. Some, seeing no hope
of a satisfactory adjustment, throw up their hands
in despair and begin to drift in the easiest way.

Ichihashi writes that "discouraging experiences in
job-hunting have converted a number of Japanese-
Americans into pessimists, adopting the 'what's-the-
use' philosophy."[9] The majority of the young people
have hard problems to face in this period of transition.   These pioneers have no precedents to follow;
they must work out every step by themselves.

It would seem that the most serious problem confront-
ing the United States in its relationship to the young Japanese within its borders is that of furnishing an incentive toward higher education and well-directed, aggressive leadership.
Just a few evenings ago I was talking with a very promising
young man who had repeatedly taken honors for scholarship in
his high-school courses; who has splendid ability from the
athletic standpoint; who exercises a remarkable influence
among his friends in the social world, and who can be counted
upon to lead in the musical line, especially community singing
and choral work.
In this conversation, the tragedy of the situation
was forcibly brought home to me, for I was urging upon him the
value of a college education. With rather unusual frankness he
stated: "You know as well as I do that a Japanese, although
well-educated, never has an equal opportunity with an American
no matter how uneducated that American may be." This is the
attitude taken by many of our young people, and they are satisfied to follow in the footsteps of their parents as keepers
of small "emporiums" or greengrocer's stalls. The young man
with whom I was talking is a clerk in a store, selling the
usual variety of Japanese articles.[10]

There will be a relatively large number of
Japanese in this group from sheer necessity. Should
the young Japanese in America gain control of all
the preferred positions to which they aspire, there
would be comparatively few opportunities left for
anyone else. Not all will be surrendered to those
of oriental ancestry; hence a considerable number
will have to admit defeat of this sort. Many white
men in California would be glad to conduct

greengrocers' stalls--in fact, many have tried only
to fail. While many Japanese consider the conduct
of such a business an admission of defeat, there
will doubtless develop a more rational attitude as
already evident among the Chinese of Hawaii.

     6. The Philosophical Type. In the sixth
place, we may note the philosophical type, or the
creative man.[11] A number have been able to analyze
the situation and are setting about in a calm and
rational way to solve the problems which confront
them. When some realize that the scheme of life
which their parents brought to America has become
disorganized and does not present a well-defined
pattern of behavior, they go back in search of something more dependable. As a result they become more
"Chinesey" and more "Japanesey" than their parents.
When others become aware of this disorganization,
they abandon everything connected with the parental
culture as they would leave a sinking ship and adopt
wholesale, without discrimination, the conventional
American patterns of life. For some time they may
feel secure. Too often they encounter difficulties
when they are not accepted as Americans even though
they have taken over the conventions and follow them
to the letter. At times this conventionalized American pattern is abandoned and there is a reversion
to an orthodox type in the parental group where
there is a welcome with an "I told you so." In some
instances a shock or rebuff by the white group leads
to bitterness. An iconoclastic attitude develops
which attacks, in a blind and irrational manner, all
traditional beliefs and institutions, no matter if
they be oriental or occidental. Such a person does
not work out any consistent scheme of life-organiza-
tion; he is not able to adjust himself to the difficult conditions which develop on account of the contact and conflict of the oriental and occidental
cultures.[12]
     A considerable number, however, are

unperturbed by the difficult problems they have to
face. They are aware of the fact that they are living in a world of change and do not try to make an
adjustment once and for all to an immutable social
world. They study the conditions so that they may
be able to control the environment and adapt themselves to it. They use discrimination. Where they
find conflicts between the two cultural systems they
set about to make readjustments to remove the difficulties. In certain instances, some practice of the
parental group is offensive to the white group and
produces strained relationships. The young people
call this to the attention of their elders and improvements result. At times when the white group
misunderstands and misinterprets some custom which
means much to the immigrants, they endeavor to present an adequate interpretation that sets the practice in an entirely new light. A number appreciate
the point of view not only of the immigrant generation but that of the young people of oriental ancestry and the American white group as well. Thus
they are in a position to act as mediators. They do
not reject wholesale the culture of their parents
and adopt everything American; they work out a life
organization that embraces elements selected with
discrimination from both cultures. Thus they are
able to adjust themselves with considerable success.

This philosophical type may be broken up
into several subdivisions.

(a) The Accommodative Type. A number
appreciate the conditions under which they are living and adjust themselves to the situation in which
they must participate in the two cultures. They are
alert and make use of any opportunities which present themselves. At the same time they are careful
not to push themselves too far lest they be responsible for the development of unfavorable attitudes
which will react against themselves as well as other
members of the group. Furthermore, they are careful

not to shock the parental group too much. A certain
Chinese girl in Hawaii had worn the Chinese dress in
the grammar school, but when she reached the upper
grades and was getting ready for high school she came
to the conclusion that she would have to adopt American dress. Her mother insisted that she continue
to wear the Chinese costume. The girl opposed this
idea and finally won her mother over. She completed
high school and went on to the University. At the
end of her college course she told one of her professors that she admired her mother. She understood
her mother's position, but knew that it would be impossible to carry out her wishes. She adjusted herself gracefully to the situation and was able to
work her way through without any break with her
mother.

(b) The Go-Between Type. This subdivi-
sion is made up of those who appreciate the several
points of view and are thus able to serve as ar-
biters between them and bring them to a better understanding of each other. They may serve to bring a
better understanding between the first and second
generations, between the white Americans and the entire oriental group, both immigrant and alien, and
also between the East and the West. [13]

(c) The Self-Confident Type. A number
realize full well that their lot is not an easy one,
but they are confident that if given a fair chance
they will be able to win, even in the face of the
stiffest competition. While some come to the conclusion that prejudice is so strong that no person
of oriental ancestry can make any satisfactory adjustment in America, those of this type are confident that they can succeed. A number of them have
met the Whites and in fair competition have been
able to win. This has given them an enhanced value
of their own abilities. A young man of Japanese ancestry, who was born and educated in California,
looks to the future with confidence.

Everything else being equal, the second generation should be able to become assimilated into American society just as soon, for example, as the second generation German or Frenchman. But, obviously, everything is not equal. To use a broad classification, man is composed of two aspects, the physical and the mental. In the eyes of the average American in California, the Japanese is regarded in a light different from that of the German or Frenchman in his physical make-up, just as the American is viewed by the average Japanese in Nippon as peculiar physically when compared with people more like himself. The Japanese realizes that he cannot change his outward appearance, that he will always have black hair, that he will have a physiognomy characteristic of the group to which he belongs, and the like, so long as he keeps his race pure.

However, at the same time, he is aware of the fact that his mental equipment can be changed, that the one way to equal the place reached by the German or Frenchman in the estimation of the average American is to develop his mental aspect to a degree far in excess of that demanded of other races. Hence more is required of the Japanese for the assimilation into American society than is asked of other racial groups. Not a curse but a blessing is this for, as the sturdy oak, the more the Japanese is buffeted the stronger he becomes.[14]

This feeling of confidence is more evident in Hawaii than on the Coast because of the relative absence of race prejudice. A number of young persons have said that color will not be the determinative factor but that the best man will win; if they lose in a fair struggle they will offer no alibis. This attitude of confidence is no mere childish whim; certain white people are beginning to give it serious consideration. A prominent sugar man in Hawaii said with some feeling that unless the white boys "buck up" they will soon be taking orders from the American-born Japanese.

(d) The Altruistic Type. Certain persons

see the problems which others have to face and decide to devote themselves to their solution, even
though it may mean great personal sacrifice. Some
look forward to service for their own groups. Some,
appreciative of the advantages they enjoy in America,
have decided to render service in the Orient where
conditions of life are less favorable. Oftentimes
the persons who have succeeded in making fairly satisfactory adjustment gain confidence in themselves
and then begin to think about helping others who
have made less headway in the accommodative process.
A number who enter the teaching profession have much
to say about service to others. Much of that, to be
sure, they imbibe from the atmosphere of the teacher-
training institutions. With some it may be a matter
of rationalization to defend their choice of profession, but many are genuinely interested in rendering
service to others.

   Conclusion. In large measure these personality groupings may be considered transitional types.
As the situation changes and these citizens of oriental ancestry accommodate themselves to American
life, there will be significant modifications in the
factors which condition their personalities. As the
immigrant group gradually passes out of the picture,
there will be a decline in the oriental influence
with an increase in the control exercised by the behavior patterns of the American group. Inevitably,
personality types which vary widely from those of
the present will be developed.

REFERENCE NOTES

Chapter I

[1]"A young Japanese, about thirty years, ill shaven and disconsolate, sat sipping his coffee and looking forlornly about him in a dingy restaurant. . . . His was the saddest and loneliest figure I ever saw. . . . I sat opposite him and tried to pick up a conversation. He eyed me with a preoccupied stare and kept silent. . . . Suddenly he waved his trembling hands and shot out a question which startled me. There was an inspired note in his voice, and his eyes gleamed. 'Have you ever experienced a fierce longing?' he uttered pointedly. 'You know a tre-tre-mendous yearning?'. . . . It's a desire that transcends everything. I'd desert my parents, I'd cheat my sister, I'd do anything to achieve it. . . . I desire to go to Japan! I hate San Francisco, I hate the noise, the feverish excitement, the aimless blundering. . . . You have nothing but change here--new job every month, new house, new wife, new dangers! Life is always insecure; and distressing. Everybody is seeking pleasure, running after it, and never finding. Walk the streets, and you find people as lonely as I am, walking, walking, but nowhere to go. But they must be moving, forever moving. . . . Yes, to Japan! I want to go to Kagoshima, and eat sweet potatoes. . . . Japan is wonderful. . . . There is peace and quiet there, even though one has to eat sweet potatoes three times a day. . . .

His mournful face had the expression of a man who had just exhausted himself from ecstatic emotion."
Japanese American News, October 17, 1929.

[2]Etsu I. Sugimoto, A Daughter of the Samurai, p. 163. Copyright 1925 by Doubleday, Doran and Company, Inc. Quoted by permission.

[3]The official title was "The Chinese Consolidated Benevolent Association."

[4]Cf. C. N. Reynolds, "The Chinese Tongs," The American Journal of Sociology, XL (March, 1935), 612-623.

[5]Cf. Carol Green Wilson, Chinatown Quest, for the activities of Donaldina Cameron of the Presbyterian Mission Home of San Francisco. She rescued several hundred slave-girls in her thirty-six years with the mission.

[6]Cf. C. C. Wu, Chinatowns, Unpublished doctor's dissertation, University of Chicago.

[7]D. H. Kulp, Country Life In South China, p. 187. Quoted by permission of the author.

[8]George W. Knox, The Spirit Of The Orient, p. 185.

[9]Cf. Ibid., pp. 183, 185.

[10]"It was the filial piety of China that rendered possible the completion of the Panama railroad, where to strike the soil was to liberate death; where the land devoured laborers by the thousand, until white and black labor could no more be procured in quantity sufficient for the work. But labor could be obtained from China--any amount of labor--at the cost of life; and the cost was paid; and multitudes of men came from the East to toil and die, in order that the price of their lives might be sent to their families."
Lafcadio Hearn, Japan: An Attempt At Interpretation, pp. 57-58. Quoted by permission of The Macmillan Company, publishers.

[11]In the Orient a man is dominated not only by the living present but by the dead past. In China fate has much to do with the choice of mates. No one can go against this. Children have heard that fate rules all and that those who have tried to go contrary to this destiny have gone on the rocks. Children adopted these ideas and lived according to them. They came to believe that their dead ancestors were responsible for this mysterious guidance. This spiritual sanction behind the expressed opinions of the community exercises a tremendous control over domestic affairs. When the will of the ancestors,

operating through the guiding hand of fate, has selected two
marriage mates, there can be no thought of divorce. In America, far away from the graves of their ancestors, where these
religious sanctions do not function in the same manner, it is
easier for disorganization to set in.

[12]John MacGowan, Men and Manners of Modern China, p. 91.

[13]The system of parentally-arranged marriages was so deeply
intrenched that not even young men from America could escape
it. The following letter was written to an American woman in
1922 by a California Chinese who had accompanied his father to
his old home in China. "I promised all my friends and you too
that I won't marry in China and I'll be in America again within six months time. My plan was all right to me when I sailed
from America on January fourteen and until I reached the village on February 20 with my father, but it is all broken by my
folks in China.

"I refuse to marry when folks inquire of my purpose in
coming to China. For I had one reason and that is just to accompany my dad, and no other. But it was all useless for my
refusal and everyone was a stranger and against me, too, on
the point of marriage and religion in this village away in the
inland of China. Had I known the conditions that exist in our
village I would not have gone into the tangle. But it was
rather hard for me to avoid it, for I must accompany my dad to
his destination. On arriving in the village everyone was
quite glad to see me. But in those few days my life companion
was fixed for me by my folks before I knew anything about it.
I cannot even see the girl because tradition here rules that
boys should not see the girl before marriage. So I am rather
afraid of taking such a step. But I got to do it anyway for
to refuse will cause trouble on both sides."
Survey of Race Relations, 20-B. (20-B is the number of the
document in the depository of the Survey at Stanford University.)

[14]Knox, op. cit., p. 181.

[15]Arthur H. Smith, Village Life in China, pp. 248-249.

[16]A Chinese bride related the story of her engagement: "My engagement was celebrated in the month of May. It will seem strange to Americans that in China every one comes to an engagement party except the two people for whom the party is given. We were neither of us to appear, nor indeed had I ever seen this young man who was destined to become my husband. He was still in Canton, where he was to remain until the time of our marriage, which had not yet been set or even discussed."
Good Housekeeping, November, 1925, p. 207.

[17]Arthur H. Smith, Village Life in China, p. 237.

[18]Ibid., p. 258.

[19]Herbert A. Giles, The Civilization of China, p. 99.

[20]A Chinese woman wrote: "I was born in America, but was raised in oriental fashion. My mother died while I was quite young and I was raised by my grandmother. My father was dominated by the Chinese idea that the man was the head of the family and that the children were to be entirely submerged in the family--we were not considered as having any individuality of our own. When I was in school I was told that my position was a subordinate one even in instances where I had more information than father on account of my school work. I was kept closely at home and restrained until I began to revolt against this situation."
Survey of Race Relations, 102-A.

[21]"In China the New Year is preceded by a universal season of debt-paying from which no one is exempt."
A. H. Smith, Village Life in China, p. 304.
        "New Year must not be violated by duns for debts, but the debt must be collected New Year though it be. For this reason one sometimes sees an urgent creditor going about early on the first day of the year carrying a lantern looking for his debtor. His artificial light shows that by a social fiction the sun has not yet risen; it is still yesterday and the debt can still be claimed."
Ibid., p. 208.

[22]Adapted from Hawaii Chinese News, January 20, 1928.

[23]C. C. Wu, op. cit.

[24]Giles, op. cit., p. 162.   Quoted by permission of Henry Holt and Company.

[25]Survey of Race Relations, 228-A.

[26]Cf. Charles R. Shepherd, The Ways of Ah Sin, pp. 212-215.

[27]Unpublished Document.   Used by courtesy of Dr. Romanzo Adams.

[28]"Japan needs no poorhouses for her worn-out laborers and their widows, thanks to the family system. The family system provides an ideal shock-absorber for unemployment during industrial fluctuations. When lack of orders thins out the factory workers, the poorer streets are not cluttered with workless and resourceless men. They return to the farms whence they came; they share out their poverty with the family; all have less, but none starves. The Japanese merchant in the time of depression is not an isolated unit struggling for existence. He is a knot in a great web of people bound together by the family system, and he gets credit and backing. The mercantile class, lowest in the social scale of old Japan, mutually prevented the ruin of their families. When a ship is lost if the owner alone bears the loss, his whole estate is gone and his family is ruined. Hence, as such a disaster may in the course of time fall to the lot of any family, it is for the interest of each and all to unite and share the risks. In business the family system furnishes an important and imponderable asset. When a merchant goes to his banker for credit, the banker not only wants to see his balance-sheet; he asks about the family. Who are his relatives? Who are his wife's relatives? Is he the head of a family or a member of his father's family or of his wife's family? Will the family council back him up? The reputation and resources of the family are as important in the domain of business as the reputation and resources of the firm. If the family is a good one,

there will be little difficulty about credit. This fact helps
to explain why Japan got through the catastrophic 'slump' of
1920 with a remarkably small number of bankruptcies."
Hugh Byas, *Asia*, April, 1924, pp. 291-292. Quoted by permission of *Asia* magazine.

[29]See "Hand-vine" system, pp. 232.

[30]A certain Japanese on the Pacific Coast offered his younger brother several thousand dollars if he would not go into a
certain business. He entered the business, nevertheless, and
failed. The elder brother then paid about twice the amount of
his original offer to settle with the creditors; it was obligatory upon him to uphold the family honor.

[31]A Japanese teacher in Hawaii, who considered herself a
failure in her first experience, wrote home that she was planning to quit. She received the reply, "Don't quit now; the
townspeople will be surprised and laugh at you, and we also
will be disgraced."

[32]Cf. Sugimoto, *op. cit.*, pp. 148-152; *Asia*, April, 1924,
p. 291.

[33]*Op. cit.*, p. 27.

[34]*Ibid.*, p. 38.

[35]Cf. Nobushige Hozumi, *Ancestor-Worship and Japanese Law*.

[36]Cf. Hearn, *op. cit.*, pp. 66-69.

[37]"The children must not only obey the parents and grandparents, but must observe among themselves the domestic law of
seniority: thus the younger brother should obey the elder
brother, and the younger sister the elder sister. . . . At
meal time, the elder boy is served first, the second son next,
and so on,--an exception being made in the case of a very
young child, who is not obliged to wait. This custom accounts
for an amusing popular term often applied in jest to a second

son, 'Master Cold-Rice'. . . . as the second son, having to
wait until both infants and elders have been served, is not
likely to find his portion desirably hot when it reaches him."
Hearn, op. cit., p. 73. Quoted by permission of The Macmillan
Company.

[38]R. B. Perry, The Gist of Japan, p. 74.

[39]Wallace Irwin, Seed of the Sun, p. 56.

[40]On July 1, 1899, their first child, a son, was born to
them. Their joy was inexpressible, for traditionally Japanese
always wish to have a son for their first child. He was named
Hikio, which means "child of strength." Four years later, a
girl was born to them. Their joy was perfect now for, besides
having saved quite a sum of money, they were proud parents of
two children. The second child was named Suna, which means
"kind and gentle"--On the twelfth of May, 1909, I, the fifth
child, Misao, was born to them. My parents were disappointed--
not because of the number of children, but because I was a
girl. You see, there were four girls and only one boy now!
Unpublished Life History.

[41]Unpublished Life History.

[42]Survey of Race Relations, 64-B.

[43]Perry, op. cit., p. 75.

[44]Sugimoto, op. cit., p. 89. Quoted by permission of
Doubleday, Doran and Company, Inc.

[45]J. H. Longford, Japan of the Japanese, p. 106.

[46]Hearn, op. cit., p. 79. Quoted by permission of The
Macmillan Company.

[47]Unpublished Life History.

Chapter II

[1]Throughout this monograph the mainland situation is considered largely in terms of California. It was the area of first settlement by immigrants from the Orient; most of the Orientals live in this state; the California situation has been in the limelight more than any other and has largely determined the policies of the United States with reference to the Oriental; and more data are available for California than for any of the other Pacific Coast areas.

[2]A California Japanese published his first impressions of Honolulu as follows: "Such extravagant costumes some of the ladies from the land of the cherry blossoms wear; kimonos and obis [broad sashes worn by Japanese women] direct from the Ginza [the main street] of Tokyo, and in the most shrieking colors, red, yellow, orange, blue and green! Kimonoed women with dozing babies tied loosely to their backs, scuffling through the narrow streets nonchalantly in wooden getas [the wooden street shoes of the Japanese] was a surprise or, shall I say, shock to me. Such would be a fascinating scene if sketched in Dai Nippon where majestic Fujiyama, scenic tea gardens, and gleaming temples reign supreme; but painted against a background composed of rattling Ford automobiles, Hawaiian policemen, and concrete buildings, the display appears distinctly out of place. At times one unconsciously wonders whether or not he is still in American territory." The Japanese American News, May 12, 1927.

[3]Japanese American News, May 13, 1927.

[4]Unpublished life history.

[5]We may, in passing, call attention to the irrationality of the color line. The largest white barber shop in the business district of Honolulu draws the line against American Negroes but will serve Porto Ricans, even though they may be coal black. Even though many Porto Ricans are decidedly negroid, they are classed as Caucasians in Hawaii. An illustration from

California also bears out this idea of irrationality. The
principal of a state school was taking a group of visitors
through his institution when the writer, on seeing several
races represented, inquired about the color line. The principal replied that there was no color line and that there was no
discrimination against the colored boys. He went on to say,
"The people of California are big enough to take a better attitude than the people of the South." When asked about those of
yellow color (the Japanese) he said, "Well, I was talking about
human beings."

[6]Governor of the Territory of Hawaii from July 5, 1921, to
July 5, 1929.

[7]In contrast we may note the experience of a Chinese boy in
Chicago. A tall, athletic boy graduated from the University of
Hawaii with a splendid basket-ball record and as a commissioned
officer. He entered Chicago Theological Seminary where, for
his practical field work, he was sent to a metropolitan church
to coach basketball and do boys' work. Although an experienced
boy's worker and basketball player, an American citizen and a
cadet officer, he was rejected. It was felt that the Chicago
boys would not accept a "Chinaman" as a club leader.
A. W. Palmer, Orientals in American Life, p. 115.

[8]The "Eta" class was hopelessly below the lowest class of
commoners. They were not considered Japanese and were commonly
referred to as "things" not as "persons." They were outcasts
who followed lowly occupations which were beneath the dignity
of the commoners. (Cf. Lafcadio Hearn, op. cit., pp. 271-274.)
According to Winifred Raushenbush, the feud which has existed
in the Japanese town of Florin, California, has been due in no
small measure to the presence of a considerable number who are
of Eta origin. A number have settled there in the hope that
they might lose their identity in a foreign country. But the
Eta farmer in California has not been able to escape. As a
consequence one, at least, is working hard to send his sons
through the university in the hope that they, as professional
men, may escape from the traditional stigma in one of the large
cities.
Cf. Survey Graphic, May, 1926, pp. 271-274.

[9]"Haole" is the Hawaiian word for "stranger." In popular usage it has come to be applied to those of north European ancestry. This word has become naturalized in the English language of Hawaii and is found in many of the documents in this volume. Since it is a very convenient word, the author has adopted it in his own discussions.

[10]This behavior on the part of the oriental students, however, is explained in considerable measure by the remainder of the document.

[11]Unpublished document.

[12]Unpublished life history.

[13]From an interview.

[14]See p. 18 for influence of the native Hawaiians on race relationships.

[15]In India the Eurasian, or person of mixed European and Indian blood, is practically an outcast, accepted by neither parental group. He is very sensitive as to his origin and does not speak of his mixed blood.

[16]Cf. W. C. Smith, "The Hybrid in Hawaii as a Marginal Man," American Journal of Sociology, XXXIX (January, 1934), 459–468.

[17]Survey of Race Relations, 309-A.

[18]From an interview with a teacher in Honolulu.

[19]A white student was the winner for the first time in the sixth annual contest which was held on February 13, 1928.

[20]Unpublished life history.

[21]Survey of Race Relations, 424-B.

Chapter III

[1]The Chinese are selected because they can be observed over a longer period than the Japanese.

[2]According to The Eighth Census, Population of the United States in 1860, "405 male and 20 female Chinese are included in the white population" of Oregon (footnote, p. 404); "1 male Chinese" in Nevada (p. 565); "1 male Chinese" in Utah (p. 577); "1 female Chinese" in the Territory of Washington (p. 583); "14 male and 7 female Chinese" in Pennsylvania (p. 438); "1 male and 2 female Chinese" in New Jersey (p. 318).

[3]The following data from The Fifteenth Census, 1930, Population, Vol. II, p. 34, show what has taken place in the Chinese group in the United States from 1890 to 1930.

CHINESE GROUPS IN THE UNITED STATES
FROM 1890-1930

Year	Total	Native Born	Foreign Born
1890	107,488	2,930	104,558
1900	89,863	9,010	80,853
1910	71,531	14,935	56,596
1920	61,639	18,532	43,107
1930	74,954	30,868	44,086

The native-born group increased steadily from 1890 to 1920 but from 1920 to 1930 the increase was greater than in any of the preceding decades. The foreign-born group had been decreasing from 1890 to 1920 but then took an upward swing. Several factors could have been responsible for this increase: (1) the entrance of aliens not in the excluded classes, such as merchants, professional men, and students; (2) children born in China of alien mothers but whose fathers were American citizens; (3) the reëntrance of aliens who had returned to China during the previous decade; (4) illegal entries, principally from Mexico and Canada. There was an increase in the foreign-born group of 979. When this is subtracted from the

increase of 13,315 in the total group, there are 12,336 to be
accounted for through an increase in the second and third generations born in America.

[4]These figures are from Romanzo Adams, The Peoples of
Hawaii, pp. 26-27; and The Annual Reports of The Governor of
Hawaii.

[5]At present there is comparatively little prejudice against
the Filipinos in Hawaii, even though they are the second group
in point of numbers. They are almost exclusively engaged in
manual labor on the plantations and have not become a factor in
any of the preferred occupations. To be sure, there is abundant
evidence that the "Other Caucasians" consider the Filipinos as
distinctly inferior and behave toward them in many ways that
coincide with that belief, but as yet their behavior has not
become highly emotionalized. The Portuguese and Japanese are
more prejudiced against the Filipinos because their status is
more precarious than that of the "Other Caucasians." According
to the Census of 1930, the Chinese, Japanese, Koreans, and
Filipinos constituted more than 64 per cent of the total population of the Territory of Hawaii. Still there is comparatively little prejudice against them because they do not compete
seriously with those of north-European ancestry. The effect of
numbers on prejudice is shown remarkably well in the Dominion
of Canada. According to the census of 1921, British Columbia
had 59.4 per cent of all the Chinese, 94.6 per cent of the
Japanese, and 93.6 per cent of all East Indians in Canada. The
Orientals are concentrated in this one province where they enter into competition with the Whites, and prejudice is probably
stronger there than anywhere else on the Pacific Coast.

[6]For some time the sugar men of Hawaii have been uneasy on
account of the Japanese who constitute the largest population
group in the Territory. Because the Japanese have shown considerable ability in organization and coöperation, the planters
have feared that the sugar industry was at their mercy. In the
post-war period the sugar interests directed a campaign of
propaganda at Congress for the purpose of bringing a modification in the Immigration Law that would permit the importation

of Chinese labor to break the grip of the Japanese. (Cf. Labor
Problems in Hawaii. Hearings Before the Committee on Immigration and Naturalization, House of Representatives, 67th Congress,
First Session on H. J. Res. 158 and H. J. Res. 171, Serial 7—
Part 1, 1921.) The shrewdness of the Japanese became evident
in the strike of 1920. The workers went out on one island
only, while on the other islands they continued at work and
paid benefits from their wages, thus practically forcing the
sugar planters to finance the strike against themselves.
(Albert W. Palmer, The Human Side of Hawaii, pp. 106–07.) Because of this, the Japanese are considered less desirable than
others who have been more docile.

[7]In continental United States, in 1860, there were 33,149
Chinese males and only 1,784 females or 1,858 males to 100
females. The greatest imbalance came in 1890 when there were
2,679 males to 100 females. In 1884 there were in Hawaii
17,243 Chinese males and 1,011 females or 1,706 males to 100
females. In 1900 there were 23,341 Japanese males and only
985 females in continental United States or 2,370 males to 100
females. This was the peak of the imbalance among the Japanese.
The 1900 figures for Hawaii were 47,508 males and 13,603 females or 349 males to 100 females. In 1890 there were 427
males to 100 females in the Japanese group in Hawaii. Several
causal factors enter into this sex disparity. The economic
situation was not one of great security in the earlier years
of the migration. Nearly all the men planned to return home
after a comparatively brief stay and did not bring their wives.
According to the Biennial Report of the Board of Immigration of
Hawaii for 1890, about one-half of the first lot of Japanese
who arrived in Hawaii on February 8, 1885, and about one-third
of the second and third lots returned to Japan on the expira-
tion of their three-year contracts. In the ten-year period
1885-1894, 21,881 Japanese men had arrived in Hawaii and 4,507
had returned to Japan and 692 left for the United States.
The conditions in Hawaii were more favorable to the coming of
women; the plantation worker was assured of a regular wage and
a house for his wife and family, together with certain other
privileges such as free medical attention and free fuel. Furthermore, his wife could work on the plantation and receive a

regular wage. This stability encouraged the coming of Japanese
women to the Islands. In 1885 an agreement was made with the
Japanese government that with every one hundred men there should
be thirty women. The planters advanced the passage money to the
male workers which was repaid in monthly instalments, but the
entire expense of the females was paid by the Government of
Hawaii and no repayment was required. This agreement relative
to the proportion of women was not followed to the letter, however. In the period 1885-1897 there were 39,720 male arrivals
and 9,232 females. The net result of this assisted immigration
was a comparatively high ratio of Japanese women in Hawaii. It
was much higher than on the Coast. With the annexation in 1898,
assisted immigration and contract labor from Japan came to an
end. Then the ratio of women dropped very greatly until the
Japanese Government applied the Gentlemen's Agreement of 1907
to Hawaii thereby stopping the immigration of laborers. The
Gentlemen's Agreement excluded Japanese laborers from Continental United States only, but the Japanese Government, on its own
initiative, extended its provisions to cover Hawaii as well.
After that the female arrivals exceeded the males as the men
were sending for their wives, a considerable number of whom
were "picture brides." There was also an accumulation of
Japanese women in Hawaii through the process of selective emigration. A larger percentage of the men emigrated to the
United States. It was the foot-loose, unmarried men who left.
In the period 1905-1907, there were 24,853 Japanese males mi-
grating from Hawaii to the Pacific Coast and only 1,704 females.

[8]The excess of males has been responsible for the importation of prostitutes or "slave girls." On this problem and its
resultant interracial feeling, see C. G. Wilson, Chinatown
Quest; C. R. Shepherd, The Ways of Ah Sin; C. R. Shepherd,
"Chinese Girl Slavery in America," Missionary Review of the
World, Vol. 46, pp. 893-898; C. C. Wu, Chinatowns, unpublished
manuscript, University of Chicago Library.

[9]According to a computation by Dr. Romanzo Adams of the
University of Hawaii, in 1900 less than 10 per cent of the
Chinese men had wives in Hawaii and less than one-fifth of
this group of married men had non-Chinese wives. Out of a

total of 1,759 wives in Hawaii 375 were non-Chinese. When
Hawaii was annexed to the United States in 1898, the Chinese
came under the Exclusion Act of 1882 and the supply of wives
was thereby cut off. Since the sexes have become more nearly
equal in number, outmarriages among the Chinese have decreased.
See Romanzo Adams, "Further Developments of Race Contacts in
Hawaii," Pacific Affairs, October, 1929, pp. 627-630; Romanzo
Adams, Interracial Marriage in Hawaii, the Macmillan Company,
1937.

[10]They urged that the Chinese be included in the Dyer Bill
(H.R. 2404). This bill made certain provisions for the uniting
of the families of immigrants. According to this, certain members of the family would not be counted in the quota allowed to
each country. On June 13, 1930, Congress approved the admission of Chinese wives of American citizens where marriage occurred prior to May 26, 1924, the date when the quota law was
approved.

[11]"The health officer of Los Angeles County has estimated
that, on the basis of the birth rates quoted and assuming that
all immigration of every kind into the state would be barred
for the future, the Japanese already in California would increase so rapidly that in one hundred years they would outnum-
ber the whites." Japanese American Relations: Causes Which
Produce Friction, leaflet published by Japanese Exclusion
League of California, 1921, p. 6. See also Japanese Immigration and Colonization, pamphlet by V. S. McClatchy, Japanese
Exclusion League of California, 1921, pp. 46-52; California
and the Oriental, by the State Board of Control of California,
1920, pp. 35-41; and Japanese Immigration, Hearings Before the
Committee on Immigration and Naturalization, 66th Congress,
Second Session, 1920. For a criticism of some of these state-
ments, see Y. Ichihashi, Japanese in the United States, pp. 36-
37.

[12]A. W. Palmer, Orientals in American Life, p. 38.

[13]"The different races have lived side by side without seriously competing against each other. The white man has been

the capitalist, the manager, the clerk, the teacher, the 'white-
collared' clan generally. The various races began as plantation laborers and have gradually made their way out into farming, mechanical trades, and retail business. In doing this
they displaced no white working men, for there were no white
men in these positions and the brown men have kept them so
well filled that few white men have come in. All this adjustment consists of what a scientist might call 'symbiosis,' where
two groups live side by side but separately, and in a relationship of mutual accommodation that has made for racial peace in
Hawaii. But will it continue?"
A. W. Palmer, Orientals in American Life, pp. 118-119. Quoted
by permission of the Friendship Press.

[14]This competition is already being felt and has led to a
radical change in the policies of at least one business establishment in Honolulu. A member of the musicians' union in
Honolulu said that the young Orientals, trained in the high
school orchestras of Hawaii, would soon be an important factor.
When that time comes, prejudice will develop against the musicians of oriental lineage.

[15]Op. cit., p. 116.

[16]Cf. W. C. Smith, "The Hybrid in Hawaii as a Marginal Man,"
American Journal of Sociology, XXXIX, 459-468.

[17]There is, however, an exception in the case of some
Chinese. An American-born Chinese man may go to China and
marry, but his alien wife will not be permitted to enter the
United States. His children, however, who are born in China
are American citizens and have the privilege of entry. A boy
could remain with his mother until full grown and then emigrate
to America. Under such conditions he would be Chinese through
and through even though an American citizen. He could then
return to China, marry and have children who also would be
American citizens. The law (Sec. 1993 of the Revised Statutes)
was amended on May 24, 1934, (H.R. 3673) to read: "Any child
hereafter born out of the limits and jurisdiction of the United
States. . . . is declared to be a citizen of the United

States. . . . In cases where one of the parents is an alien, the right of citizenship shall not descend unless the child comes to the United States and resides therein for at least five years continuously immediately previous to his eighteenth birthday and unless, within six months after the child's twenty-first birthday, he or she shall take an oath of allegiance to the United States of America as prescribed by the Bureau of Naturalization.

[18]For a further discussion, see Chapter V, "The Riddle of the Future," in A. W. Palmer's Orientals in American Life, pp. 138-164, especially pp. 161-164.

Chapter IV

[1]This chapter was first written in 1928 and remains practically unchanged in order to present the situation as it was at that time.

[2]By way of contrast, we may call attention to the young men of Anglo-Saxon parentage. In 1928, when a Y. M. C. A. secretary in Honolulu suggested that a group of Punahou High School boys discuss their vocational problems, one boy spoke up and said: "What do we care about these vocational discussions?" "Yes," commented another, "It's all settled; we, the Punahou boys, (The Punahou Schools admit only ten per cent non-whites) will be the lunas (foremen) and the McKinley fellows will carry the cane." (McKinley High School is public and the majority of the pupils are of oriental ancestry.) All in the group gave their approval by laughing heartily.

[3]In 1875 a treaty of reciprocity was entered into between Hawaii and the United States which was favorable to Hawaiian sugar. This arrangement, however, could not inspire the sugar men with the same confidence as did the fact of organic union with the United States through annexation.

[4]Unpublished life history.

[5]Story of Sugar in Hawaii, p. 71. Mr. John K. Butler, secretary-treasurer of the Hawaiian Sugar Planters Association, stated on February 13, 1929, that eighty-five to ninety per cent of the work was done on the piecework system. Cane is hoed by row or acre. Irrigation is done by term contract. In cutting, the man is paid by the number of tons cut. Loading is also paid in the same way. These conditions mark trends of development within the last five or six years. From mimeographed document of Committee on Hawaiian Environment, Division of Research, Department of Public Instruction, Territory of Hawaii.

[6]Ibid, p. 69. See also E. W. Greene, Concerning Oahu Sugar Company, Honolulu, 1928 (pamphlet), pp. 11, 19; Annual Report of the Governor of Hawaii, June 30, 1927, p. 48.

[7]Cf. "Give Hawaii a Square Deal," Address by E. Faxon Bishop, president Hawaiian Sugar Planters Association, to the Delegates to the Press Congress of the World on October 25, 1921. See also W. A. Du Puy, Hawaii and Its Race Problem, pp. 60-73.

[8]Cf. Du Puy, pp. 64-68, for a brief description of certain irrigation projects.

[9]Pp. 49-50. See also E. W. Greene, op. cit., p. 9.

[10]Mr. Victor Ilahibaksh of India said in an address on April 5, 1928: "You do not grow sugar in Hawaii; you manufacture it. You put on a certain amount of fertilizer, a certain amount of water, a certain amount of labor and then you take off a certain amount of sugar."

[11]Since the Republicans do not hold a title in fee simple to the White House, there is considerable uneasiness in Hawaii at the time of a presidential election. The big sugar men are Republicans.

[12]The following quotation from an editorial in The Friend of January, 1930, gives an insight into the situation. "What of the future of sugar? The future of our second basic industry, pineapples, seems assured, but what about sugar? Will the present low price of sugar keep up? No one knows or even dares prophesy what will be the status of sugar five years from now. There are too many variable factors to be taken into account, the political situation both domestic and foreign, the tariff, the undue expansion of the industry, the climatic conditions, economic considerations, sluggish markets, etc., to permit of a safe and sane answer. We may all guess. We may all be hopeful, but how many of us are sure?"

The Jones-Costigan Act which limited sugar production caused much uneasiness in 1934.

[13]This is made very evident by the attitude of the sugar planters at the time of the strike in 1920. Before the strike, workers requested a conference to consider conditions on the plantations but they were met with a flat refusal. The secretary replied, "The Hawaiian Sugar Planters' Association will settle its own industrial troubles." This attitude is revealed in the Hearings Before the Committee on Immigration and Naturalization in 1921.

[14]Nippu Jiji, August 6, 1927.

[15]In public esteem, the farmer follows close upon the heels of the literati. "They are successful farmers and with them farmers have been ranked high in the social scale, far above the soldier and even above the merchant." Kenneth S. Latourette, The Development of China, p. 87. With such a heritage it should not have been difficult to hold the Chinese boys on the plantations, if the conditions had been reasonably satisfactory.

[16]Unpublished life history of a college student.

[17]This idea is discussed further in the chapter on "The School."

Assistant Attorney General Seth W. Richardson reported: "It was everywhere conceded that the more schooling which such

boys were given, the less inclined they were ever to go back
and perform common labor upon a plantation. Many experienced
persons professed entire disbelief that any considerable number
of such boys would ever go back on the plantations, while
others had more or less hope that future years might bring a
change in that regard.

"Not only was the claim that the educational advantages
thus given the pupil were inclining him against plantation
work, but it was vigorously asserted that the parents of the
children of Polynesian or oriental blood were united against
either the return of their children to the plantations or any
change in the educational system calculated to produce that result. All these parents were anxious to get away from the plantations, both for themselves and their children. Curiously
enough, the labor itself does not seem the real objection. The
fact is that such labor is looked on as menial and degrading,
and the racial parents want none of it for their offspring."
(Underscoring mine.) Law Enforcement in the Territory of
Hawaii, Senate Document No. 78, 72nd Congress, 1st Session,
1932, p. 38.

[18]An extract from an article by Riley H. Allen sets forth in
some measure the problem created in Hawaii by the attitude of
the white people toward manual labor. He wrote: "An ideal
held steadfastly in mind by the Territory's educational leaders
is that Hawaii's youths shall recognize the dignity and value
of manual labor. In this sub-tropical country, the inevitable
habit of the white man is to ease existence by the employment
of servants for much household, yard, and stable or garage
work (not to speak of labor in the fields). Just as inevitable
is the reaction upon the minds of young Japanese, Chinese,
Koreans, Filipinos, or Porto Ricans. They see that their parents make up the servant class, and their natural wish is to
get away from that class. Teachers in Hawaii's public schools
who have assisted the newspaper of which I am editor in its
annual home garden and school garden contests have told me many
incidents to illustrate the difficulty of convincing the small
Oriental that he would not 'lose face' (originally a Chinese
expression meaning to lose caste or prestige) if he did manual
labor around the school or in any public place. The best

argument was that of example. When the teachers themselves
took shovel and hoe, or swept the school yard, the pupils
realized that representative Americans were not ashamed of
manual labor, and once learned, that lesson was not forgotten."
American Monthly Review of Reviews, December, 1924, p. 622.
Quoted by permission.

[19]From an interview.

[20]Unpublished manuscript.

[21]The sugar planters did try to secure white labor for the
plantations and a number came from Europe, principally from
Germany, but they did not continue long at ordinary field work.
A number of white men from continental United States started a
farm colony for growing vegetables at Wahiawa, about twenty
miles from Honolulu but the venture was not successful. In
1901, as this project was in process of failing, James D. Dole,
later president and general manager of the Hawaiian Pineapple
Company, planted his first pineapples there. Mr. Dole brought
with him the New England tradition that labor was honorable
and he actually worked in the fields.

[22]The Hawaii Hochi, August 13, 1928.

[23]A question relative to agricultural education was asked of
a group of college students in Hawaii with the following result: the Anglo-Saxons, Chinese, and Hawaiians were almost
unanimously in favor of agricultural education, but practically
all of them were quite far removed from plantation labor. The
Japanese were about equally divided for and against. The significant point was that those in favor lived in Honolulu, while
those in opposition came from the rural districts. Some, who
have expressed an interest in agriculture, have worked on plantations during vacation periods to earn money for school expenses; that was only a means to an end--to the end of making
possible a break from the cane field as soon as possible. Furthermore, summer work of this sort differed from a regular job,
year in and year out.

[24]It is probable, however, that in time an impression will
be made. The Hawaiian Sugar Planters' Association, the most
powerful agency in the Territory, has been hammering away per-
sistently. Restrictions of various kinds are being placed on
the opportunities for a cultural education while efforts are
being made to make technical, particularly agricultural education, more attractive. During the depression the so-called
"frills" have been slashed. If this process continues, there
will be slight opportunity for making any choice—it will be
an education to fit one to be contented on the plantation, if
that is possible, or none at all. See chapter on "The School."

[25]In the spring of 1927, the University announced a two-year,
short course in agriculture and sent notices to all the schools
of the Territory in February and March. On August 3 President
D. L. Crawford stated that out of three hundred applications
for admission to the Freshman class only two applied for the
short course in agriculture and fourteen for the full four-year
course.

One writer endeavored to make the situation with reference to the courses in agriculture appear somewhat more favorable than these figures would indicate by stating that 110, or
30 per cent of the 379 who had taken degrees from the University since 1912, were in agriculture. (Honolulu Star Bulletin,
May 22, 1928.) An examination of the directory of the graduates as published in the University of Hawaii Alumni Magazine
for May, 1928, reveals the fact that only two in this total
were actual "dirt" farmers in the Territory. On the other hand
there were several "verbal" farmers, or those engaged in agricultural extension work or in the teaching of agriculture. The
sugar chemists and technologists, the surveyors on the plantations, those connected with the Pineapple Experiment Station at
the University, and even the manager of a plantation store were
included. In this list of agriculturists there are comparatively few Chinese and Japanese names. The Orientals evidently
have come to the conclusion that the best positions on the
plantations are reserved for those of north-European ancestry;
there is little use for those of color to specialize in agriculture.

[26]*Honolulu Star Bulletin*, January 28, 1928.

[27]Unpublished life history. Used by courtesy of Professor Romanzo Adams.

[28]Cf. Romanzo Adams, *The Education of the Boys of Hawaii and Their Economic Outlook*, p. 29.

[29]*Honolulu Star Bulletin*, September 8, 1922.

[30]According to E. Faxon Bishop, "The industry was pioneered by individuals who either went broke from the financial strain, or consolidated their interests in the companies that are operating today." *Op. cit.*, pp. 6-7.

[31]There is the alternative of governmental ownership and operation of the basic industries. Because of the serious problems to be faced by the sugar industry, this may be the only solution.

[32]"The proportion of citizen laborers on the sugar plantations of Hawaii is not as yet very large but it is growing." A. W. Lind, *Social Process in Hawaii*, May, 1935, p. 3. See Chapter V for the changes taking place.

[33]"The Philippine Problem," *Pacific Affairs*, February, 1929, p. 50.

[34]*Proceedings of the Twenty-eighth Annual Convention, California State Federation of Labor*, September 19-23, 1927, pp. 63-64.

[35]*The Honolulu Star Bulletin*, March 8, 1928.

[36]As an example we may point to a young man of Chinese ancestry who was vice president and general manager of an important automobile sales establishment on the downtown "Automobile Row" in Honolulu. A white man was president of this corporation, and the concern had a number of white employees under the direction of the Chinese manager.

[37]Cf. W. A. Du Puy, op, cit., pp. 73–82 for a brief description of the pineapple industry.

Chapter V

[1]The writer is indebted to Dr. Romanzo Adams of the University of Hawaii for the bulk of the information in this chapter relative to the recent developments in Hawaii.

[2]The figures on employment in the pineapple industry are not available. In 1931 the pineapple pack reached a peak of 12,726,291 cases. The Governor's Report for 1934 (p. 5) states that the pack was "slightly over 5,000,000 cases" in 1932. Many thousands of tons of pineapple have been left in the fields and the planting of new areas has been restricted. This condition has inevitably thrown many out of employment. In 1933 7,815,540 cases were packed.

[3]"The last two years have witnessed considerable change in the attitude of parents toward vocational classes, particularly in agriculture. There is now evidenced a greater interest on the part of both students and parents in vocational agricultural classes." Biennial Report of the Department of Public Instruction of the Territory of Hawaii, 1931-1932, p. 19. See also pp. 13, 27, 39.

[4]Table X indicates that there has been an increase of 148.1 per cent among the Japanese women with American citizenship on the plantations in the period 1931-1934. An increase of Hawaiian-born women on the plantations will be an added attraction to the young men. According to Edgar T. Thompson, the planters are paying serious attention to the matter of attracting the young women. They consider that without them they cannot hold the young men.

[5]See Chapter IV, reference 27 for a description of the old-time plantation foreman. Even though we make considerable

allowance for exaggeration, the resultant foreman would not be
acceptable to the American-born workers.

[6]For a description of the pidgin, see chapter on "Language."

[7]The Governor of Hawaii devoted the first three pages of
his 1923 report to a defense of the Territory. He wrote (p. 1):
   "The people of the Territory of Hawaii have observed with
increasing concern a growing tendency on the part of their fellow citizens of the mainland to classify this organized Territory of the United States as a part of the group of colonies or
possessions that first came under the beneficent influence and
jurisdiction of the United States as a result of the Spanish-
American War or by more recent purchase."
   In the summer of 1934 an item appeared in the Star Bulletin of Honolulu urging that the letters "U.S.A." be stamped on
mail matter to call attention to the fact that Hawaii is a part
of the United States. The same paper had an editorial entitled
"The Possession Obsession." It referred to a number of articles
that listed Hawaii among the possessions. It continued, "may
it be remarked again that Hawaii is not a !possession'? Is
Alaska a 'possession'? Is there not room in a mainland brain
for the concept of TWO territories of the United States?"

[8]Cf., Law Enforcement in the Territory of Hawaii, Senate
Document No. 78, 72 d. Congress, 1st Session.

[9]Undoubtedly Secretary of the Interior, Ray Lyman Wilbur,
assisted materially in calming the troubled waters. Secretary
Wilbur was acquainted with and interested in Hawaii on account
of his connection with the Institute of Pacific Relations which
had its headquarters in Honolulu. He sent his executive assistant, William Atherton Du Puy, to Hawaii in 1932 to study the
racial situation. The Department of the Interior published
his report, Hawaii and Its Race Problem, in 1932. This report
of 131 pages is a fair picture of the situation Hawaii. It is
evident that the author was not swept off his feet by the
"scare" headlines in mainland newspapers.

[10]An extract from a report on the subject of the employment
of citizen labor by the Oahu Sugar Company, written in December,
1931, is as follows:

"There are doubtless a number of factors which have tended
to improve conditions regarding employment of citizens. Some
of these are as follows:

1. Gradual improvement in attitude toward plantation field
work on the part of parents and boys.

2. More local boys growing up to working age.

3. Saturation of various types of employment in Honolulu
which were regarded as socially preferable to plantation work.

4. Wide application of piece-work system to field work.

5. Emphasis on improved living conditions and reasonable community life on plantation.

6. Year-round employment with opportunity to make good earnings.

7. General policies and the interest which has been taken by
a number of the men in our operating staff in encouraging cit
izen labor.

8. The development of methods of training boys for field
work and helping them through the transition period from school
to work. . . .

"A brief statement in regard to item 8 may be of interest.
About 18 months ago we organized a citizens' training gang for
field work made up of boys, mostly local, who were finished
with school, ranging from 16 to 18 years of age. They work as
a regular piece-work field gang at the usual piece-work rates,
sharing the gang earnings on the regular group piece-work system. It is necessary to have a luna who will deal with them
fairly but without mollycoddling. After a suitable period in
this gang they go out into cultivation contracts or regular
field piece-work gangs. After such training a boy goes into a
regular gang knowing how to handle a hoe, pick, shovel, or
fertilizer, gun, etc., knowing how to work, and able to hold
up his end of the work and group earnings with the men in the
gang. We believe that with this method of training there is a
marked improvement in the morale of boys starting work and also
in their chances of finding a reasonable contentment in their
work and staying with it. This training gang is made up mostly
of local boys, although we are now getting a few boys from

Honolulu. I believe that there may be a gradual increase in
the number of Honolulu boys seeking work on plantations, but I
believe that it would be a mistake for a plantation or the association as a whole to attempt to rush any such movement."
Richardson, op cit., p. 193.

[11]For a considerable period of time the conditions in Hawaii
were not conducive to the development of calm thinking and
clear insights on the part of the Japanese. In connection with
the plantation strike in 1920 much unfavorable propaganda was
spread far and wide. While the Filipinos participated in the
strike and actually took the initiative, the planters were
prone to call it a Japanese strike. They declared that it was
a nationalistic movement on the part of the Japanese to gain
control of the sugar industry. The Emergency Labor Commission
that went to Washington emphasized the idea that Chinese were
needed on the plantations to break the control of the Japanese
and thus keep Hawaii American. About the same time certain
conclusions drawn on the basis of a biassed statistical manipu-
lation in a government bulletin declared that in 1940 the electorate would be in control of the Japanese. (See Chapter X.)
From all appearances, the planters reiterated this idea so much
that they came to believe it and became fearful. Under such
conditions they could not be expected to do things to attract
these dangerous aliens and their sons to the plantations. The
Japanese reacted normally to this condition. This situation
was not conducive to calm and clear thinking.

[12]Cf. Exclusion of Immigration from the Philippine Islands:
Hearings Before the Committee on Immigration and Naturalization,
House of Representatives, 71st Congress, 2nd. Session, on
H. R. 8708, pp. 219-220, 266-267.

[13]Assistant Attorney General Richardson said: "I made every
effort to find out what the citizens of the Territory had in
mind to meet such problems but, speaking frankly, I was unable
to find much crystallized thought on this subject. The territorial inclination to 'mahape,' meaning 'put it off until tomorrow,' seems to be particularly applicable to the consideration of the future of the employment problem."
Op. cit., p. 39.

But more to the point is another statement by Mr. Richardson: "Even the controlling business interests of the Territory, in spite of their success in the administration of the industries of the Territory, were also subject to the charge of laxity. For years they have permitted the importation of foreign labor of the lowest grade into the Territory to continue without, until recently, considering any serious attempt to establish an educational system for the island youth suitable to island conditions, and without working out any real employment program for the purpose of carrying on the island industries with island labor. Today I found many of them without any particular ideas on this vitally important subject."
Ibid., p. 20.

[14]Mr. Richardson brought out the following in his report: "Moreover, as was suggested by some of the employers, sheer necessity, in order to prevent starvation, may ultimately cause the island youth to return to plantation work. The fact that the island youth, upon leaving school, can find no other employment, and needs must live, might cause him to return to the plantations."
Ibid., p. 41.

[15]See Presidential Address of John Hind for the planter attitude, Chapter XII, note 3.

[16]Op. cit., p. 41.

[17]A few excerpts will give the tone of the editorial: "When college professors in public utterances enter upon the discussion of serious problems connected with important industries they tread upon dangerous ground and they should use the utmost care even when such problems are connected with sociology. Questions which have baffled men who have spent a lifetime in a business or industry can seldom be solved by a theorist who looks on from the outside and the theories of solution often can do serious harm. . . . It would be well for the University to educate its professors as well as its pupils before permitting members of its staff to make public addresses on economical questions that so vitally concern the Islands....

It is suggested that Dr. Adams be granted leave of absence to
study the sugar industry and pine industry and the homestead-
ing projects with a proviso that he will refrain from further
expressing himself until he knows more about what he is talking
of. He would then be less likely to do harm to Hawaii's industry and to the University of Hawaii."

[18]In 1910 a prominent planter in Hawaii "expressed an earnest desire for a return of the days of the penal contract system when the planters could compel their workmen to live up to
the letter of their contracts. He also said that under the old
regime women had worked all day in the field with infants
strapped to their backs and, if either men or women refused to
obey orders, they were arrested and the court would fix the
penalty--a fine or imprisonment which could be worked out in
connection with the confinement in jail or on the plantation on
which the prisoner had originally been employed." Industrial
Conditions in Hawaiian Islands, House of Representatives, Document No. 53, 63rd Congress, 1st Session, p. 8.

Chapter VI

[1]Access to these trades, however, is somewhat restricted
by the labor unions. See chapter on "Discriminations and Racial Consciousness."

[2]At the University of Hawaii in 1927-1928 twenty-one, or
8.9 per cent of a total of 236 Japanese, chose civil engineering and seven, or 6.3 per cent of a total of 110 Chinese, elected this course.

[3]On the basis of 102 replies from the 1922 graduating class
of McKinley High School of Honolulu, the average monthly
salary for each group was: Anglo-Saxon, $100.00; Portuguese,
$75.00; Chinese, $68.00; Japanese, $67.50; Hawaiian and Part-
Hawaiian, $60.00.
Hawaii Educational Review, June, 1923.

[4]Cf. Curtis Shields, "Industrial Opportunities in Hawaii,"
The Friend, September, 1926.

[5]At the University of Hawaii, out of a total of 236 Japanese students registered in September, 1927, thirty-four, or
14.4 per cent, were taking the pre-medical and pre-dental
courses, and of 110 Chinese, twelve, or 10.9 per cent, had
chosen this course.

[6]This condition is reflected in the registrations at the
University of Hawaii; only two Japanese out of a total of 236
were taking the pre-legal course in 1927-1928 as over against
sixty-three in education and thirty-four in the pre-medical and
pre-dental courses. Three Chinese out of a total of 110 were
in the pre-legal group.

[7]On January 1, 1929, there were 2,483 teachers in the pub-
lic schools of Hawaii and more than a fourth were of Chinese,
Japanese and Korean ancestry. The reports of the Department of
Public Instruction no longer give the ancestry of the teachers.
In the 1932-1933 catalogue of the University of Hawaii six
Chinese and five Japanese names appear in the faculty list. In
the extension division and in the Agricultural and Pineapple
Experiment Stations there are in addition five Chinese and ten
Japanese names.

[8]The Territorial Normal School was merged with the department of education of the University of Hawaii to form the
Teachers College of the University in September, 1931.

[9]See Chapter XII, footnote 2.

[10]The entrance salary in the elementary schools for teachers
with first class certificates is $110.00 per month. The en-
trance salary of a few who hold second grade certificates is
$95.00. The maximum is $150.00. The salaries for high school
teachers range from $130.00 to $200.00. The salaries of regular teachers are paid for twelve months. Under date of August
31, 1934, a letter from the Department of Public Instruction,
states that no new salary schedule has been adopted, but since

1929 two radical changes in practice have taken place. (1) All salaries have been subjected to a flat 10 per cent reduction. (2) The automatic annual increase has been abolished.

[11]Unpublished life history.

[12]Report of the Governor of Hawaii, June 30, 1929, p. 73.

[13]Report of the Governor of Hawaii, June 30, 1932, p. 94.

[14]The writer examined the list of principals of schools in the School Directory for 1935-1936 and in a total of 200 principalships detected what appeared to be twelve Japanese names and fifteen Chinese and Korean.

[15]The following document from a Chinese girl reveals the family opposition. "I became a teacher through the influence of my family. The idea I had uppermost when I was in high school was to become a nurse. My father objected to it very much. He said that a nurse's life was very hard and tiresome. He brought in all kinds of examples to show how terrible it was to become a nurse and how wonderful it was to become a teacher. I tried very hard to convince my father that a nurse's life was just as good as a teacher's life and in fact better because a nurse helped the needy and sick. At last my father·was disgusted with my ideas and said I could do what I pleased about it. This changed my idea a little. On the other hand, my mother said that I should become a teacher because I was weak and not strong enough to become a nurse. She said that a nurse should be strong. She also stated that if I became a teacher I could help them all. I wanted to help them very much and I knew that they all needed my help. At last I asked my brother which was better, a teacher or a nurse. My brother gave me a ready reply saying that a teacher's life was ten times better than a nurse's. I said to myself that maybe a teacher's life was better so, after a great deal of thinking, I changed my mind and went to the Normal School."
Unpublished life history.

[16]Honolulu Star Bulletin, November 4, 1921.

[17]It is reported that on one of the sugar plantations in
Hawaii Chinese were employed in some of the higher positions,
usually reserved for white men. The manager's wife was not
"lily-white"; she was part-Hawaiian. Because of this fact,
the manager could not develop the usual white aristocracy in
the preferred positions for then his wife would feel out of
place. Hence, he could not draw the race lines in the usually
rigid manner.

Chapter VII

[1]For a discussion of the occupational problems of the Japanese, see E. K. Strong, Second Generation Japanese Problem,
pp. 1-22, 208-251; E. K. Strong, Vocational Aptitudes of Second
Generation Japanese in the United States.

[2]The anti-oriental feeling culminated in the Congressional
Act of May 6, 1882, whereby the immigration of Chinese laborers
was suspended for ten years and by several reënactments resulted in actual exclusion.

[3]A Chinese writes: "The young people, educated and trained,
no longer wish to follow their forebears in three-legged economic pursuits, such as being cooks or runners of chop-suey
houses and laundries." Missionary Review of the World, June,
1934, p. 295.

[4]In 1870, out of 2,069 laundrymen in San Francisco 1,333
were Chinese. Census of the United States, 1870, Vol. 1. In
1930 there were 2,343 laundry operatives, owners, managers,
and officials in San Francisco. The figures were not given
for the Chinese launderers in San Francisco, but there were
only 1,188 males and 81 females engaged in this occupation in
the whole state of California in 1930. Census of the United
States, 1930, Population, Volume V, pp. 97, 209.

[5]The Pacific Citizen, quoted in E. K. Strong, The Second-Generation Japanese Problem, . 234.

[6]According to the California Fish and Game Commission (letter of February 21, 1929) the peak year for Japanese fishermen in the state was the license year 1919-1920 when 1,280 licenses were issued to them. Doubtless, the Alien Land Law was responsible for shifting a number from agriculture to fishing. In the year 1927-1928 the number had dropped to 956. According to a letter of August 16, 1934, from the California Department of Natural Resources, Division of Fish and Game, there were 787 licensed Japanese fishermen in the state in the year 1933-1934. The total number of fishermen for the state was 4,991.

[7]It is true that the movement of the second generation into fishing has been slow. But since some have turned to that occupation, others undoubtedly will enter it when old enough. It is highly probable that the uncertainties about fishing have been a retarding factor. Repeatedly bills have been introduced in the California legislature to restrict the Japanese in fishing. Assembly Bill No. 754 was introduced in the Legislature early in 1937 providing that commercial fishing licenses shall be issued only to citizens of the United States. If such a restriction is made effective, the alien Japanese will be forced out of this occupation and will be unable to hand over well-established businesses to their sons.

[8]When George Shima, the "Potato King" of California, died in 1927, the newspapers held him up before the young people as a conspicuous example of a successful man who had started at the very bottom by developing waste lands.

[9]The California Anti-Alien Land Act of 1920 stopped all leasing of land to aliens. A similar law was passed by the state of Washington in 1921. In 1927 the California legislature amended the Land Law to make it possible to investigate the validity of titles to land used by Hawaiian-born Japanese.

[10]"The typical Japanese farmer lives in what is pretty close to a mere hovel. He is clad in dirty overalls. . . . He rises about four-thirty or five in the morning and is out working in the fields before the clock strikes six. . . . He. . . . labors until darkness prevents him from doing any more. Tired from the week's work, he usually rests on Saturday, the farmer's holiday, with apparently no interest in seeking recreation. On Sunday he goes back to the same routine. The farmer's son lives in this atmosphere year in and year out. . . . He knows that the profits of his father are small compared with the amount of time he spends at work." Strong, Second-Generation Japanese Problem, pp. 232-233. Quoted by permission of the Stanford University Press.

[11]Strong writes: "Agriculture offers the greatest opportunity for employment, the establishment of homes, and the chance to prosper. Here the Japanese are wanted, for they are among the best workers and come into the least competition with the Occidental elements of the population. The second generation can lease and buy land and thus establish permanent homes and prosper according to their industry." Second Generation Japanese Problem, p. 233. Quoted by permission of the Stanford University Press. Strong also writes that "agriculture is first choice of Japanese high-school boys." Ibid., p. 219.

[12]According to figures released by the Consulate General of Japan in San Francisco for October 31, 1926, out of a total of 467 American-born Japanese who were employed in the Pacific Coast and Rocky Mountain States 140, or 30 per cent, were engaged in agriculture.

It has been interesting to note that the Japanese-American citizens' leagues have been encouraging the second generation to go into farming. They have urged that young farmers study scientific production and distribution and that they develop coöperation between growers and shippers. Some have concluded that second generation boys in particular would profit more from training in agricultural colleges than in professional schools.

[13]Y. Ichihashi, Japanese in the United States, p. 206. Quoted by permission of the Stanford University Press.

[14]A newspaper editorial in 1927, which presented facts relative to the large amount of pork shipped into California, urged the Japanese to raise hogs for the local market.

[15]According to the Japanese-American Courier of December 29, 1934, the second generation Japanese are becoming increasingly important in the fruit and vegetable markets of Seattle. "Where once almost all the stands were operated by first generation men and women with a few youthful second generation assistants, there are now more and more of these young assistants who are growing up and taking over their parents' duties. Clear, youthful voices, enunciating almost perfect English are replacing the halting syllables of the older generation. . . .
Not only are the second generation fellows entering the field of shipping, but they are also operating their own packing houses. Stressing quality in their fruit and vegetable packing, a few second generation youths are already winning reputations among the city's produce men as packers who can cater to the quality trade.

[16]This chain system operates factories which employ several hundred Chinese in the manufacture of certain lines of their merchandise.

[17]Japanese have long been noted for their manual dexterity and a considerable number of young men have gone into repair work. At first the automobile provided opportunities for repair work and later came the radio.

[18]Survey of Race Relations, 350-A.

[19]A merchant on Market Street in San Francisco said of the Chinese girls: "They dress in native costumes, they attract attention, and they can meet the public. That is why many of them are working as elevator girls and salesladies in big department stores, some as secretaries and others in clerical positions. One girl is a secretary in a radio station and she, too, wears Chinese dress."

[20]"Whereas six years ago there was only one Chinese beauty parlor on Grant Avenue, now there are at least half a dozen in Chinatown."
The Chinese Christian Student, March–April, 1931, p. 5.

[21]In the spring of 1934 the First National Bank of Seattle opened a branch bank in which both Chinese and Japanese tellers were employed.

[22]Letter from Harry M. Shafer, Assistant Superintendent of Schools, Los Angeles, January 8, 1931.

[23]Letter from Willard E. Givens, Superintendent of Schools, Oakland, California, September 19, 1934.

[24]Letter from Worth McClure, Superintendent of Schools, Seattle, Washington, August 28, 1934.

[25]The Registrar of the Territorial Normal School of Honolulu stated in an interview that several Japanese had come from the coast to teach in Hawaii because of the greater opportunity.

[26]According to a letter from the Superintendent of Public Instruction for the state of Oregon, dated August 22, 1934, "So far as this department is informed, there are no teachers of Chinese or Japanese ancestry employed in any of the public schools in Oregon."

[27]There is some indication that their social service activities will extend beyond their own group. According to the Japanese-American Courier of May 19, 1934: "Miss Teru Uno, a member of the Tacoma General Hospital faculty staff, received recognition and reward for six years of courageous up–hill struggle this week when it was announced by Dr. Terry of the Tacoma institution that she had been chosen from a select group of nurses to take up observation work in pathological cases at the internationally famed Mayo Clinic, at Rochester, Minnesota.

This is the first time that the Tacoma hospital is sending a nurse east, and the fact that the first selection is Japanese is an especially high honor, according to hospital officials.

Miss Uno won her first big fight for the right to be a
nurse in this state when she was accepted at the Tacoma General
Hospital Nursing School after being rejected by Seattle Hospital
nursing schools.

At that time both American and Japanese friends rallied to
her cause. As an outcome of that incident, other Japanese
girls who followed in her footsteps have been welcomed at the
various nursing schools."

[28]Unpublished manuscript. On September 1, 1930, the writer
of this document began her service in a Y. W. C. A. on the
Coast. For two years before this she served as director of
religious education in a Japanese church.

[29]Japanese American News, February 27, 1929.

[30]According to the Japanese-American Courier of March 10,
1934, Dr. Hisao Weharo is a second-generation Japanese optom-
etrist who has an American clientele in Oakland, California.

[31]According to the Japanese-American Courier of December 14,
1935, a second generation Japanese girl from the Northwest is
Assistant Director of Bacterial Research with a pharmacological
firm in Cincinnati. After graduating from the University of
Washington, she earned a Ph. D., degree from the University of
Cincinnati. Since 1932 she has been carrying on research on
hay fever pollens.

[32]For the experience of a Japanese electric welder in Long
Beach, California, see Strong, Second-Generation Japanese
Problem, p. 3.

[33]In a letter of October 9, 1934, Mrs. Lily Satow Fujioshi
writes: "I feel that the ambitious second generation who is
seriously training for a business or professional career must
master the Japanese language and also must acquire training
along specialized lines as well as general knowledge.

[34]Japanese American News, September 13, 1928.

[35]Opportunities in the metropolitan dailies, to be sure, are
limited. The gradual growth of the English sections of papers
that were once printed entirely in Japanese, however, is providing an opening for a considerable number of journalism students. This has been responsible for an increasing number of
second-generation students in the school of journalism of the
University of Washington.

[36]In the neighboring Canadian province of British Columbia
the occupational outlook for the young Orientals is not promising. They may not practice law, pharmacy, or dentistry, but
they may practice medicine because the licensing of physicians
is under Dominion control. A recent law is gradually crowding
the Orientals out of the fishing industry. There is a law
which places a handicap against them in agriculture. In this
instance, it is not so much the law as the administration of
it which is vested in a commission that exercises discriminatory powers.

Chapter VIII

[1]Kazuo Kawai, "Three Roads, and None Easy," Survey Graphic,
May, 1926, p. 165. Quoted by permission of the Survey Associates, Inc.

[2]One youth concluded, "even if your college education gets
you nowhere, you can still start a fruit-stand." A. W. Palmer,
Orientals in American Life, p. 143.

[3]For statistical data on the movement to the Orient see
J. F. Steiner in E. B. Reuter, Race and Culture Contacts,
pp. 168-173.

[4]Survey Graphic, May, 1926, p. 165. Quoted by permission
of the publishers.

[5]Cf. Strong, Second-Generation Japanese Problem, pp. 229-230.

[6]_Ka Leo O Hawaii_, May 11, 1927.

[7]Several of these American-born Japanese remained in the Orient. Miss June Goto became a regular member of the faculty of the Doshisha Women's College. Dr. Raymond K. Oshimo assumed the pastorate of the Bancho Kyokwai in Tokyo. Kensuke Kawachi joined the teaching staff of Kwansei Gakuin, Kobe. George Sakamaki has been city editor of the Manchurian Daily News, Dairen, Manchoukuo.

[8]Since the initiation of the Doshisha experiment, several announcements have appeared in the papers both in Hawaii and on the Coast that several mission, as well as government, schools were offering inducements to American-born Japanese to teach English in Japan. Heretofore they have employed American and British teachers but this arrangement has not been entirely satisfactory. High salaries were necessary to attract these instructors. Furthermore, there have been certain difficulties because the majority of them did not know the Japanese language. The editorials urged the young Americans of Japanese ancestry to accept these positions, even though it be for periods not to exceed five years.

[9]A representative of the Tokio Y. W. C. A. said to a group of American educators: "We strongly advise against the coming of great numbers of second-generation Japanese-Americans to Japan where opportunities for work or success are rare in this over-populated country. However, there are always some who must return for some reason or another. All those who return meet great difficulty in finding work, entering schools, or in adjusting themselves to conditions here." _The Japanese-American Courier_, July 21, 1934.

[10]The American-born Chinese are generally of peasant ancestry and encounter a certain amount of class prejudice in China. The Chinese, born in China but educated abroad, usually come from higher social strata and have fewer obstacles to face when they return home.

[11]Survey of Race Relations, 20-B.

[12]Kazuo Kawai, op. cit., p. 166. Quoted by permission.

[13]Cf. Ichihashi, op. cit., p. 391.

[14]Cf. J. F. Steiner in Reuter, op. cit., pp. 168–173 for statistical data. See also Strong, Second-Generation Japanese Problem, pp. 230–231.

[15]The "cockroach doctrine," while perfectly clear to anyone who has ever lived in Hawaii, may be repellent to mainland people to whom a cockroach is not a large and amusing bug, an inevitable accompaniment of life in the Islands, but a small, dirty, repulsive insect indicative of unsanitary conditions and bad housekeeping. From a letter by Dr. A. W. Palmer.

[16]Romanzo Adams, The Education of the Boys of Hawaii and Their Economic Outlook, p. 47.

[17]Hawaii Chinese News.

Chapter IX

[1]"If a boy shows any tendency to give up the quest for a better jób and accepts the job that is always open, field labor, his parents and friends express their disappointment in no uncertain terms. His father tells him that since he has an education he must accomplish something that will honor and help the family. To take a field labor job is to confess failure. The Japanese parents tell their boys that they must be 'Erai hito' (great men) that is, upper class men." (By "great man" the Japanese mean anyone who has a status superior to that of an unskilled laborer. A carpenter, a plumber, or skilled artisan is considered "great.")
Romanzo Adams, The Education of the Boys of Hawaii and Their Economic Outlook, p. 39.

[2]Cf. Kimball Young, Source Book for Social Psychology, pp. 374-378.

[3]Mr. Morishita is a California-born and educated Japanese.

[4]New Japan, January, 1928, p. 26.

[5]For some Chinese girls the names Mrs. White or Mrs. Taylor seem to have more value than Mrs. Chong or Mrs. Lum. Many Portuguese girls prefer Mrs. Jones or Mrs. Scott to Mrs. De Souza or Mrs. Pereiro.

[6]Cf. Mears, op. cit., p. 366, for a case of a Japanese boy who was elected captain of a college baseball team in California.

[7]A Chinese, who was signed by the New York Giants' baseball team of the National League in the spring of 1928, married a white girl. The Hawaii Chinese News of October 8, 1927, reported that the Chinese "Paddock," a noted sprinter had returned to Honolulu with a "quantity of medals, gold watches, and a blushing bride of sixteen."

[8]In California, a person can occupy a position which gives him standing even though he is not at the very top. Oriental labor comes into direct competition with white labor. Furthermore, many Japanese farmers hire white workers in the busy seasons. Hence, not all Orientals are inferior to all white men.

[9]Unpublished life history.

[10]Unpublished life history of a Japanese social worker.

[11]See Chapter II, note 9.

[12]"Kanaka" is the Hawaiian word for "man," but colloquially it is applied to any Hawaiian, old or young, male or female.

[13]"Pake" is the Chinese word meaning "old man," but in the vernacular of Hawaii it is now applied to any Chinese, old or young, male or female.

[14]Unpublished life history.

[15]According to studies made by Dr. A. W. Lind of the University of Hawaii, the Japanese and Portuguese in Honolulu appear to repel each other; in several areas of the city when one group increases, the other decreases by moving out.

[16]Cf. A. W. Palmer, Orientals in American Life, p. 136.

[17]"Home and village life also must be improved so that the plantation worker, instead of being looked down upon as the mud-sill in the economic structure, may come to feel that his life has advantages superior to those of the 'white-collar' worker in town."
Palmer, op. cit., p. 136.

[18]To be sure, some of them might actually be starved back to the plantation where they would be compelled to carry on the status-destroying routine of their fathers. That may be considered the characteristic attitude of the planters a few years ago. A marked change, however, has become evident. See Chapter IV. Very few of the younger generation would accept employment under such conditions.

[19]The Chinese reverence literature and learning above all else. Consequently, men of letters are given a position of dignity and honor; they are ranked highest in the social scale. "Every Chinese boy may be said to have his chance. The slightest sign of a capacity for book-learning is watched for, even among the poorest. Besides the opportunity of free schools, a clever boy will soon find a patron; and in many cases, the funds for carrying on a curriculum, and for entering the first of the great competitions, will be subscribed in the district on which the candidate will confer a lasting honor by his success. A promising young graduate, who has won his first degree with honors, is at once an object of importance to wealthy fathers who desire to secure him as a son-in-law and who will see that money is not wanting to carry him triumphantly up the official ladder."
H. A. Giles, The Civilization of China, pp. 129-130. Quoted by permission of Henry Holt and Company.

[20]See Chapter XVIII.

[21]It has been said that the Japanese meditate about painting pictures that will bring them recognition in the white
group, while the Chinese, with their feet planted more firmly
on the earth, are far more interested in the practical endeavor
of painting their own houses.

Chapter X

[1]Japanese in California, p. 47. According to Strong, Second-Generation Japanese Problem, Table 12, p. 143, there were
2,500 citizens 21 years of age and over in California in 1930.

[2]The group should gradually increase until a peak is reached
in 1943. In 1922 the births among the Japanese in California
reached the highest point and those born in that year will be
of voting age in 1943. According to the Japanese-American
Courier of March 6, 1937, "It is believed there are between
1,400 and 1,500 Americans of Japanese ancestry in King County
of eligible voting age, more than 1,000 of whom are in Seattle.
This contrasts with an estimated 104 in Seattle in 1928, indi-
cating the number coming of age within the past few years."

[3]Personal letter, dated March 25, 1932.

[4]Dr. Romanzo Adams has written relative to the change from
1930 to 1932: "The number of adult citizens, nearly all eligible to vote, has increased by 7,936, as estimated, the number
of registrants by 11,679, and the number of votes cast by
14,030. Male registrants increased by 18 per cent, female by
28 per cent.
    "In 1930, 89 per cent of the men and 73 per cent of the
women were registered, for 1932, 94 per cent of the men and
82 per cent of the women. In 1930, 69 per cent of the "mainly
eligible" (both sexes) voted, and in 1932, 80 per cent.
    "The data relative to registration and voting according to

race are not yet available, but since the Hawaiian and part-
Hawaiian participation was so nearly complete in 1930 the improvement must have been mainly for the white, the Chinese, and
the Japanese, and especially for the women. These striking increases in the vote may be explained by reference to four
things:

"1. There was unusual interest in the 1932 election in
Hawaii.

"2. Certain racial groups, such as those of Chinese or of
Japanese ancestry, have come to participate in politics pretty
recently and there seems to be a steady gain in their interest
as they increase their experience.

"3. Equal suffrage stands for a status for women that is
more or less contrary to tradition and the people are gradually
changing their attitude in such a way that more of the women
vote.

"4. The reduced movement of people, especially of the white
people, means that fewer citizens lost their vote as a consequence of insufficient residence." Administration in Hawaii:
Hearing Before the Committee on Territories and Insular Affairs,
United States Senate, Seventy-Second Congress, January 16, 1933,
p. 106.

[5]Dr. Henry Takahashi of San Francisco, President of the
National Japanese American Citizens League, wrote: "On the day
before the last San Francisco city election my office looked
like the supervisor's room in the city hall. There were five
incumbent supervisors asking me as president of the San Francisco League to endorse them in the next day's election. In
so doing, they promised everything from planting cherry trees
on Post Street to supporting our coming League convention financially.

"It is said, that only Tamotsu 'Floyd' Murayama, our
crack press reporter was granted audience by Pres. Franklin D.
Roosevelt on his election tour of the Pacific Coast last year
when he remarked, 'We have 90,000 (This figure is too high;
see Table VI--W. C. S.) citizens of Japanese ancestry on the
Coast.' The President, who had ignored his remarks until this
time, turned around with a flash and listened intently to
Murayama."
The Japanese-American Courier, January 6, 1934.

[6]From an interview.

[7]The second generation is receiving increasing attention from the politicians. In the spring of 1936 Mayor Smith of Seattle appealed to the Japanese for their votes. He said in a paid advertisement in the Japanese-American Courier of February 22, 1936, that if reëlected he would continue the same fair treatment of the Japanese people that had made them his friends during his first term. On December 17, 1936, the second-generation Japanese of San Francisco held a "victory dinner" celebrating the reëlection of Mayor Angelo Rossi. The Mayor was guest of honor and a considerable group of officials attended, one of whom was Judge Curtis Wilbur of the Circuit Court of Appeals. It is also significant that the Japanese-American Courier of March 6, 1937, has almost a whole page of political advertising in connection with a city campaign.

[8]A Survey of Education in Hawaii, United States Bureau of Education, Bulletin, 1920, No. 16, pp. 12-25.

[9]The Japanese in Hawaii, pp. 20-22.

[10]Administration in Hawaii, p. 107. See note 5 for complete reference.

[11]Despite the fact that the plantation system is so organized that the management exercises widespread control over the workers in the several aspects of life, the employers are left comparatively free in their political activities. "Contrary to current opinion, the plantation lends support to popular democracy in the Islands by encouraging its employees to exercise their rights as voters. They frequently provide transportation for their employees to the polling places. . . . Whatever the political pressure upon the plantation voter may be the balloting seems to indicate that he relies upon his own judgment within the privacy of the voting booth. This emancipation from plantation influence may be expected to increase as the numbers of citizen laborers grow." A. W. Lind, Social Process in Hawaii, May, 1935, pp. 3-4.

[12]The Nippu Jiji, November 7, 1926.

[13]Unpublished life history.

[14]In the campaign of 1928 the secretary to a prominent part-Hawaiian telephoned an Anglo-Saxon that they had decided to crowd Mr._____ off the Republican slate; they were urging all to vote for the Hawaiians on the ticket.

[15]According to several observers, the success of one Haole politician in Hawaii has been due in no small measure to the fact that his Hawaiian wife accompanied him during the campaigns and would sit by his side on the speaker's platform.

[16]Administration in Hawaii, p. 111. See note 5 for complete reference.

[17]These same Chinese have been reëlected twice since then and several others of oriental ancestry have also been elected.

[18]Dr. A. W. Lind has written relative to racial blocs: "The fear, so frequently expressed, that each of the racial groups will vote as a unit is without foundation judging by the experience thus far. No candidate for office would think of campaigning on a racial basis; to do so, even in a district with a high concentration of voters of his own ancestry, would be to court disaster. A study of the last four biennial elections in Honolulu reveals the fact that although the political novice may draw support specifically from his own racial group, he cannot be elected upon the basis of such support. The experienced and successful politician, on the other hand, inevitably alienates many voters of his own racial ancestry. The most active opposition to Chinese and Japanese candidates in recent elections has come from organizations within the same ethnic groups. There is clear evidence that in the case of some of the more experienced Haole and Hawaiian politicians, a majority of the citizens of their own ancestry voted against them. This is particularly true of the Haole Democrats and the Hawaiian Republicans in Honolulu." Social Process in Hawaii, May, 1935, p. 5. Cf. also Administration in Hawaii, pp. 110-112, 128-130.

[19]*The Pacific Herald*, November 5, 1928.

[20]*Japanese American News*, October 23, 1927.

[21]The anomaly is set forth by a Japanese college man in Hawaii: "I am an American citizen of oriental ancestry. One of the things which hurts me deeply is the attitude that some 'white' Americans have taken towards us in this R. O. T. C. controversy. Simply because we object to a system which to our thinking is un-American and comparable to the Prussian military scheme prior to 1914, these white men say that we are 'ungrateful, traitorous Japs.' God knows we are moved to oppose compulsory military training by as deep a love for the stars and stripes as any man can have. I, for one, have expatriated myself from Japan, and my whole heart and allegiance goes to the United States. We Americans of oriental ancestry are in a precarious situation. There are some people who are continuously trying to ferret out something to charge against us. Our speech, our actions, everything comes under their strict surveillance, and great is the joy of these self-righteous critics whenever they can pounce on something that they can twist into a race issue, challenging our assimilability and our loyalty. Well, I suppose we can't expect life to be a bed of roses without thorns." *The Christian Century*, April 1, 1926.

[22]*The Boston Transcript*. For a further statement from Governor Farrington see Ichihashi, *Japanese in the United States*, p. 376.

[23]This system was followed by the United States up to 1907. Cf. U. S. 34, Statutes, 1929.

[24]Cf. Ichihashi, *Japanese in the United States*, pp. 323-324.

[25]Contrary to much of the popular propaganda, the government of Japan has facilitated the expatriation of the American-born children. The amendment to the Law of Nationality in 1924 made it difficult for the children born in America to retain Japanese citizenship. The children had to be registered

within two weeks and for some Japanese living in out-of-the-
way places on other islands or in rural places on the mainland
this would be almost impossible. Doubtless, the Japanese Government saw in this an opportunity to remove a source of irri-
tation. The Japanese consuls resident in America have been
advising expatriation from Japan.

[26] In recent years the Japanese American Citizens League has
been urging the young people to expatriate themselves from
Japan.

[27] On the other hand, a considerable number of parents failed
to register their children with the consulates before the law
was amended in 1924. According to R. L. Buell, "Out of a total
of 2,345 Japanese births in the State of Washington for the
years 1915-1917, only 1,770 were registered with the Japanese
consulate."
American Journal of International Law, Vol. 17, p. 34.

[28] "Why Japanese Parents in Hawaii Register Their Children
as Citizens of Japan," The Universal Review, August, 1928,
pp. 10-11.

[29] Adams, loc. cit.

[30] The political ideas of the second-generation Japanese on
the Pacific Coast give evidence of quite thorough Americanization. It appears that they vote the Republican ticket and,
like good Republicans, they are painfully distressed by the
Reds and Communists. The third biennial convention of the
Japanese-American Citizens League, which was in session in San
Francisco the first week in September, 1934, passed the following resolution: "Be it resolved that the Japanese-American
Citizens League coöperate with and support any organization
or governmental agency to expel and deport from the United
States such undesirable alien communists who are found guilty
of subversive acts toward our nation regardless of race, creed,
or nationality." Could anything be more Republican or more
American!
     In the summer of 1935 one of the leaders among the young

Japanese of the Northwest made a tour of western Washington in
company with a party of Republicans when he made many speeches
in support of "the back to the Constitution" movement.

[31]Unpublished life history.

[32]The value which many girls place upon their citizenship
may be realized in some measure in connection with their marriage choices. Many will not select foreign-born mates who
are ineligible to naturalization because they would then lose
their citizenship. This is not a mere matter of theorizing;
they have seen what has taken place in a number of instances.
Several did not realize at the time what it meant to lose their
citizenship but later came to regret the loss. A change has
now come in this respect. The Cable Act, signed by President
Hoover on July 3, 1930, and amended in the Third Session of the
Seventy-First Congress, provides that an American woman shall
not forfeit her citizenship, even though her alien husband may
be ineligible to citizenship because of race, nationality, or
other causes. It also permits women who have previously lost
their citizenship by marriage to ineligible aliens to become
repatriated without submitting to a long naturalization process.

[33]Unpublished life history.

[34]Unpublished life history.

[35]Ralph S. Kuykendall, Hawaii in the World War, pp. 41-42.

[36]Cf. ibid., pp. 176, 320-321.

[37]By way of contrast to the Pacific Coast area of the United
States, we may note conditions in British Columbia. The Canadian-born children of oriental parentage do not have the privilege of voting in that province. Many consider this a serious
handicap. Because they do not have the franchise, many discriminatory laws have been passed against them and they have
no defense. This denial of the franchise makes the future uncertain. The young Chinese in Vancouver appear to be sullen
and bitter because of this condition. Since they are not

permitted to participate as Canadian citizens, they cannot take
any vital interest in local affairs.

Some in both Chinese and Japanese groups have suggested
that the matter of franchise be carried through the courts
where they believe the denial of suffrage would be declared un-
constitutional. British Columbia will not surrender without a
hard fight, for they have taken a strong stand against granting
this privilege to Orientals and their Canadian-born descendants.
On several occasions, moves were made in the Dominion Government at Ottawa to grant the franchise, but British Columbia
has been able to block everything thus far. About ten years
ago the Labor Party began a consideration of the enfranchise-
ment of the Orientals, but such strong opposition developed
that it was abandoned. The net result of this situation is
that there is considerable feeling between the races in British
Columbia.

This situation tends to direct the attention of the
Chinese to China. A young professional man in Vancouver said:
"The Canadian-born children of oriental parentage are not given
the franchise in British Columbia and this is a very serious
matter. As I see things now, the only hope is in doing our
best to help develop a stable government in China and then secure her support in a boycott on British Columbia in order to
gain the franchise. The people of China know how to use the
boycott and, doubtless, will be willing to help us. If the
longshoremen in China refuse to unload ships that clear from
British Columbia ports and the Chinese people refuse to buy
their goods, that would exert a great influence. The oriental
trade of this province is a very important factor; without
that Vancouver would dwindle away. Ships from other Canadian
ports would be handled and that would place British Columbia
at a great disadvantage. A number of young men have been considering this course of action, and it seems to be our only
hope. This would not be disloyalty to Canada, but it would be
merely a means to compel British Columbia to give the Canadian-
born Orientals the same treatment that the other provinces accord them, for this is the only province that denies them the
franchise."

Within the last few years The Japanese Canadian Citizens
Association has initiated a movement to win recognition as

full-fledged citizens of Canada. The Canadians of oriental ancestry are nominal citizens only, without the right to vote.
With several lines of economic endeavor and several professional
fields closed to them they are pushed into the category of
aliens. This situation, quite naturally, has retarded expatriation of the young Japanese. According to a survey conducted by
the Japanese Association of Canada there were more than 11,600
Canadian-born Japanese in British Columbia handicapped by the
lack of full citizenship rights.

[38]In the campaign of 1928 there was one discordant note when
a stump-speaker for the Democratic party said: "Why elect this
Jap to the house? It is bad enough to have a Jap for the deputy
city and county auditor. He ought to be deported to Japan where
the rest of the Japs belong. Besides it is un--American to have
him on the job. Are we Democrats to stand for a Jap in the
house?" This, however, is not to be considered typical, but
rather a part of the "mud-slinging" in which the Democrats indulged rather freely during the campaign. Furthermore, an independent paper declared that this particular stump-speaker
was a source of embarrassment to the Democratic leaders and was
not truly representative of the party.

Chapter XI

[1]It is very much as a Chinese who was educated in England
said of himself when asked if he was a Christian: "I was con-
firmed at Public School--they made it a part of the course as
they did cricket and footer--and I took it all as part of the
English I was there to learn."
Louise Jordan Miln, Mr. and Mrs. Sen, p. 191.

[2]Unpublished life history.

[3]Unpublished life history.

[4]Unpublished life history.

[5]Unpublished life history.

[6]In this new community, an Englishman was giving a series of talks on Buddhism. One might conjecture what was the effect on the boy when he saw a <u>white</u> man professing the unpopular religion. Did that give him courage to come out openly?

[7]The Japanese people have been remarkable for their spirit of religious toleration. Shintoism is uniquely tolerant in its attitude toward other religions. Buddhism, which came from India, has historically exemplified in a high degree its ability to make accommodations to other religions.

[8]A Japanese daily newspaper published in Honolulu.

[9]Unpublished life history. Used by courtesy of Dr. Romanzo Adams.

[10]From an interview.

[11]Unpublished life history. Used by courtesy of Dr. Romanzo Adams.

[12]From an interview.

[13]A Japanese college graduate in Honolulu has made the suggestion that the whole problem of these dormitories be made the subject of a thorough-going study.

[14]A Japanese social and religious worker said that the Hi-Y will have to change its methods or it will not meet the needs of the boys and young men in Hawaii. A secretary who has been trained in a mainland Y.M.C.A. college and in the summer conferences will not necessarily fit Hawaiian conditions. When he tries to make live and boisterous American boys out of the quiet Japanese and teaches them to throw their hats to the ceiling and "make whoopee" when they enter the Association building, he is developing in them traits which will create friction between parents and children. Some Americans advocate activities such as "Father and Son Banquets" in order to develop a better understanding between parents and children.

When one considers the situation in the Orient where, among
other formalities, the children must address their parents with
certain honorific terms, one can imagine the expression on the
face of a Japanese father if his twelve-year-old boy, in American fashion, slapped him on the back and called him "Dear old
dad." Programs manufactured in New York City are often misfits
in Hawaii!

[15]There is no adequate statistical measure available to show
the actual situation with reference to the religious affiliations of the young people. Some figures are available for
Hawaii, but they are so inadequate that any presentation would
confuse rather than clarify. On the basis of observation, we
may conclude that Buddhism has a stronger grip on the Japanese
of Hawaii than on the Coast. In Hawaii the Japanese form the
largest group; they can continue more of the old country practices and there is less break in their religious life. The
second generation in Hawaii can use the mother-tongue more
fluently and, on the whole, are not so far removed from their
parents as on the Coast. In Hawaii there is less danger of en-
countering ridicule on account of professing Buddhism.

[15]An Hawaiian-born Japanese, for three years resident on the
mainland as a student at the Chicago Theological Seminary,
wrote of this:

"The interest of the new generation in Christianity is not
in speculation relative to its religious terminology. The tension does not lie in the definition of God. The new generation
is not concerned with speculation about God. Whether God is
made real or less real through the scientific interpretation of
the universe and the modern psychological interpretation of
man's mind and body is not a question that will stir him to
any violent emotion. The new generation is ethically minded.
His life is motivated by the conscious desire of living in
harmony and coöperation with the white Americans and to understand the other groups of American citizens of other racial
descent. Consciously or unconsciously the new generation faces
the problem of bringing about interracial amity and understanding. This attitude will approach religion, therefore, ethically. The new generation believes and affirms that in the name

of Christianity the diverse groups of people with different
cultures and traditions, living under the same flag, can understand each other. He hopes positively that Christianity offers
the key to spiritual understanding which otherwise cannot be
had."
Ken Kawachi, "The Second Generation and Religion in Hawaii,"
New Japan, January, 1929, p. 20.

[17]Unpublished life history.

[18]For a further discussion, see Palmer, Orientals in American
Life, pp. 63-64, 165-197, especially pp. 179-184.

                          Chapter XII

[1]For certain detailed information see Reginald Bell, Public
School Education of Second-Generation Japanese in California,
Stanford University Press, 1935.

[2]According to Bulletin 16, 1920, of the U. S. Bureau of
Education, tuition fees have been charged. We quote from p. 66:
"At present (1920) a tuition fee is charged all those who attend the Maui High School. The purpose of charging such a fee
is thereby to exclude children of plantation laborers who, it
was thought, could not or would not pay the tuition. This practice, the commission must point out, is discriminatory and un-
justifiable and should be abandoned. A public high school must
be kept open to the poorest and humblest boy or girl of the
territory, and his way made as easy as possible if the school
is to accomplish the work which it is organized expressly to
do. Charging a tuition fee in order that the school may be retained largely for the children of the more prosperous people
is a plan which will defeat the very purpose for which our public schools are established."

[3]The address by John Hind presents the point of view of the
planters, as follows: "In order to meet the demands of our

agricultural developments, laborers in large numbers have,
from time to time, been brought into the territory, thereby en-
abling its industries to operate and expand. The offspring of
these laborers, have, however, absorbed different ideals from
those of their parents, and while it may be considered un-American to criticize by a word any phase of education, it seems
very evident particularly in view of the fact that the welfare
of this territory is dependent upon agriculture, that our system of education is not all that it should be." [He goes on to
tell about the mounting costs for school buildings and teachers,
and that this situation should be alleviated by other means
than by adding to the tax burden.] "The responsibility should
be up to the parents, and without doubt a closer contact with
life's actual problems would, in the end, prove of much greater
value to them than an indefinite continuance in school. This
is a question, it seems to me, for the laymen to decide. . . .

"Furthermore, the student by spending many years in free
schools and each day parading the streets with an imposing ar-
ray of books under his arm, in time believes himself the superi-
or of any but the few who, by special ability, or good fortune,
occupy the higher positions, and he naturally expects, by his
assumed qualifications, to occupy such positions, taking it for
granted such positions will be waiting for him when he is
ready. . . . The final results, in many cases, will be the 'big
head'. . . . The solution, as I see it, is that the taxpayer
be relieved of further responsibility after the pupil has
mastered the sixth grade, or possibly the eighth grade, in a
modified form. This does not imply by any means that education
necessarily ceases, but the boy and girl are placed on their
own resources and with such talents as they possess will gravitate to the positions or employment for which they are best
fitted or may qualify. . . . My point is, why blindly continue
a ruinous system that keeps a boy and girl in school at the
taxpayers' expense long after they have mastered more than sufficient learning for all ordinary purposes, simply to enlighten
them on subjects of questionable value. . . . By entering some
field of employment they will, besides earning wages, be gaining in experience and efficiency, and above all learn to appreciate the value of a dollar by working for it; and at the age
when boys under our present school system are supposed to

graduate, he will have established a position for himself,
while the boy of more extended book learning may require a long
period in which to unlearn. . . .

"It is sometimes assumed, the young man, failing to secure
the gentlemanly occupations, for which presumably his schooling
has qualified him, will gravitate to occupations of less dignity. Some of them undoubtedly will, but you can rest assured
there will be large numbers constituting a disappointed, dissatisfied and disgruntled class, with hopes of any easy living
blasted, many of them will become wasters or worse, and with
nothing to lose, are ready followers of any rabid agitator.
The sooner the public appreciates the possible results of this
extremely expensive free education and realizes, besides book
learning, it is necessary that actual experience be acquired
in the school of 'world's hard knocks,' the better. . . . The
prevailing system of having the young people occupy a position,
free from any thought of responsibility, up to the age when
they should properly have some of their life's problems definitely settled, is wrong, for besides being a heavy burden on
the taxpayer, in a great many instances, it places the young
people at a very considerable disadvantage. . . .

"I may appear rather pronounced in my criticism of our educational system, but with all due respect to the learning,
ability and honesty of purpose of our educators, the alarming
increase of our budget for public instruction certainly calls
for some pronounced measures to get it down to a more practical
and business basis, a basis conforming nearer to what the
people really need, and what the country can reasonably support.
To accomplish this it will undoubtedly be necessary to have the
interest, coöperation and assistance of some of our practical,
conservative men, rather than to depend too much on men, who
by their training and devotion to learning, have become unduly
idealistic and hence extravagant."
Honolulu Star Bulletin, November 16, 1925. For an interesting
comment on this address, see The Nation, December 23, 1925,
p. 722.

[4]At a public hearing conducted by the educational committee
of the Territorial Legislature in the spring of 1929, a man
stated that he had paid $42.50 in fees for two children in a

public junior high school. This was admitted as being correct
by the principal of the school.

[5]According to the Governor's Report for June 30, 1932, provision was made "for a tuition fee of $100 a year, placing
within the board of regents, however, the discretionary power
to waive entirely or to reduce such fee in case of students upon whom the payment of such fee would work undue hardship, p. 9.

[6]A recent proposal to adapt the schools to the plantation
system has been made by President D. L. Crawford of the University of Hawaii. He accepts the present plantation system without any question as being the best for Hawaii. He admits that
the schools have not fitted the young Orientals for the prevailing system of agriculture. According to his scheme, all
the youth are to work on the plantations. The educational opportunities for the majority are to be greatly restricted while
a few outstanding ones are to be given opportunities to train
for the professions and certain preferred occupations.   The
plantation work will not be attractive, but continuation
schools are to be provided to make these workers more satisfied
with their lot. He writes: "The continuation school must not
be a vocational school. It must be a means of getting away
from one's job temporarily, rather than learning more of the
techniques that are supposed to go with the job. The best
place to learn those techniques is while one is at work. Let
the continuation school be a brief excursion into another
world, and it will be found that the laborer works better and
more effectively as a result of it. . . .
    "There is no good reason why the social order should not
provide a means of gratifying this natural craving for excur-
sions into another mental world throughout the entire period
of adult life. This, of course, must be on a voluntary basis."
Paradox in Hawaii, The Stratford Co., Boston, 1933, pp. 246-
247 and passim.

[7]Honolulu Star Bulletin, November 17, 1928.

[8]Dr. Ng Poon Chew in Japanese American News, January 1,
1928.

[9]_Annals of the American Academy_, January, 1921, pp. 111-112.

[10]Nevertheless, a large number of Japanese wish to return to the homeland, provided they can locate themselves well. The fact that on the average some five hundred men, three hundred women and one thousand children per year go to Japan and remain there would bear this out. In the minds of most of the Japanese immigrants there is a state of indecision and they are holding a return to the old country as one of the possibilities. In many ways they would have a better status in Japan. In the American communities they are nobodies,--and to this they are quite sensitive. When many return to the Orient, however, they are disappointed because the actualities do not measure up to their idealizations. Furthermore, the children have difficulties in making adjustments in the Orient. All these uncertainties have their effect on the education of the second generation. These problems will be present in some measure until the immigrant generation shall have passed off the scene.

[11]Unpublished life history.

[12]Survey of Race Relations, 116-A.

[13]Letter written to school official.

[14]Since the school attendance figures for the Chinese and Japanese are not tabulated by nativity they include some temporary students from the Orient. Nevertheless we may assume that the vast majority of the oriental population in the school-age group are native-born. Hence the data concerning school attendance may be applied to this group with slight, if any, correction.

[15]Cf. Winifred Raushenbush, "Their Place in the Sun," _Survey Graphic_, May, 1926, p. 203.

[16]_Ibid._, p. 143. Quoted by permission of the _Survey Graphic_.

[17]The year 1920 is the mid-point in Table XV.

[18]According to the <u>Annual Report of the Governor of Hawaii</u> for 1927, p. 78, the larger pineapple canneries of the Islands employed 2,461 school boys and 2,802 school girls, a total of 5,263, during the summer of 1927. The school children constituted 36 per cent of the total number of employees. The same report also states that 476 school children were employed part-time on the sugar plantations during the year 1926 and 4,308 were employed full-time during the summer vacation.

[19]Unpublished life history.

[20]Thirteen Japanese in the University of Washington appeared on the honor roll of the winter quarter of 1933-1934. In the spring of 1934 eight Japanese earned either valedictory or salutatory honors in the high schools of the Pacific Northwest.

[21]<u>The Pacific World,</u> Vol. 1, pp. 74, 92.

[22]<u>Comparative Psychology Monographs</u>, Vol. III, No. 15, p. 56.

[23]Unpublished life history.

[24]In our democratic schools, pupils are taught, in theory at least, that one person is as good as another. When this idea is carried into practice by the children of Orientals in America it may often be quite shocking. When the Japanese of Honolulu gave a reception to the Japanese crown prince as he was returning home from America in 1928, according to a report, an American-born Japanese girl rushed up to the prince, held out her hand, and said, "Oh, I'm so glad to see you." The Japanese Consul said that she ought to be shot. This act outraged the immigrant Japanese who were accustomed to the formalities and ritual of the Orient.'

Chapter XIII

[1]Pidgin or pidgin-English is the name applied to the

language of trade in many Chinese and other oriental ports.
It is a jargon made up for the most part of corrupted
English words, but having a small number of Chinese, Portuguese,
and other words. In Hawaii, English and Hawaiian words pre-
dominate, but the Portuguese, Chinese, Japanese, and Filipinos
have made contributions.

[2]For a further discussion of the Hawaiian pidgin, see
W. C. Smith, "Pidgin English in Hawaii," American Speech,
February, 1933, pp. 15-19; J. E. Reinecke, "Hawaiian-Island
English," Mid-Pacific Magazine, March, 1933, pp. 273-278;
J. E. Reinecke, "The Competition of Languages in Hawaii," So-
cial Process in Hawaii, II (May, 1936), pp. 7-10.

[3]Honolulu Advertiser, May 11, 1924.

[4]The following letter from a Japanese was published in the
Honolulu Advertiser, December 15, 1931.
"Excuse ples sir:
Des tame too much like paper talk. Other man too much no
pololei talk-talk. Whasa mater thes man 'SUBURBANITE! speak
no gurra roads outside gotch.
     Roads too much gurra this time, we all time eggs hapai
no one time broke. Dis tam truck too fast go, bottle no broke.
     Maybe thes man 'SUBURBANITE' too jealous—he quick speak
like job work on road for Territor, what you call this kin
'Kapakahi Haole,' he speak no pololei talk. Only money like,
think so.

                    Yours truly, truck haul man."

[5]In a vocabulary test given to the seniors of McKinley
High School in Honolulu in the autumn of 1928, a student of
oriental ancestry made the highest score.

[6]The following is a specimen of the language heard in some
Chinese homes in America. "Long teem before (a long time ago)
mi hab see one piece Melican (American) joss pidgin man (missionary) Canton side. He talkee mi Melica side one man alla
same 'nother man, maskee (no matter if) he poor man, richee man,

white man, black man, Chinaman, any fashion man, he can stop
this side, mandolin (government) take care he alla same. Mi
fear he talkee lie pidgin (told a lie). Melica side no ploppa
(proper) maskee (never mind). Spose Ilishman (Irishman) no too
muchee bobbery, mi can stop two, three year, catchee littlee
chancee, takee that dollar, buy shilling billee (exchange)
takee steamer, go back Canton side." (C. C. Wu, <u>Chinatowns</u>,
unpublished Ph. D. dissertation, University of Chicago, p. 278.)

[7]<u>A Survey of Education in Hawaii</u>, United States Department
of the Interior, Bureau of Education, Bulletin, 1920, No. 16,
pp. 37-38.

[8]Henry J. Allen, ex-governor of Kansas, after a visit to
Hawaii, published the following statement: "Sociologists, race
students, international philosophers, and practical politicians
will seek in vain to alarm us in the future about the Japanese
situation in Hawaii. We've found the last proof of the assimil-
able qualities of the Japanese. We discovered in a Japanese
newspaper, the immortal comic strip, 'Bringing up Father.' No
people can read the daily story of 'Jiggs' and 'Maggie' unless
they take on our culture."
<u>The Binnacle</u>, newspaper of the University Cruise on S. S.
Ryndam, October 27, 1926.

[9]In the summer of 1924 an American college professor took
a party of students to Japan. There were several American-born
Japanese in the group and the director thought that one in particular would be useful for making speeches in the vernacular.
He did make a speech on one occasion, but it was in English and
an American missionary translated it into Japanese.

[10]A college girl in Hawaii wrote of herself: "I have suffered humility and timidity because of my lack of Japanese.
The Haole friends I have raise a skeptical brow when I admit
to them that I am not able to translate a simple sign or advertisement for them. And to save me the embarrassments and
regrets I am facing now, my parents, though far from rich,
spent money on my tuition and supplies and they were willing
and eager to give more if I had desired more knowledge."
Unpublished life history.

[11]According to an editorial in the Courier of January 1,
1934: "It was on January 1, 1928, that The Courier set sail
on uncharted seas. Today, after six years The Courier is sail-
ing on but many of the seas have been charted through bitter
experience. Four years of the Courier's short life have been
passed during one of the worst economic depressions in the history of the nation. Coming comparatively unscathed through the
depression has given the Courier greater confidence and
strength." According to an editorial in the issue of January 1,
1937: "The Courier outgrew its five-columned dress of gloss
paper and by 1930 had taken on seven-column newsprint dress.
On May 19, 1934, The Courier expanded to its present eight
columns."

[12]The following table gives the data for the Language
Schools in Hawaii.

ORIENTAL PUPILS IN LANGUAGE SCHOOLS IN HAWAII, 1922-1934

Racial Descent			Year			
	1922	1924*	1926	1928	1932	1934
Chinese	1,314	1,162	2,220	2,176	2,478	2,714
Japanese	21,448	15,687	26,768	33,607	40,017	41,192
Korean	126	225	468	732	522	646

*These figures are not necessarily correct. The language
schools were in litigation and not all made reports to the Department. Some of the figures were estimated.

     Data from Biennial Reports of the Department of Public
Instruction.

[13]"Serious study of the oriental language is not likely to
be undertaken until with approaching maturity there comes a
realization of the value of this linguistic knowledge in securing positions in the business world. Those who can afford
to do so may return to the Orient for such language study while
others make belated efforts to gain the needed proficiency in
this country. The courses in the Japanese language offered at
the University of Washington are attended by considerable

numbers of second generation Japanese who for one reason or another made little progress in this language during their earlier
childhood. Ordinarily a thorough knowledge of the Chinese or
Japanese languages is gained only by those American-born Orientals who have had the advantage of residence and study in the
Far East."
E. B. Reuter, Race and Culture Contacts, pp. 175-176. Quoted
by permission of the McGraw-Hill Book Company.

[14]Unpublished life history.

[15]For a brief discussion of the Japanese Language Schools,
see Bell, op. cit., pp. 17-26; 98-103; Strong, Second-Generation Japanese Problem, pp. 201-207; Romanzo Adams, The Friend,
August, 1925, p. 178; September, 1925, pp. 197-198.

[16]Annual Report of the Governor of Hawaii, 1922, p. 6.

[17]Orientals in American Life, p. 54. Quoted by permission
of the Friendship Press.

Chapter XIV

[1]Survey of Race Relations, 332-A.

[2]Unpublished life history.

[3]Survey of Race Relations, 81-A.

[4]In the lower grades of the schools there is practically
no difference as between Hawaii and California. Because of the
comparative absence of race prejudice and the free intermingling of the races in Hawaii, they arrive at the parting of the
ways at a later age. Furthermore, the social distance between
the two groups increases at a more rapid rate in California
than in Hawaii.

[5]This stands out more strikingly on the Pacific Coast where the pupils of oriental ancestry form small minorities in the student bodies of the schools.

[6]Home influence is an important factor in the development of attitudes. Certain homes, no matter of what race, harbor traditional prejudices which they transmit to the younger generation. Even in Hawaii, many parents are adverse to their children's association with those of other races. Certain oriental homes also develop prejudices against the white group. A young Chinese in Hawaii whose father had lived in California for some time wrote of the influence in his home: "When I was in the lower grades my parents strongly objected to my acquaintance with Haoles. They had the foolish idea of calling foreigners 'devils' and they called the white race the 'white devils.' They said that I should not make the acquaintance of these 'white devils' because they were dangerous."

The attitudes which the parents have toward other groups and races in America are often determined by conditions elsewhere. Many Koreans are bitter against the Japanese on account of the situation in the homeland. There is also considerable evidence of feeling between many Chinese and Japanese. A Chinese college girl in Hawaii reveals this fact. She wrote: "At this time China was staging a war with Japan over the Shantung Province. The Japanese children in school jeered at me so much that I could have killed everyone of them. I told them that if the United States should ever fight Japan I would shoot every 'Jap' on the island of Oahu. Expecting the answer they said that they would kill every Chinaman and Haole in Waipahu so they could be admirals in the Japanese navy. That made me so furious that I have never forgiven the Japanese yet." On the other hand, many homes are responsible for the development of attitudes which are favorable to other groups and races.

[7]The Hollywood Daily Citizen, November 27, 1922.

[8]The Hollywood Daily Citizen, November 29, 1922.

[9]The Hollywood Daily Citizen, November, 1922.

[10] Survey of Race Relations, 266-A.

[11] Pan-Pacific Youth, December, 1927, p. 12.

[12] It is interesting to note the subsequent career of this boy.

"Another honor was won by a Japanese student on the eastern coast when John F. Aiso, a Hollywood boy and now a junior at Brown University, was elected into the Inter-Fraternity Governing Board. He is probably the first Japanese to receive such a distinction. He is a member of the Delta Upsilon fraternity which has given to the United States four secretaries of state. The last being Charles Evans Hughes. . . .

"The Sphinx fraternity, an honorary fraternity for undergraduates for high scholarship, elected Aiso into one of its offices. Last year he was given the honor of being chosen All-Eastern debater when only a sophomore and this year he heads the Forensics as president and is debate captain for this year. . . . Aiso is also a member of the Delta Sigma Rho, national honorary debating fraternity.

"Aside from being deputation chairman of the Brown University Christian Association and active in the debating field, Aiso has also gone out for athletics. He has won a couple of letters, being on the cross-country and track teams."
The Los Angeles Japanese Daily News, November 4, 1929.

The same paper on July 7, 1930, gave this additional information: "More honors have been piled upon John F. Aiso, who has just finished his junior year at Brown University. For the second successive year he was privileged to serve as the President's aide. Last year he served in this capacity to the late Dr. Faunce and this year he was aide to Dr. Clarence Barbour, the new president. . . . Once again John Aiso was elected captain of the debating team and in addition, the coaching staff voted to give him one of the two Hick's prizes of $50.00. While as captain last year, Aiso guided his team to third place in the east and another successful year is being anticipated."

The following information concerning John F. Aiso was received from the Secretary of the Alumni Association, Brown

University, Providence, R. I., under date of August 18, 1934.
(The numbers in parenthesis indicate the years in college,
sophomore, junior, and senior.) Freshman Cross Country Team;
Freshman Debating; Freshman Track; Cross Country Team (2, 3, 4);
University Track Team (2, 3); Debating Union, Executive (2),
President (3); Delta Sigma Rho, national honorary debating
fraternity, (2, 3), President Brown Chapter (4); Chairman Depu-
tations Brown University Christian Association (3); Candidate
for Final Honors in Economics (3, 4); International Club,
President (3); Interfraternity Governing Board (3); First
"Class of 1880 Prize" given for public discussion of topics of
interest to undergraduates (2); First Hicks Prize Interclass
Debate (2); First Hicks Prize Intercollegiate Debate (3);
Carpenter Prize for Elocution (3); Sphinx Club, Steward (3);
Treasurer (4); Commencement Speaker (4). The letter says further: "John F. Aiso. . . . is recognized as one of the foremost
debaters in college circles. . . . he. . . has been outstanding
in the Eastern Intercollegiate Debating League for his work as
a debater. Last year (1929-1930) the Brown team, largely
through Aiso's efforts, won eight out of nine intercollegiate
debates, and carried off the title. Among the teams defeated
were those of Harvard, Yale, Pennsylvania, and Dartmouth."
He received the A. B. degree from Brown University in
1931, entered the Law School of Harvard University and received
the LL.B. degree in June, 1934.

[13]The Japanese-American Courier, June 16, 1934. In the
spring of 1936 there were twenty valedictorians, salutatorians
and commencement speakers in the high schools of the Northwest.
Ibid., May 23, 1936. A second-generation Japanese was elected
editor-in-chief of a high-school paper in Seattle. In Port-
land a Japanese was elected president of the Hi-Y Club for the
first time. Ibid., February 1, 1936.

[14]This situation, in considerable measure, applies to the
high schools as well.

[15]The attitude toward the Negro in the southern states car-
ries over and draws the line against other races of color.
The ruling of the United States Supreme Court in November, 1927,

on the Martha Lum case brought forth considerable comment in
the Chinese and Japanese papers in America. Martha Lum, an
American-born girl of Chinese parentage was refused admission
to a white school in Mississippi. The case was carried through
the state courts which ruled against the girl and the United
States Supreme Court declared that the Mississippi law barring
the colored races from white schools was not in conflict with
the Constitution of the United States. (Gong Lum vs. Rice (1927),
275 U. S. 78; 48 Supreme Court Report, 91.)

[16]From an interview.

[17]Unpublished life history.

[18]Because of this situation, a member of the University of
Hawaii faculty has proposed that in selecting white students
for the University, only those with high scholarship records
in high school be admitted.

[19]Unpublished document.

[20]An examination of the Census data makes it evident that
this invitation was very little more than a noble gesture. The
Chinese and Japanese are very few in the occupations that are
highly unionized. They are found in unskilled labor, agriculture, etc. Where they are found in the more skilled trades,
it would appear that these occupations are plied in their own
communities and are not under white control. There is a considerable number of bakers, but probably the majority of this
group serves the oriental community. There are very few plasterers because the Orientals do very little building--they
settle largely in the older sections of the cities. Cf. Fifteenth Census of the United States, Population, Vol. V, Occupation Statistics, Chapter 3, Table 6.

[21]According to one Japanese, the majority of the young
women in their group who wear kimonos are engaged in domestic
service. They wear this particular garb at the request of the
employers in order to maintain a distinction.

[22]Unpublished life history. Used by courtesy of Dr. Romanzo Adams.

[23]The Japanese admitted to "The Hui Lokahi" was reared in Kona. See p. 196.

[24]Survey of Race Relations, 350-A.

[25]E. B. Reuter, Race and Culture Contacts, p. 177. Quoted by permission of the McGraw-Hill Book Company, Inc.

[26]There are two types of Portuguese in Hawaii, the "white" largely from the Madeira and Azores Islands and the "dark" from the Cape Verde Islands.

[27]A white man in California made this comment on the church situation.

"I didn't pay much attention to this Methodist Church affair over here, so I don't know much about it. But why don't they take them into their own churches? Why make them build a church of their own? There are six or eight churches around here. They are educating the Japanese in our language and preparing them to go to the same heaven, and why not let them go to the same churches?"
Survey of Race Relations, 111-A.

In the same neighborhood, however, a white woman would not even have them in heaven.
"You want to know, if they [the Japs] are to be subjected to this same restriction in case they decide to go to hell. No! for hell will be occupied exclusively by the Japs, and they can run it to suit themselves. Their immorality, disbelief and cunning hypocrisy, particularly in the case of those professedly "converted" (and which hypocrisy is designed to pull the wool over the eyes of kind-hearted but unthinking Christians, its ultimate aim to establish a Jap foothold here) assure them of dominating the nether regions. In Heaven, however, restrictions will be unnecessary, for no Japs will be there."
The Ledger, Los Angeles, Oct. 5, 1923.

[28]Resident Aliens on the Pacific Coast, pp. 370-372.

[29]No. 40,815, amended by Ordinance No. 41,382, February 16, 1921.

[30]The Friend, February, 1932, pp. 323-324. Cf. A. W. Palmer, Orientals in American Life, pp. 131-133 for additional information.

[31]A comment was made that this high charge was much like the prices Chinese fix for Americans in China. It also reminds one of the treatment Americans receive in India. The situation in America, however, is entirely different. On the Pacific Coast the barber sets his price high in order to keep the Oriental away. In India and China they want the American to come to their establishments; he is considered to be very rich and therefore able to pay high prices.

[32]Survey of Race Relations, 263-A.

[33]At times one encounters somewhat puzzling situations in Hawaii. In Honolulu the manager of a certain steamship agency stated that they could not afford to have Orientals in their ticket office to wait upon the public, made up largely of tourists from the mainland. Many curio stores in the city depend largely upon tourist trade; a number of these are conducted by those of oriental race while others have salespeople from this group. Evidently there is no objection here; it may even be economically advantageous to have such persons lend "atmosphere" to these establishments.

[34]The Los Angeles Times, October 7, 1925.

[35]It is evident at times that the Koreans may receive preferential treatment over the Japanese. This may be due to the fact that many know nothing about Korea and Koreans. Hence they have no fixed attitudes against them; they are at a loss as to how the Koreans should be classified. Perhaps, too, the anti-Japanese feeling of the Koreans helps them in some measure in securing better treatment from the white people in California.

[36]Survey of Race Relations, 243-B.

[37]Raymond K. Oshimo, unpublished master's thesis, University
of Chicago.

[38]We have also the phenomenon of the "white Negroes," a considerable number of whom have been able to lose themselves in
the white group. Juanita Ellsworth, "White Negroes," Sociology
and Social Research, May-June, 1928, pp. 449-454.

Chapter XV

[1]The school has given the young people contact with American
life and with a world largely unknown to their parents. They
have learned the English language and often become interpreters
for their parents. The children rise to positions of importance and the parents come to be dependent on them in many ways.
The children have not been slow to appreciate their importance
and this has tended to dislocate the traditional relationships
between parent and child. This situation has resulted in a
certain precocity on the part of the children who have assumed
an indubitable air of superiority in dealing with their elders.
A Japanese boy in California asked his father for twenty-five
cents to buy candy. When the request was not granted, the boy
told his father that he would not read the letter he had just
received from an American. Conscious of the advantage they
hold, there is an inevitable tendency among the youth to regard
their own opinions and knowledge as better than those of their
parents. Such a situation is not conducive to the maintenance
of the traditional family control over the children.

[2]Social disorganization may be defined as "a decrease of
the influence of existing social rules of behavior upon individual members of the group."
Thomas and Znaniecki, The Polish Peasant in Europe and America,
Vol. IV, p. 2.

[3]"A disorganized person is one who does not act efficiently in the situation in which he finds himself."
Krueger and Reckless, Social Psychology, p. 387.

[4]A calculation based on the number of delinquents for the years 1929-1930 and the total number in each population group in the age group 10-19 years from the census of 1930 (The figures were not available for 10-17 years as used in Table XVI.) gave these three groups the same relative positions as in Table XVI.

For additional data see Romanzo Adams, "Juvenile Delinquency in Honolulu," and Andrew W. Lind, "Some Measurable Factors in Juvenile Delinquency in Hawaii," Report of Governor's Advisory Committee on Crime, 1931, pp. 161-177; 183-192.

[5]"Prof. Romanzo Adams, of the University of Hawaii, went to the community in Japan from which many of them came, in an attempt to find the secret of their good behavior. He believes that ancestor worship and a regard for the maintenance of a clean family record, which is a dominant passion among them, is responsible for it.

"In Japan, he says, when a young man is ready for marriage, a union is arranged for him by his father. The family record must be set up. If there is a flaw in it his chance for a good marriage is lessened. Maintenance of this flawless family record is considered the most important of all considerations. It exercises a constant check on every member of the family.

"In Hawaii, when a Japanese boy under western influence becomes a problem, it is no uncommon thing for him to be sent back to his grandfather. There he lives in an atmosphere in which the attitude toward waywardness is so strong that he cannot stand against it. In a few years he returns to Hawaii, disciplined into propriety."
W. A. Du Puy, Hawaii and Its Race Problem, pp. 125-127.

[6]The Filipino, Hawaiian, and Porto-Rican girls have high delinquency ratios. The records show that sex offenses run high in these three groups. The problem in Hawaii is accentuated on account of the disproportionate number of men,

particularly among the Filipinos, and by the large number of
men in the army and navy service. White men take advantage of
women of the colored races; they have no regard for the public
opinion of these groups. A case has been reported where an
Anglo-Saxon widower had a Japanese school girl call regularly
at his house and remain for the night. After this life had
continued for some two years, the girl told her story. A medical examination revealed the fact that she was an "old timer"
but not diseased. This life had made it possible for her to
have good clothes and fine jewelry. After she had been visiting this man for some time, a group of white married men—all
about thirty-five or forty years of age—began to visit this
house for wild parties which were attended by five other Japanese girls.

[7]The Portuguese and "Other" Caucasians do not occupy the
same relative position in divorce and delinquency. The fact
that they are better adjusted to the social environment of
Hawaii and are not forced to make great changes in language,
religion and mode of life makes it less difficult for the
young people to adjust themselves. Furthermore, they are in
a position to give their children advantages which tend to reduce delinquency. In the main, they live in better neighbor-
hoods where the conditions are more wholesome.

[8]From a paper read before the Hawaiian Academy of Science,
May, 1928. See also A. W. Lind, "Some Ecological Patterns of
Community Disorganization in Honolulu," American Journal of
Sociology, XXXVI, 206-220.

[9]According to the Report of the Chief Justice of the Supreme Court of Hawaii for 1931-32, of the convictions in the
courts of the Territory for violations of the National Prohibition Act 159, or 22.1 per cent out of a total of 720 Japanese were
citizens.

[10]For certain data, see the following: N. S. Hayner, "De-
linquency Areas in the Puget Sound Area," American Journal of
Sociology, XXXIX, pp. 314-328; W. G. Beach, Oriental Crime in
California; E. K. Strong, The Second-Generation Japanese

Problem, pp. 175-182. The mimeographed Annual Reports of the
Los Angeles County Probation Department show no new cases filed
against American-born Chinese or Japanese in 1928 or 1929; two
cases against Chinese and seventeen against Japanese in 1930;
no cases against Chinese and seventeen against Japanese in 1931;
no cases against the Chinese and nineteen against the Japanese
in 1932.

[11]Clifford R. Shaw made a study of Seattle in 1929 with the
following results:
"Gazert district. . . . has 262 boys and only 15 delinquents,
with a rate of 5.7. Area 26, exclusive of the Gazert district,
has a total of 295 boys and 82 delinquents with a rate of 27.7,
which is somewhat higher than any other area in the city. Upon the basis of the limited information now available, it is
not possible to explain the extremely low rate of delinquents
in the Gazert district. It may be pointed out, however, that
the male juvenile population in the district is predominantly
Chinese and Japanese. Of the 262 boys from 10 to 17 years of
age, living in the district in 1928, more than 90 per cent were
Chinese and Japanese. (Norman S. Hayner says, "Ninety per cent
of the boys in this school district are Japanese." American
Journal of Sociology, XXXIX, p. 319.) National Commission on
Law Observance and Enforcement, Report on the Causes of Crime,
Vol. II, p. 184.
        Of this situation Dr. Palmer wrote: "On the Seattle map,
it was noticed that. . . . at one point the black dots grew
thin where, by all the normal expectations, they should have
been thick. . . . A prominent Seattle citizen is quoted as saying. . . . 'So Seattle was white, where it ought to have been
black, because it was yellow.'" Orientals in American Life,
p. 57.
        "Studies in Vancouver, B. C., show results similar to
those in Seattle. During the last nine years an average of
fifty-one per cent of the 1,241 children in the Strathcona
public school were Japanese, nineteen per cent Chinese, and
thirty per cent white. Since 1922 the Oriental population has
increased 112 per cent and the white population has decreased
24 per cent. This school district includes the original business center of Vancouver, the present center being about one

mile to the west. Average rates for boy and girl delinquency
in Vancouver for two successive five-year periods from 1925 to
1934 give this area a rate about one half that of the district
to the east and about one third that to the west.

"In an unpublished study of The Oriental Delinquent in
Court Judge Helen Gregory MacGill of the Vancouver Juvenile
Court has found that during the ten-year period from 1926 to
1935 the rate for white juvenile delinquency in the city of
Vancouver was thirteen times as great as that for Orientals.
Of the 26 Oriental children appearing in court during this
period 13 were Chinese and 13 were Japanese. Since there have
been during the ten-year period about three times as many Japanese school children in Vancouver as Chinese, the delinquency
rate for the Japanese has been about one third that of the
Chinese.

"After graduation from school the Chinese boys of Van-
couver-- disdaining the menial work of their fathers and prevented by race prejudice from securing better positions—frequently develop a grudge against society, take over the common
Chinese attitude that it is all right to evade the white man's
law and forthwith get into trouble. Some of them show a spine-
lessness that permits them to be supported by the wages and
tips of white waitresses working in the little cafes that are
the social centers of Chinatown."
Norman S. Hayner, "Family Life and Criminality Among Orientals,"
paper presented at the annual meeting of the American Sociolog-
ical Society, December 29, 1936.

[12]"Many Chinese girls on the Pacific Coast have trouble because their parents are old-fashioned. When a certain girl
wanted to go with a boy, her father wanted to send her to the
reform school. She went out a few times with a Chinese boy
who was a sailor. When he was away, he wrote letters to her as
a boy would to his sister, but her father intercepted the letters. Some time later he tried to place her in a girl's home
in San Francisco, but she ran away to her grandmother. Her
father, however, brought her home, whipped her and locked her
up. From time to time they had outbursts and then she would
go to her grandmother. Survey of Race Relations, 244-A.

[13]A section from the by-laws of the Japanese Mutual Betterment Association in a California city exemplifies this.

"To overcome the prejudice and to maintain our reputation
for cleanness and further to be always better neighbors in the
district in which we reside, we, the residents of Hobart Avenue
pledge mutually to make our best efforts:

1. To keep the front lawn and back yard always green and
clean and most beautiful.

2. To wash the windows at least once in every three months
and to hang clean curtains.

3. To take utmost care not to give any disturbance to
neighbors. Strict quietness after 10 P.M. and before 6 A.M.
. . . . no music, singing or phonograph or playing on any
musical instruments or dancing or starting of automobiles during the afore-described hours. (Exception to be made in cases
of emergencies and some other occasions recognized by the custom of the community and the country at large such as Christmas,
New Year's eve, Halloween, etc. . . . or when the neighbors consent on a special party to be held.)

4. To watch so that no children shall play on the neighbors' lawn.

5. To dress decently according to the American custom.
Laboring apparels must be changed with decent street clothes
when one goes out except in time of actual working.

6. Not to gather together in one's front steps for gossiping."
Survey of Race Relations, 71-A.

[14]It must not be assumed from this that rural life was ideal
among the Japanese. In California, the short-term leases on
land made for uncertainty and provided no incentive to develop
a community life of a high order. A letter from an Hawaiian-
born Japanese in California to a friend in Honolulu gives an
insight into the rural situation. "The environment particularly of the rural Japanese community is demoralizing and pitiful
to the extreme. The life of the Japanese laborers is gloomy
and hopeless. Their primary interest is gambling and the subject of their conversation day after day is gambling and women.
Now most of the young Hawaiian-born who choose to live a country
life and many of them must, whether they prefer it or not, live
among this group just described, no matter where they go.

Consequently the effect of such an environment upon them is not hard to imagine and those who are morally weak will certainly succumb. I can cite case after case where sad things have happened to Hawaiian-born boys."

[15] It has been reported that a young Japanese on the Coast was employed as a detective and was very successful in apprehending bootleggers. In a comparatively short time he built a large house in the town. Coincident with this his effectiveness as a detective decreased. He was the son of a poor farmer. It was inferred that he fell in line and accepted the usual hush-money.

[16] H. H. Guy, Mid-Pacific Magazine, March, 1928, pp. 241-242.

[17] According to Professor C. N. Reynolds of Stanford University: "The percentage of the total Chinese population in parasitic occupations is diminishing in size and the reason for entering such occupations is changing. . . . The younger generation, with more or less conscious American standards, are being forced into such callings by economic necessity—and they are correspondingly less happy in them." Palmer, Orientals in American Life, p. 149. Quoted by permission of the Friendship Press.

[18] An American attorney on the Pacific Coast who has done much legal business for the Orientals said that the American-born Chinese were the ones who did the "dirty work."

[19] Survey of Race Relations, 244-A.

[20] Any group that is denied political participation suffers from discrimination by the police. It is a common practice for police officers to improve their rating with their superiors by making a large number of arrests. This leads them to single out those who are disfranchised because they have no defense. Bribery is then the only way out. Disfranchised groups in a population are dangerous because they are fruitful soil for the development of corruption.

[21]The Chinese in Hawaii have a great many. The Japanese, a younger group, have fewer organizations, but they are gradually on the increase, both on the Coast and in Hawaii.

[22]As an example, one of the prime duties of the Japanese Association in Seattle is to aid in the annual community fund drive. The Association undertakes to raise the quota assigned to the Japanese community. In return the Association receives a certain portion of the community fund which it expends for welfare purposes. At present, social welfare work is one of the major activities of the Association. The Association also sponsors educational lectures, moving pictures, and entertainments. Many Americans attend these programs and thus learn to understand and appreciate Japanese culture.

A number of associations on the Coast have sought to perpetuate themselves through the organization of Junior Divisions, composed primarily of the American-born youth. A number of the second generation are unfavorable to this organization. Because of its tie-up with the older organization it will not adapt itself so readily to the needs of the younger group. Furthermore, some of the "red-seeing" white Americans look upon this as a tool of the "nationalistic" Japanese Association of the immigrant generation. The second generation is interested in being American and prefers to avoid this charge, even though it be an unfounded one.

[23]Cf. Ichihashi, op. cit., pp. 224-227, for a brief statement relative to the origin of the Japanese Association of America.

[24]The Chinese-American Citizens' Alliance sent representatives to Washington to appear before congressional committees on several occasions. The Japanese-American Citizens' League in 1934 brought pressure to bear in congress in connection with the Kramer amendment to the Dickstein bill, H. R. 3673.

The Japanese-American Citizens' League is a younger organization which is beginning to make its influence felt. Early in 1937 a program was drafted which included, among other things, a study of anti-Japanese bills introduced in the various legislatures with a view to the adoption of constructive measures to counteract such legislation.

[25]W. I. Thomas and Florian Znaniecki, The Polish Peasant in Europe and America, Vol. IV, p. 178. Quoted by permission of Dr. W. I. Thomas.

[26]Ibid., p. 204.

[27]In considering the Chinese of Honolulu this statement needs some qualification because of the prominence of certain of their men in the community.

[28]There are two classes of Chinese in Hawaii, the Punti and the Hakka from the Canton area. In the homeland the Punti are considered a superior class, but in Honolulu a number of the Hakka are outstanding men in the Chinese community. In the older generation the Punti and Hakka did not intermarry, but the young people have begun to break over these lines. Only a few years ago when such a marriage did take place there was much gossip about it, but a gradual change is in evidence. Since many of the Chinese of marriageable age are now of the third generation, class distinctions of the old country mean but little to them.

[29]Japanese American News, March 27, 1929.

[30]See Chapter II, footnote 8.

[31]Survey Graphic, May, 1926, p. 142.

[32]See Chapter XII.

[33]The Chinese-American Citizens Alliance edits The Chinese Times in San Francisco, a paper which has a national circulation. It is entirely in Chinese because it has been very largely addressed to the older generation in an endeavor to get them to understand the younger group. The Japanese-American Courier which began publication Jan. 1, 1928, states on May 19, 1934, "The Courier has been regarded as the voice of the second generation principally, and the organ of the Japanese in the United States in general." This paper is controlled by second generation Japanese.

Cf. Palmer, Orientals in American Life, p. 172, for a further
statement from the editor of the Courier. Several other
papers have entered the field since this first venture.

Chapter XVI

[1]A number of immigrant women, who have experienced a greater freedom in the new environment, have done much to set aside
this old tradition.

[2]Survey of Race Relations, 322-B.

[3]When a Chinese man marries, he brings his wife to his
father's house, or rather she is brought to him, where she becomes a servant to his mother. Very often the mother-in-law
tyrannizes over the young wife and makes her lot a hard one.
The bride's relation to her mother-in-law is far more important than to her husband, and her subjection continues so long
as his mother lives. The young wife belongs not to her husband, but to his parents.
Cf. Knox, op. cit., p. 182.

[4]In California the young Chinese are eager to leave the old
Chinatowns and move into single residences. But the anti-oriental prejudice has made it very difficult to secure houses
outside the oriental ghettos. In Honolulu this movement is
very noticeable and the old Chinese system of three or four
families in a three or four room house is rapidly declining.
In a number of instances, the usual situation has been re-
versed in that a number of Chinese parents live with their married children in the newer cosmopolitan areas of Honolulu. The
young people with their better incomes have become the heads of
the households. Some of the elderly Chinese, however, have
longed to return to the old Chinatown.

[5]According to Japanese custom, the eldest son is responsible
for the care of the parents and so it is not easy for him to

break away; the younger sons can leave more readily. For some
time one of the Japanese papers in Honolulu has been advocat-
ing that the young married couples move into their own homes
as rapidly as possible.

[6]A college boy in Hawaii said, "If I were forced to marry
a bride of my father's selection who did not suit me, I would
sooner sacrifice my family tie than be forced into a life-time
misery."

[7]The Los Angeles Record of July 14, 1928, carried the following item relative to this case: "Bobby was American-born
and a flapper at heart. Given in marriage by her parents to a
man three times her age in return for a handsome dowry, she
soon rebelled and turned to youths like herself, who loved jazz
and parties and bright lights. Her indulgent middle-aged husband showered her with jewelry, costly jade and Chinese gold
. . . . Openly she scorned her husband. And the end of the
trail found her, inevitably brought to death by violence and
her lovely body thrown on a lonely roadside. Lee Bor in the
county jail shakes his head sadly. 'She was too much like
American girl,' he murmurs in a grief-broken voice. 'If only
she had stayed with me. If only she had been real Chinese
wife.'"

[8]Survey of Race Relations, 363-B.

[9]The Nippu Jiji, April 24, 1928.

[10]The Interpreter, June, 1927, p. 11.

[11]I am indebted to Mr. Dan Kane-Zo Kai for the expression
"hand-vine method." "Hand-vine" is a direct translation from
the Japanese.

[12]Honolulu Star Bulletin, April 15, 1927.

[13]Cf. Sugimoto, op. cit., p. 193.

[14]"Young Mister One Bum Brain, afterward Wunbunde Blaine
(The Chinese substitutes l for r in his English.) will stop
'junior highing' and 'go into business'—as paper basket administrator—and with three quarters of his wages paid on a
!collegiate cut,! go out studiously understudying the mannerisms—and only the mannerisms—of a bank executive. Lady Flap
Pearl Wing, after learning how to scribble love notes, will
drop her geographies to become a tea-room doll. And upon having enough wages and tips will shed her gingham and metamor-
phose into a gorgeous silken creature. . . . And when two such
!matrimonial bargains! meet, there is but one consequence. As
with the individuals, so with the family. Installment-installed
davenports and a pretentious sedan which takes up half of the
family budget go to place them among the proper and distinguished. Children are sent into this world without provision
for their care or education. Wonderful future recruits for the
army of discontent and the unemployed!" The Y - World Chinese
Y.M.C.A., San Francisco.

[15]When the family makes all arrangements for marriage, the
young people need not concern themselves. When a young fellow
has to win a girl in competition with other men, he has to develop devices for making himself known. Probably the keen interest of oriental boys in athletics is partially motivated by
the desire to win approval in the eyes of the other sex. One
Japanese boy told about training as a sprinter in order to win
a girl while in high school. The idea was suggested to him by
a moving picture.

[16]The importance, from the parental angle, of tracing the
lineage of a prospective daughter-in-law in America may be
gained from the following statement of a Japanese minister in
Hawaii. This shows how rigid the class lines were in Japan.
It also reveals very strikingly how old class distinctions
come to mean nothing when the young people have grown up in the
more democratic atmosphere of America. The second generation
will not be able to break completely with this heritage because
they are constantly reminded of it by the immigrant group.
When the third generation comes upon the scene, however, the
"Eta" (see footnote 7, Chapter IV.) class, or any other lines

of distinction in Japan, will be so far removed that they will
mean nothing. He said: "A short time ago a problem came to my
attention. A young Japanese woman, who is a teacher in the public schools of Hawaii, is in love with a young Japanese, but his
parents object to their marriage. Her parents belong to the
'Eta' class in Japan, which is the lowest class or caste, and
they do not want their son to marry such a girl because that
will bring dishonor to the family name. The class lines are
drawn very rigidly in Japan.

       "I asked the girl to come to our home so that I might talk
the matter over with her. She did not know that she belonged
to the 'Eta' class. Her parents had come from Japan and had
not told her about it. When she learned that she belonged to
this low caste she began to weep; this troubled her very much
for a whole week. I invited the young man to our home also
and talked to him since he had learned that she belonged to
this class. He said that this made no difference at all to
him; he loved the girl and since she was highly respected here
he would pay no attention to the old idea. I do not know what
will be the outcome because his parents have not yet consented,
but I believe that they are changing somewhat. The fact that
we have had the girl in our home for some time seems to be having an effect on them. This old idea comes out from time to
time in Hawaii. At one time two girls were interested in the
same young man and one of them used the 'Eta' idea to prejudice
the other girl's parents against him so that she could get him.
This resulted in correspondence with Japan, but it was found to
be a false report.

       "I, myself, have changed considerably in my attitude to-
ward the 'Eta' group, but if it were a matter of marriage I
might draw the line. When a person has been reared in Japan,
it is difficult to break with the old traditions. This, however, means very little to the members of the younger generation who have been born in Hawaii."

       (For an "Eta" girl in California who is ostracized see
Survey Graphic, May, 1926, p. 143. In one of the large California cities the proprietor of the largest department store
in the Japanese quarter was of the "Eta" class. It was reported, however, that he was having difficulty in arranging
for the marriage of his daughters.)

[17]From an interview.

[18]Unpublished life history. Used by courtesy of Dr. Romanzo Adams.

[19]Unpublished life history of a Chinese college girl.

[20]The Honolulu Star Bulletin of October 9, 1926, carried a news item headed, "Orientals Not So Slow; Learn U. S. Methods Of Domestic Quarreling." This article reported a divorce case of two Chinese in which the wife brought suit on grounds of cruelty. The actions of the woman were quite American, even to the throwing of a shoe at her husband in the court room.

[21]The influence of these modified oriental homes is heightened by the fact that the young people are not given full entrée into the white group.

Chapter XVII

[1]Japanese American News, July 17, 1928.

[2]The Japanese-American Courier, Jan. 27, 1934.

[3]Unpublished life history.

[4]A young Japanese wrote of himself; "My own home life was a queer mixture of the Occident and the Orient. I sat down to American breakfasts and Japanese lunches. My palate developed a fondness for rice along with corned beef and cabbage. I became equally adept with knife and fork and with chopsticks. I said grace at meal times in Japanese, and recited the Lord's prayer at night in English. I hung my stocking over the fireplace at Christmas and toasted !mochi! at Japanese New Year. The stories of the Tongue-cut Sparrow! and 'Momo-taro! were as well known to me as those of Red Riding Hood or Cinderella. As I look back upon it, now, I see that my parents indulged in

this oriental side of the family life with a certain amusement
and tolerance. I rather think that they were good showmen and
had no serious idea of making Japanese citizens of their offspring.

"On some night I was told bedtime stories of how Admiral
Togo sent a great Russian fleet down to destruction. Other
nights I heard of King Arthur, or from Gulliver's Travels and
Tom Sawyer. I was spoken to by both parents in Japanese or in
English. I answered in whichever was convenient or in a curi-
ous mixture of both." Aiji Tashiro, "The Rising Son of the
Rising Sun," New Outlook, September. 1934, p. 37. Quoted by
permission of The New Outlook.

A young Chinese wrote of the American-born Chinese: "They
inevitably adopt the external mannerisms, sentiments, and characteristics of Americans, while inwardly, ... 'the younger
generation leads a truly double and romantic life of the East
and the West. They study Chinese and speak English, admire
Confucius and adore Jesus, read Chinese literature and enjoy
dancing to American music; and they celebrate two New Years.'"
Quoted from Chingwah Lee in Missionary Review of the World,
June, 1934, p. 294.

[5] Unpublished life history.

[6] According to a tabulation made by the Foreign Department
of the Japanese Government, there are 16,340 American-born
young people in fourteen of the forty-six prefectures of Japan.
On the basis of this partial tabulation it is estimated that
there is a total in excess of 20,000. It is said that the
Japanese Government is in favor of their return to America
chiefly because they are primarily American citizens. (The
Los Angeles Japanese Daily News, December 12, 1929.) An American Citizen League has been organized in Wakayama, Japan. One
of the major features of the organization is to help the American-born youth to return to their native land. (Ibid., March
31, 1930.) "One of the most active organizations for the young
people of Tokyo is the Ria club (Raised in America). It is
made up of girls who were raised in America." (Ibid., April
10, 1932.) The Japanese-American Courier of July 21, 1934,
speaks of Miss Miya Sannomiya, a California girl and graduate

of the University of California, as the newly-appointed secretary for the American-born with the Tokio Y.W.C.A.

[7] From an interview.

[8] From a personal letter.

[9] Unpublished life history.

[10] Survey of Race Relations, 443-B.

[11] After the Denver-Hawaii football game in Honolulu in the 1928 season, Coach Fred T. Dawson of the University of Denver is reported to have said of a Japanese player on the University of Hawaii team: "Hawaii has a little guard who is as good as any I have seen. . . . I sent three men into the game Saturday with specific instructions to break through Toyama—to get him out of there. But. . . . they could not move him. He deserves a great deal of credit for keeping us from scoring that time we had three downs on the one-yard line." Honolulu Star Bulletin, December 18, 1928.

[12] The Japanese-American Courier of Seattle, a four-page weekly, devotes almost an entire page to sports.

[13] The Japanese American News, May 29, 1927.

[14] According to President A. W. Palmer of the Chicago Theological Seminary, "changing names is a Chinese habit. They change the names of their children or their own names at various stages in their development, quite apart from the adoption of any English names." Personal letter, May 11, 1933.

[15] The Los Angeles Times, December 31, 1925.

[16] On the other hand, there is a reversion to the oriental names. This change usually comes after the person has passed through some disillusionment. When he finds that he is no longer accepted fully as an American, he reverts to his oriental name.

[17]From an interview.

[18]Owing to the density of the oriental population, ancestral
tradition tends to persist longer in the immigrant generation
in Hawaii than in the same group on the mainland. This condition tends to retard the process of Americanization in the
younger generation. In some plantation communities the second
generation lives almost wholly in a transplanted Japan. Everywhere they go, they hear the Japanese language and see Japanese
customs followed. In Honolulu, they have more contacts with
other races and differ greatly from those residing in the rural
districts. On the Coast, the old-world traditions tend to dis-
integrate more rapidly because of the greater number of contacts.
This, however, must be qualified somewhat. Some, particularly
among the Chinese, have been isolated in certain city areas so
that a number of the American-born have grown up practically as
old-world Chinese in America.

[19]A good illustration is found in an article by Romanzo
Adams, "Laughing at the Wrong Place." "An American moving picture was presented in Honolulu to an audience made up almost
wholly of boys and girls of Chinese and Japanese ancestry.
These children laughed at the wrong place. The laughter was
spontaneous and there was no intent to be rude. It was just
the case of seeing in a situation something incongruous and
hence ludicrous while people of a different tradition saw it
otherwise. A leading character was a man of wealth and local
power. Lacking the finer sort of sentiment, he was contemptuous of the better ideals of his time. A sordid money-getter
not too particular as to methods. The one good thing in his
life was his sincere love for his daughter. The devotion to
the girl humanized him. It revealed something worthy in his
character. He was not wholly bad.

"The tragedy of the play centers around the accident that
causes the daughter's death. The father's grief is mixed with
remorse for he sees himself as partly responsible. If he had
followed a different course the accident would not have occurred. According to the way of the movies, the father registered extreme grief. He was all broken up.

"Under the circumstances most Americans would have

sympathized with the father. Even if they felt that his loss
was a sort of retribution they would not, in the presence of
such extreme suffering, have failed to be sympathetically moved
by his grief. No occasion for laughter here. But the children
of oriental ancestry did laugh. Probably, to them, the in-
congruity lay in the weakness of a man who gave way to his
feelings. To Orientals the display of grief is unworthy of a
man; it forfeits his respect. Here was a supposedly strong,
at least ruthless, leader who turned out to be only a cheap
imitation of a man. Sympathy was impossible. This false note
in the would-be tragic ending made the whole affair ludicrous to
oriental minds." Pacific Affairs, July, 1929, pp. 415-417.

[20]Cf. O. E. Rolvaag, Peder Victorious, for the American-born
generation of Norwegian ancestry; J. H. Mariano, The Second
Generation of Italians in New York City.

[21]Unpublished document.

Chapter XVIII

[1]According to some observers, the sugar interests on one of
the islands seem to be succeeding remarkably well in developing a uniform type. One man has suggested that this is an experiment worthy of study by the eugenists. If a person exhib-
its any tendency to do anything out of the usual routine, he is
moved on to some other place. One observer has said that the
sugar interests on this island may do one of three things to
this non-conformist: (1) they may transfer him to some other
position on the same island; (2) they may transfer him to another island, and at times they have actually placed men in
better positions in Honolulu and have given them farewell re-
ceptions; or, (3) they may dismiss a man so it will be practically impossible for him to secure a position anywhere in the
Territory. Through the Hawaiian Sugar Planters' Association
and the ramifications of the sugar interests into every nook
and cranny of the islands they can practically "freeze" him out

of the Territory. Life is made so intolerable for some that
they are glad to leave. There is now coming to be a type—be
they illiterate manual laborers or university graduates in the
preferred positions—that conforms to the wishes of the sugar
men. Even those who are not working for the plantations tend
to conform, because the sugar men, in large measure, control
the purse strings of the island.

[2]Louis Wirth, The Ghetto, p. 251. Quoted by permission of
the University of Chicago Press.

[3]Abbreviation for "typical." A young Japanese has written
of this type:
    "I made some attempt about this time to analyze the
strange contrast between my contemporaries' family life and my
own. I began to classify them, even coining words to satisfy
my needs. There was a class of Japanese that I called 'Typs.'
This was an abbreviation for 'typical Jap.' A 'Typ' usually
needed a haircut or had too obviously had one. He lived in one
of the drab houses near Yeslerway with half a dozen or more
brothers and sisters, all just one year separated in age. His
father ran a grocery store; his sisters finished high school
and worked in a market. The 'Typ' was enviably proficient in
Math. and in Art; totally lacking in the finer points of social
grace. His clothes were incongruous and misfit. He either
slunk timidly in the society of Americans or assumed a defiant,
truculent air. He was impervious to self-consciousness. . . .
and persisted in jabbering loudly in Japanese in the presence
of Americans. All 'Typs' cliqued together in school and out.
The timid kind went on to college and became Phi Beta Kappas
and 'Doctors.' The brazen variety became denizens of pool
halls and street corners. I decided that I was not a 'Typ.'
. . . . Despite their outward conversion to Occidental living
I knew they were basically still Japanese.
    "A typical example was George, a friend of mine who was
the son of a wealthy importer. His case was typical of the
Japanese emphasis of primogeniture, and the peculiar attitude
of Japanese men toward women. I had always thought of George
as a youth thoroughly Americanized, for he was born and reared
in America. But one day, on visiting his home, I was astounded

by the humble air in which his own mother served him and the
lordly attitude in which he ordered her about. He adopted the
same attitude toward his sisters. Even his eight-year-old
brother wielded the Japanese prerogatives of the masculine sex
by ordering his much older sisters about like a young ty-
rant. . . .

"Outwardly George and his family were as American as Bab-
bitt, from the grand piano in the living room to the electric
waffle iron in the breakfast nook. But the last remnants of a
Japanese heritage would not disappear until another generation.

"I have seen many Japanese families with native-born sons
who are no more American than their cousins in Kobe. In fact
I have envied the admirable Japanese traits which I unfortunately lack." Aiji Tashiro, New Outlook, September, 1934, p. 38.
Quoted by permission of the New Outlook magazine.

[4]Blind adherents to conventional ideas.

[5]Cf. Wirth, op. cit., pp. 122-123, for a like situation
among the Jews.

[6]Unpublished life history.

[7]The Interpreter, September, 1927, pp. 17-18. Quoted by
permission of Foreign Language Information Service.

[8]Survey of Race Relations, 225-A.

[9]Op. cit., p. 360.

[10]Survey of Race Relations, 308-A.

[11]Cf. Thomas and Znaniecki, op. cit., Vol. III, pp. 29-30, 44.

[12]As in any other group, some have not worked their way
through to develop a wholesome life organization. They have
not developed any consistent ethical standards and have preyed
upon members of their own group. In Hawaii a number have
grafted on birth-certificates by accepting high fees for which
they promised to secure the proper documents. This practice

became so bad that the Secretary of the Territory of Hawaii announced through the press that the Government had no agents in
the field and that anyone selling affidavits would subject himself to prosecution. Some have also taken advantage of ignorant immigrants. Since the passage of the alien land laws in
California, there have been temptations for the American-born
to lease land in their names and permit aliens to operate it.
Some Hawaiian-born Japanese have taken advantage of this situation. This has brought unfavorable criticisms against the
Hawaiian-born Japanese. This type of person is more adaptable
to changed conditions than is the conformist who is so rigid
that he cannot adjust himself to new situations. The grafter
sees a certain interstitial area in which he may operate and
adapts himself to that situation.

[13]One member of the group says of himself: "I think of myself, culturally a child of the Occident, understanding the
Occident as my very own; but still racially a child of the
Orient, very ignorant of the Orient, to be sure, but so constituted that with proper effort I could learn more of the Orient
than could full Occidentals. Then here is my mission in life,
to interpret the East to the West, and to contribute to America
the knowledge accruing from a proper interpretation.

To prepare myself best, I am studying the history of the
Orient, and especially the history of the relations between
the Occident and the Orient. If I can learn oriental history
and can teach it to Americans, I believe I will be rendering
some service to America." Kazuo Kawaii, op. cit., p. 166.
Quoted by permission of the Survey Associates, Inc.

[14]S. Morris Morishita, "Race Prejudice in California," New
Japan, January, 1928, p. 26.